JOËL-FRANÇOIS DURAND
IN THE MIRROR LAND

EDITED BY JONATHAN W. BERNARD

University of Washington Press
in association with
Perspectives of New Music

Copyright © 2005 by the University of Washington Press
Printed in the United States of America

11 10 09 08 07 06 05   5 4 3 2 1

Cover photo by Joël-François Durand. Cover design by Ashley Saleeba.

University of Washington Press
PO Box 50096
Seattle, WA 98145-5096, U.S.A.
www.washington.edu/uwpress

Perspectives of New Music, Inc.
Music, Box 353450
University of Washington
Seattle, WA 98195-3450, U.S.A.
www.perspectivesofnewmusic.org

Library of Congress Cataloging-in-Publication Data
Durand, Joël-François.
    Joël-François Durand in the mirror land / edited by Jonathan W. Bernard
      p. cm.
    Includes essays on Durand's music by his students Christian Asplund,
Eric Flesher, and Ryan Hare, and by colleague Jonathan W. Bernard.
    Includes bibliographical references, list of Durand's works (p.   ), and
index.
    ISBN 0-295-98574-7 (hardback : alk. paper) — ISBN 0-295-98575-5
(pbk. : alk. paper)
    1. Durand, Joël-François. 2. Composers—France—Biography. 3. Compo-
sition (Music)   I. Bernard, Jonathan W., 1951- .   II. Title.
ML410.D955A3 2005
780'.92—dc22
[B]   2005023749

Acknowledgments

I gratefully acknowledge the generous support provided toward the publication of this book from the Graduate School and the College of Arts and Sciences of the University of Washington, and from the Donald E. Petersen Endowed Professorship, all of which were instrumental in bringing this project to fruition. I also wish to thank Pat Soden, Director of the University of Washington Press, and John Rahn, Editor of *Perspectives of New Music,* for their continuous support and commitment throughout. Finally, I would like to express my deepest gratitude to our editor, Jonathan Bernard, for his remarkable patience and dedication as he shepherded the manuscript through its many stages of correction and revision.

J.F. Durand

CONTENTS

EDITOR'S INTRODUCTION

Fifty doesn't seem so old any more. It used to be regarded as something of a zenith for creative artists, even if one could hope for additional productive years—a good many more, if one were lucky—beyond that point; it was also, inevitably, the beginning of a decline. But in an era that has seen many composers continue to work prolifically well into their sixties, seventies, eighties, even (recently) their nineties, those at the half-century mark seem by comparison barely to have reached their first maturity. So, however much we may admire a composer at the age of fifty, and however appropriate, both for traditional and for other reasons, we may find it to take the measure of his or her achievements at that point, we do so now in full awareness that any portrait of the artist drawn today is likely to be, at best, incomplete, and could easily turn out to be more a sketch than a finished painting.

This is probably even truer for Joël-François Durand than for many of his contemporaries, despite his impressive accomplishments to date—for Durand, as he himself has pointed out, was a late bloomer. At twenty-seven, by which time others his age might have had the better part of a decade's worth of work behind them, Durand was producing his Opus 1, the String Trio. Coming late to music, however, has its advantages. In Durand's case, it ensured that he wasn't embarking on a career as a composer simply because he couldn't conceive of doing anything else, or because he hadn't had (or hadn't taken) the opportunity to consider alternatives.   His education, up to and beyond the point at which he began to take music seriously, was unusually well rounded and ensured that disciplines other than music would play an integral role in his developing inner life as a composer.

The circumstances of this development are abundantly exposed in the self-interview, "In the Mirror Land," included here and, indeed, of sufficient significance as a personal statement to encourage its title's adoption as the title of the book as well. The device of the "conversation with oneself" is not unprecedented in composers' writings (György Ligeti, for one, did something quite similar in the 1970s), but it may never before have been carried to such length.[1] Here, we learn of the role played by literature, philosophy, and the visual arts in helping Durand discover just what musical composition could mean to him as a thinker—and not just about music. Although music remains, inevitably, the core experience throughout this education (both within and without the classroom), it becomes clear that without these other influences, his formation as a composer not only might have been quite different, it might never have happened at all. Their importance is evident simply from the fact that it is really not appropriate to give them that traditional designation of "extra-musical" influences—for it is clear, from the way Durand talks about them, that the crucial issue here is not simply the impact they have had on the music that he has written over the past two decades-plus. It is also, to a great extent, the converse as well: learning to be a composer has affected his thinking, in fundamental ways, about the work of certain writers and painters.

One notable example of such reciprocal effect is the place of Austrian novelist Thomas Bernhard in Durand's artistic landscape. Bernhard was a serious music student before he gave up his aspirations in that direction to become a writer, and many literary critics have judged that this earlier experience played a significant part in the development of Bernhard's distinctive style, with its very long sentences, nearly complete absence of paragraph breaks (thought by some to promote a musical flow), and incessant use of repetition (often likened to motivic structure). But although Durand agrees that these qualities are important hallmarks of Bernhard's writing, for him at least as relevant is the way in which that author's prose resonates with his own, independently developed music-compositional predilections, such as the gradual progression by reduction, in almost imperceptible increments, to a final essence of understanding. Under the influence of that resonance, Durand effectively invites us to (re-)read Bernhard, not in disregard of the generally recognized stylistic traits mentioned above, but with some attention diverted from them in favor of the long-range goal: the trajectory of the narrative as opposed to the momentary impression made by its mode of conveyance.

Conspicuous in its near-absence from the autobiographical continuity of Durand's self-interview is the influence of mathematics and the sciences, a circumstance which might seem to call for some comment, since these disciplines formed the core of his first pre-professional studies. Durand even declares at one point that the manipulations of musical materials à la Xenakis (for instance) hold little if any interest for him. In fact, a distinct facility with "quantitative" matters does come through in some of Durand's analyses of his own pieces, notably of his Piano Concerto, to which one of Durand's other essays in this volume is devoted. Readers who are familiar with the analytical writings of Pierre Boulez will recognize a kindred spirit in Durand's work on his Concerto, and will also be reminded that Boulez's own educational background—specifically an early training in quantitatively oriented disciplines—bears some resemblance to Durand's. But it would be unwise to exaggerate the implications of Durand's analytic approach for his compositional approach in this regard—especially with regard to the Concerto, which as the composer makes clear in his self-interview had its genesis in improvisation, pursued (to draw an analogy, once again, to literature) almost like an exercise in automatic writing. The premise is certainly fascinating: that one might begin work on a piece by churning out reams of raw material more or less without conscious control or thought, simply for the sake of accumulating a stockpile from which one can then select, in highly discriminating fashion, a relatively small fraction for actual compositional use. One should recognize that although the devising of this specific technique to write the Concerto was a breakthrough for Durand, in more general terms the approach is not so different from the random acts that have given some of Durand's other works their initial impetus, such as cutting the score of the String Trio apart with scissors and pasting together new juxtapositions of the fragments to form string sextet textures for *Die innere Grenze*. An attraction to the arbitrary as point of departure might even serve to explain why the Trio itself was, at least to begin with, a study in integral serialism.

More recently, Durand has found a new and perhaps more flexible way to negotiate the boundary line between random act and consciously fulfilled process in his adaptation of the "diastic" technique originally thought up by poet Jackson Mac Low. At first glance, this technique seems arbitrary in the extreme: a pre-existing text is used to derive a new text that contains (some of) the same words, but in an order determined by the order of the letters in the original words. Under Durand's somewhat simplified application, the "words" become phrases, the "letters" the constituent notes of these phrases. If the diastic reading were carried out strictly, the generation of one musical line from another would proceed according to a rigid algorithm for recombining the phrases, in essentially predictable fashion; Durand's actual practice, however, allows him to alter this "received" material further as it assumes its final form in the new piece, changing its rhythm or even transposing the pitches. Thus the input to Durand's version of the diastic method is mechanically fixed, but the output exhibits a range of variation that is potentially quite large. This method is explained and discussed in detail both in the self-interview and in Durand's essay, "Melody—Three Situations"; in the latter, it takes its place among a host of other melodic techniques, revealing the importance that processes of melodic development specifically have assumed in Durand's compositional approach in recent years.

Some composers prefer to say as little as possible about their own music; some, in fact, regard time spent writing essays or giving interviews as time essentially wasted, unprofitably diverted from the far more important business of writing notes. Letting the music speak for itself, however, is not as straightforward a matter as it used to be, and those of us with an abiding interest in contemporary music are mostly grateful when living composers make a verbal effort to orient us usefully to the more enigmatic aspects of their art. Durand's own writings are not exactly abundant—besides the self-interview and the two essays included here, his only other major prose publication is a lengthy analysis of Jean Barraqué's Piano Sonata[2]—but there is certainly enough to justify building a book around them as the central texts. In the present collection, four additional essays complement Durand's contributions, each in very different ways. Three are by alumni of the doctoral program in composition at the University of Washington School of Music, all of whom studied with Durand. In terms of methodology and critical approach, these three essays are collectively a study in contrasts and stand as testimony to their authors' ability to think independently, something which they clearly owe in no small measure to their former teacher. Eric Flesher addresses the topic of what he calls "thematic adaptation" in Durand's recent music, showing how materials from older works are re-used in newer ones but are so fundamentally transformed by their new contexts that they take on an entirely new life. Ryan Hare enumerates "centers, fields, and cracks" as metaphorical sites, at which certain problems of contemporary composition emerge and must be confronted—something that, as he explains, he has been enabled to recognize (and deal with himself as a young composer) by coming to understand the ways in which Durand has grappled successfully with these problems in his own work. Christian Asplund focuses on *Lichtung*, one of the pieces in Durand's "German trilogy" of the 1980s that explicitly evokes and responds to Bernhard, and employs a form of reductive analysis—inspired by the work of Heinrich Schenker although bearing little resemblance to this model in its specific workings—to engage the process of clarification signified by the final word of Bernhard's novel *Correction*, "Lichtung" (clearing), to which at least in retrospect the entire course of the novel may be seen to have tended, and which is reflected in the piece Durand wrote at a time when he was very much absorbed by the structural implications of this novel.   (As a nice and entirely appropriate additional touch, the form of Asplund's own essay mirrors this reductive process.)

The fourth of this group of essays, "Durand, Bernhard, and Form," is my own contribution. It shares with Asplund's an interest in the connection between Durand's music and Bernhard's prose and concentrates upon the other two pieces in Durand's German trilogy, *So er* and *Die innere Grenze*. Unlike Asplund, I propose no new analytic technique to track the process of clarification and distillation that makes an ever more dominant impression as the pieces approach their respective conclusions, preferring instead to draw parallels between the scores and certain passages in Bernhard's novels (especially *Correction*). I also draw on some of Durand's own working documents for the pieces in question, where telling evidence may be found of the "structural engineering" that brings about this developing clarification.   This essay is meant as a kind of homage to Joël: not just to his music, which I have come to admire greatly, and which I admire all the more with every new work of his I hear; but equally to an admirable colleague. I first heard his music in 1991, when he applied (successfully) for a position at the University of Washington School of Music, just a few years after I had arrived there myself; already an avid reader of Bernhard, I was intrigued to come across a composer who not only shared my fascination for him but, further, thought that his work had, or might have, musical ramifications. Try as I would at the time, though, I failed to recognize any resemblance between the prose that I already knew and the music that I had just encountered. Since then, I seem to have acquired an ability to recognize the connections that escaped me at first. But this did not happen simply as the result of greater familiarity with the music, or from hearing it in a different way; I also started to emulate the composer, bringing Durand's music and Bernhard's prose into a reciprocal relationship. This development must have been very gradual, for it was not until I re-read some of the novels in preparation for writing my essay for this volume that I realized, with a distinct shock, that something had changed in my reading experience of Bernhard: subtly deepening it, making it possible for me as never before to grasp simultaneously the moment-to-moment continuity and the larger, almost glacial pace of change.

There is much more to Durand than an affinity to Bernhard, as readers of the following pages will quickly come to appreciate. Among other writers receiving attention, ranging from brief allusion to more extended treatment, are (besides Mac Low) Martin Heidegger, Theodor Adorno, and the musicologist Carl Dahlhaus; we also encounter painters Wassily Kandinsky, Kasimir Malevich, Jackson Pollock, and Francis Bacon, film-makers Werner Herzog, Andrei Tarkovsky, and Jean-Luc Godard, and the architect Christopher Alexander. And a vast company of composers is brought into discussion in the self-interview and essays: from the earlier twentieth century (Schoenberg, Berg, Webern) to the post-War years (Messiaen, Stockhausen, Boulez, Cage, Barraqué), to the more recently eminent, such as Feldman, Ligeti, Brian Ferneyhough (Durand's principal teacher), Giacinto Scelsi, and Claude Vivier. But although they are all "influences" on Durand, in the sense that they people his artistic and intellectual world, ultimately their impact on him can be felt only through the significance and originality of his own achievements as composer and musical thinker. Evidence of the latter is on display here, for all to see; as to the former, one can only hope that the contents of this book will impel the reader to seek out Durand as manifested in his published scores and recordings, and in live performances of his music.

Jonathan W. Bernard
Seattle, Washington
February, 2005

NOTES

1. See György Ligeti, "Fragen und Antworten von mir selbst" (*Melos* 38, no. 12 (December 1971): 509–16), trans. Geoffrey Skelton in *Ligeti in Conversation* (London: Eulenberg, 1983), 124–37.

2. Joël-François Durand, "La Sonate pour piano de Jean Barraqué," *Entretemps* 5 (1987): 89–117.

In the Mirror Land: Reflections on a Self-Reflection

Joël-François Durand

To Melanie, Nicholas, and Sophia,
without whom none of this would be.

I.

−T HANK YOU FOR JOINING US *today. Please have a seat in the corner there, in front of the mirror.*

All right. Say, the lights are pretty bright over here.

 - *We can turn them down a bit if you want. Is that better?*

Yes, thank you, it's better now with the shadows. You know how I dislike interviews; it always comes out wrong somehow.

 - *Well, if it comes out wrong today, there's nobody to blame but you, I'm afraid.*

No, I can blame you.

 - *Of course, and I'm sure you will. Well then, are you comfortable? Ready for the* Self-Portrait in the Mirror?

Self-Portrait and a Dream, rather. I don't promise I'll be looking straight at the mirror all the time.

 - *We'll see about that. Shall we start with a bit of chronology? You were born in France?*

Yes, and that's where I studied music, piano at the Ecole Normale de Musique and music education at the so-called Vincennes University (Paris VIII). But before that I had studied three years of mathematics and physics after high school, "Mathématiques Supérieures" and "Mathématiques Spéciales," as they are called.

 - *So you came to music fairly late?*

I had been studying piano since I was seven, but as a full-time music student, I started after those years of scientific classes. I was twenty-one. That was a difficult period because I was very drawn to music but had no contact at all with musicians, so I had no idea how to make the switch. Then I met somebody who introduced me to Vincennes, and it sounded like the right place for me, considering my background. That was in my third year of math, and it took me about six months to decide on a complete change of direction.

- You weren't interested in the more traditional approach, through the Conservatoire?

I was very ignorant of what musical studies were at the time. For the Paris Conservatoire, it was my impression that you already had to have a strong preparation in order to get in, and all I had was many years of piano and some theory. So I didn't even bother to look into that. When I heard about Vincennes, I thought it would be a more appropriate school for me, and that's when I realized that it would actually be possible for me to go into music in a serious way.

- Were you already composing then?

I had written a number of pieces, mostly tonal, small movements for piano, that sort of thing.

- Did Vincennes offer you what you expected?

At first, yes, because their main emphasis was modern music and that was really what I had come for. I took all the traditional classes they offered: harmony, analysis, ear training, orchestration, and so on. Also some less traditional ones, such as electronic music, aesthetics, and philosophy.

- That university had a rather progressive reputation back then, didn't it?

Yes, that's when people like Deleuze were teaching there. The place had been put together pretty quickly following the events of May '68,[1] so there was a lot of momentum for change, for doing everything differently. The whole system was like that. In music there were some classes with very little planning, just discussion forever on this or that subject. I remember an argument I had with another student who thought I was too straight and challenged me to answer the question of how many times the main theme in the first movement of Beethoven's Sixth Symphony appears. I was supposed to know because I had studied piano! I think the subject of the course was minimal music (this was the mid-'70s, so it was a hot topic at the time) and the teacher was straining to demonstrate that the concept of minimalism was already found in Beethoven! Pretty basic, as you can see—it was rather loose.

Another important aspect of my experience at Vincennes was the exposure to non-Western musical cultures. There were a few instructors there who were very involved in ethnomusicology, and I remember doing ear-training exercises in class from recordings of the Dagar brothers. As I said, the general attitude favored things that were new, that challenged the dominant paradigms. For example, there was also a lot of interest in American music of the 1960s and '70s, Cage and the early minimalists (thanks primarily to the chairman of the department, Daniel Charles), as well as their European counterparts. That kind of interest was not found in any other Parisian institution at the time. So, in spite of some of its shortcomings, the department was anything but academic, musically speaking. And because of its particular isolation from the rest of the Parisian music scene, I was not really involved in the questions that the young composers coming out of the Conservatoire were asking themselves: to them the big problem at the time was how to choose between neo-serialism and spectral music. Although I was aware of these trends because I was going to a lot of concerts, I felt no such pressure; I didn't feel the weight of History on my shoulders the way students in the Conservatoire did. Since I had very little contact with those composers, I could move freely among all the aesthetics of the day and try whatever I wanted. It was really a period of all-out experimentation. I remember working on pieces in graphic notation (à la Stockhausen, Haubenstock-Ramati, and Earle Brown), music theater bordering on pranks (pseudo-Kagel), improvisations at the piano, text-based compositions (again, à la Stockhausen); all that at the same time as more traditional types of pieces. Except for these, I didn't really attach much value to the musical results of my experiments, and I didn't show them to anybody. I was just exploring the whole landscape.

- Did you study composition there?

No, the department was mostly geared toward music education. There were some composers on the faculty, but they didn't teach composition. Fortunately one of them in particular, Francis Bayer, helped me a lot at that time. I would show him my music every now and then—the pieces I considered more valuable—and he would give me his opinion. He was reluctant to give me lessons, though, because of his natural reserve; he said that he hadn't composed enough yet to be a teacher, which was remarkably honest. But he looked at my pieces and we talked. I don't think he was very impressed with me because I was working with a very analytical attitude, trying to elaborate all kinds of tables and grids to construct my pieces; I liked to plan things carefully, to have an overview of what I was going to do from the start. He was coming from a much more intuitive approach, based strongly on the sensuality of sound.

- Were you following the model shown by Boulez, for that kind of intellectual approach?

At that time, Boulez had just come back to France to start IRCAM, beginning a long-term process of modifying the musical landscape to the state that is totally dominant today. But in the mid-'70s he was still viewed with a lot of skepticism among the older generation. He represented a new kind of approach to music, especially through his book *Penser la musique aujourd'hui*, which I studied in class at Vincennes (in Bayer's class, in fact).[2] Bayer, on the other hand, had studied with Dutilleux, so he was not among the "progressivists." I must have given the impression of being on the "other side," the intellectual one, with Boulez and the other "calculators," as they were seen at the time. But I didn't really care much for Boulez's music, and I couldn't make much use of the specific techniques he had outlined in his book. My reasons for working like that were mainly that I didn't know better, and my way of thinking just happened to be similar to the kind of analytical approach Boulez had shown in his book; that's probably the extent of the influence it exerted on me, which in itself was important of course. I had just spent years studying math and science and I naturally brought that experience with me into music. It's the only way I could imagine doing things. But that was certainly not the most important reason I went into music in the first place. It was more emotional than anything.

- Do you remember what motivated you to go into music? Was it a particular event, perhaps?

As I just said, it was an emotional affair. The idea had been brewing in my mind for years, but I couldn't imagine actually doing it, because of my upbringing. I was supposed to become an engineer or something of that kind, and music was not a "job," just a hobby. That's the typical middle-class mentality. I'm not blaming anybody, mind you, they're all trapped in their environment and can't imagine anything else.

But beyond this emotional attraction, there was a very specific need: I remember that often when I heard music, either from the past or the present, I would think: "Oh, no, he shouldn't have gone this way here, that's not what I would have done in his place." I often found that I didn't agree with the decisions made by composers. This obviously didn't mean that what I would have done would have been better (and, of course, I never tried), but often I felt that sort of dissatisfaction, that frustration. So that might have triggered the decision to write music myself, so that at least I, if no one else, would be happy with the outcome. Little did I know then that doing it yourself doesn't guarantee either that you'll be satisfied!

Before that, I remember a black-and-white movie on Beethoven that I saw on TV when I was a kid, which made a deep impression on me. I don't remember who made it or anything about it, except a scene in the street, outside of Beethoven's house, and the composer was walking toward the house, his back to the camera. For some reason, it was quite a sad scene, with piano music in the background; but the character of the composer was very heroic, he was strong and was going to survive in spite of it all because he had his music. I thought: "I want to be a composer!" I must have been quite the melancholy type at the time. It was a bit of the same mood that incited me to escape from the scientific world in which I was immersed until college, and to create an inner environment, a world of dreams over which I had more control, as far as its independence from the outside world was concerned. Certainly that conflictual relation between inner and outer worlds played a great role in my thinking until fairly recently.

- When you finally decided to go into music, was your family supportive?

It was rather awful, at the beginning. Actually, I think my parents didn't really start to accept what I was doing until I got the teaching job in Seattle, about fifteen years later; so the first years were not very good, to say the least. They just wanted me to have a steady job, and they couldn't imagine that this was possible in music. They were not against music as such; my father in particular was very fond of classical music, and my parents used to subscribe to orchestral concerts in Paris and take me along. But as a full- time activity, it was totally unacceptable.

The fact is, I wasn't working at all during my third year of science studies. I was spending a lot of time playing the piano, reading books on music theory and history, trying to learn as much as I could on my own—so much so, in fact, that I ended up flunking the exam at the end of the year and getting kicked out of school. That was dramatic, but now there was no turning back. In spite of it all, my parents still supported me financially throughout my studies, even though they were really concerned that I'd have to stop at some point because I wasn't good enough and would have nothing to show for myself. Those were not the easiest years of my life, to be sure.

- With your scientific background, you could have been attracted to Xenakis . . .

But I really didn't like his music at that time. I could see that it was possible to use my background in that direction, of course, but I didn't like the musical results. So I had no reason to go there. In fact, this was my main problem, so to speak. I had nowhere to go: on the one hand I was brought up in the sciences and had a hard time making any use of it because I couldn't find anyone to help me; and on the other hand, I didn't belong to the "great" French tradition because I hadn't started in the Conservatoire as a child. And that also exacerbated my aesthetic dilemma: I admired the elaborate way of thinking that was exemplified in Boulez's and Stockhausen's writings, but I didn't care so much for the music itself. On the other hand, the composers whose music I liked were a bit out of reach: Dutilleux (whose Cello Concerto I really liked), Berg (who was dead, obviously).

- You could have studied with Dutilleux, though. He was still active as a teacher then.

That's true, but again, I thought I would be turned away for not having the proper background. I also think that I basically rejected what I perceived as the stuffy French tradition, after reading the music theory books that were in circulation at the time. All that created conflicts in my head, of course, because I admired Dutilleux's music, but I didn't want to participate in the tradition that he belonged to. On the other hand, I felt very close to Berg's music, so that must have been what got me started thinking about leaving France.

- That's when you went to Germany to study with Brian Ferneyhough.

I spent three years at Vincennes, got my "License,"[3] then started the master's program and felt more and more at odds with the Parisian milieu, mostly for the reasons I just mentioned. Even after Vincennes, I didn't belong anywhere because I had very little contact with other composers, and I saw most of Parisian musical life revolving about the Conservatoire. At the same time, I was absorbing an enormous amount of culture, in all directions: literature, cinema, painting. Not surprisingly, I suppose, I was especially attracted to German culture, mostly because a number of German and Austrian writers and filmmakers mirrored the feeling of alienation I had in Paris: Peter Handke, Thomas Bernhard (I read almost all of Bernhard at the time), Wim Wenders, Werner Herzog, Herbert Achternbusch. But I also read all the books by and about James Joyce I could put my hands on, as well as Ibsen. Duras and Artaud were probably my only steady connections to French literature.

- Were you also interested in contemporary German music?

Not particularly, not in its most recent manifestations, in any case. I was deeply involved with Berg's music, as I said before. I saw the production of *Lulu* at the Paris Opera in 1979, with the newly completed third act, no fewer than seven times; I think I saw it from all possible vantage points in the opera house! I liked Webern also, but to a slightly lesser extent, because I had a problem with the brevity of most of the pieces; but these were composers from the older generation. Honestly, I don't remember being really enthralled by any living composer at that time— not until I heard Ferneyhough's music, that is. I liked lots of things, for different reasons, but nothing that seemed to me as strong as Berg's music. Nothing else had as deep an effect, emotionally speaking.

- Could you talk about your decision to study with Ferneyhough?

That started after I heard the Sonatas for string quartet, which just blew me away: Webern's sensuality of sound, with real excitement, and a breadth of formal design that I hadn't suspected was possible. Soon after that, I summoned all my courage and, with the help of a few friends, arranged to meet with Ferneyhough, who was in Paris preparing the programming of his music for an upcoming festival in La Rochelle. I didn't know anything about him. He wasn't very well known at all then. I think he had had his first performances in France the year before, at the Royan Festival. I met him at the home of the director of the La Rochelle Festival, in Paris around Easter 1980, and showed him a little set of songs for countertenor and harpsichord that had just been premiered. He asked me several questions about the piece, my approach to writing for voice and so on; I had no idea how to answer most of his questions! I was totally baffled. At the end I vaguely muttered that I'd like to study with him if that was possible. I don't even remember if he answered; maybe he didn't hear me. I walked in the streets of Paris for several hours, totally confused, thinking I had just missed my one chance of getting somebody interested in me and at the same time feeling uplifted by some of his comments about general musical subjects. I wrote to him a few days later and he offered to take me on privately and then see if I could apply to the school in Freiburg. So I spent the following year commuting once a month to his home near the Swiss border. Then he decided that I was ready to be admitted to the Musikhochschule in Freiburg, so I took the entrance exam, passed it, and moved to Germany.

- You mentioned the shock of Ferneyhough's Sonatas. But you didn't really absorb any of the purely technical aspects of it: the formal organization for example.

No, that's true. As you know, Ferneyhough's music is tough to analyze in detail. But the Sonatas should have been within reach, analytically speaking. No, I didn't spend much time looking into it in great depth. I wasn't interested so much in the formal strategies as in the surface aspects: the gestures, inside the phrases as well as on a larger scale; and the sense of continuity over long spans of time.

- That's the time of your Op. 1, the String Trio?

The Trio was written during that year of private study. It was already finished when I entered the Hochschule. I worked on it for about eighteen months, one of the most intense periods of my life. It was the most complicated thing I had done up until then. I think I was trying to impress Ferneyhough, by working in a way that I thought he was working! In retrospect, it's funny for me to realize that, elaborate as the planning was, the result sounded rather spontaneous in many ways.

This piece was written at a time of resolution of many psychological issues and frustrations that I had endured since my switch to full-time music study. Entering the class in Freiburg was an extraordinary experience. I remember the first time I met with all the other composition students from Huber's and Ferneyhough's class: we had a weekly meeting of both studios, with individual presentations by the students. For the first time, I was in a group of composers, and that gave me a sense of identity as a composer. What a relief! I think I was really born there, in Freiburg. The music school at the time was certainly one of the best schools in the world; besides Huber and Ferneyhough, they had Nicolet, the Holligers (both husband and wife), and many other famous instrumental teachers. So the level was quite high, and there was a good amount of attention given to modern music, thanks to the many teachers who had been actively involved, at one time or another, in its performance. It was really exciting to become a part of this community.

- Let's stop at the String Trio for a minute. It's a serial piece. That was something of an odd choice at that time, wasn't it? Serialism was on the way out.

Well, it was still quite popular with a number of younger composers, even with the rise of spectral music, which was challenging it. But I realized clearly that serialism was controversial precisely because it was already a bit old-fashioned. My reason for trying it out at the time was that I wanted to push myself into a really tight corner, to force something to come out, and serial technique appeared to be the best suited to the task. It wasn't really an aesthetic choice. I wanted to test myself against the constraints of a system. The other reason was that I didn't actually like any of the integral serial music that had been written in the '50s. I was intrigued by the idea of integral serialism, but I thought the results were just awful. So I thought I'd give it a shot and see if I could come up with something I liked.

- But it's not really integral serialism. You cheated!

Yes, I did, in the sense that I didn't control all the parameters with serial tables. In a way, as soon as I started, the focus shifted a bit. I realized that in the domain of rhythm in particular, the use of small rhythmic patterns (the types that Boulez mentions in his article "Possibly . . ."[4]), was precisely what created that discontinuity so typical of that period. And that was exactly what I was trying to get away from: the discontinuity, the little bits and pieces glued together. So I couldn't really use that technique in the same way. What I did that was similar to integral serialism was to use a very systematic way of generating rhythmic phrases (rather than small patterns), and then apply the serial pitch forms to them. So these two parameters were worked out separately, then brought together. I hadn't done that before, so it still qualified as rather constraining.

- Did that help you avoid the discontinuity you referred to?

If you listen to the beginning of the Trio, you'll notice that it flows quite continuously, in spite of the constant and sometimes extreme changes of registers in each instrument (Example 1). That continuous flow resulted in part from the way I worked out the rhythmic patterns from the start in long phrases rather than small modules. The other main technique I used to ensure continuity was to emphasize certain pitches by assigning them long durations and keeping them in the same register, even when they passed from one instrument to the next. So some of these pitches create a sort of pedal; the C, for example, is used like that a lot at the beginning. Afterwards, in the second section and even more so in the third, discontinuity comes in more forcefully. But it had a dramatic role then, it wasn't the result of a change in the basic technique. I could have had the same type of texture and continuity all along, but I started to break it up, to tear apart some phrases, by forcing in other material or measures of

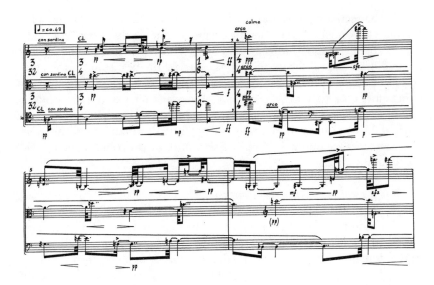

EXAMPLE 1: DURAND, STRING TRIO, OPENING

silence. It was really for dramatic effect, to create contrasts and conflicts. It also had to do with the way I was modifying my rhythmic phrases. I had a system to generate long drawn-out phrases with long durations, shorter phrases with very short durations, and the whole range in between. The system gave me all possible choices, from very long to very short. So depending on what I wanted to have happen at any given time, I could choose from my reservoir of phrases and apply them. That system was very flexible, within the constraints I had chosen.

- Did you have a similar way of working with the other parameters?

No, I wasn't about to become a "Reihen-Ingenieur"![5] The only other dimension that was treated serially was pitch. There, I used more traditionally serial techniques (inversion, retrograde, and so on). An interesting point here is that the serial forms were very limited: in the first section, the row had only two different intervals, the minor second and minor third, so there wasn't much point in using more sophisticated techniques such as segmentation or subsets. This limitation, in turn, also motivated me to introduce a new row (based on the major second and major third) in the second section, in order to create a new sound. I think that in the third section I mixed the two rows together. I don't remember exactly.

- You don't remember? But didn't you write your own analysis of the piece? You must have been quite proud of these systems to have spent all that time afterwards writing about them! Or were you simply too self-involved?

Yes, it's true, I did write all that prose afterwards. I'm not sure I did it because I was especially proud of the technical aspects—although I was quite happy with the piece itself. The reason I wrote that analysis was that I was trying to hang on to the experience of writing the piece. It had been so intense, so difficult, because of the restrictions I had imposed on myself. And it had also been my first year of study with Ferneyhough, which was quite exhilarating. I remember an anecdote about that, actually, which illustrates my frame of mind. I was reading a book by the German director Werner Herzog at the time—it must have been early spring '81, before Easter. Herzog was talking about how important it is to travel on foot, instead of by machine, to experience nature the hard way, so to speak. He related how he had traveled a great distance, from Munich to Paris, to visit an old friend of his who was very sick. He had made this trip on foot as an offering to her, as a sort of sacrifice in the hope of helping her get better. It was very beautiful.[6] That gave me the idea of making the trip to Germany, to my monthly lesson, on foot, to offer my finished Trio to Ferneyhough. I was really excited by the idea: walking through the countryside, trying to find a place by the road for the night, and so on. Then I hurt my ankle a few days before the trip, so I never did it. I don't know if I was more sorry or relieved! That's why for several months after I finished the Trio, I wanted to stay with it a while longer. I wrote that analysis in the first weeks after I arrived in Freiburg, in September 1981.

- You could have just written another work along the same lines.

Well, after expending so much energy on that one piece, I needed to go look for other problems to solve. And as I said, I was emotionally attached to the piece, or maybe just to the period I had spent writing it. In any case, I had done my serial piece, so that was that.

- Maybe it was also because you're so slow at writing music; do you tend to be overattached to the results?

At that time, that must have been true also. When you don't write much, you become a bit too attached to the little you do. That's also why I have revised most of my pieces after the first performances.

- You can't let them go?

If there weren't any practicalities to deal with, I'd probably keep retouching my pieces all my life, even the older ones. But maybe that's changing, because I think I now have a few pieces that I don't need to revise.

I remember that at the time I was writing the Trio, I thought I should spend all my life just rewriting the same piece over and over, until I got it right. The fact is, I had this feeling that just when the piece was done, I finally had a grip on what it was about, so if I did it again, it would be more focused, more in line with what it needed to be. Of course you must remember that at this time I was engrossed with Bernhard's *Correction*, which retraces the path of an architect who is writing a book and keeps correcting the manuscript over and over, by reducing it each time, until he commits suicide—the final correction. But, apart from that dubious ending, I thought that it would be interesting in music to go through this process of forever correcting because I would learn better and better all the time what it was that I was trying to do in the first place. It's a good thing I didn't follow that path. I think I would still be wondering what it is I'm trying to do.

- Do you know, now that you've gone the other way?

Well, at least I know what I don't want to do!

II.

- Let's move on to 1984. Why did you leave Germany? Didn't your life there satisfy your expectations? Or do you have an urge to keep moving on all the time?

I'll ignore that last question, if you don't mind. Yes, Freiburg certainly offered me all I expected, much more in fact, on a human as well as musical level. As I said, I really felt as though I were finally being born to what I needed to become. But it became progressively more stifling, because I put too much pressure on myself, on the way I was composing. By my last year of study at the school, I wasn't able to write anything but a few pieces for single instruments, after the Trio. It's quite odd; I'm not sure why that happened. I first wrote the violin piece, *Roman*, which was somehow a consolidation of my interest in string writing, after the Trio. Then I tried to write an ensemble piece: didn't get very far. The following year, I wrote the piano piece *...d'asiles déchirés...*, very quickly, for a competition in Italy. Then nothing for months; I was trying the ensemble-piece idea again, without success. Then, finally, in the last year I wrote a flute piece that was supposed to end all flute pieces, for bass flute! That's when things started to go wrong. There I was, trying to work out every single detail of the whole construction: time proportions, pitch organizations (several different ones), rhythmic patterns, registers, sound production, and trying to do it according to some kind of unitary, overarching system. But the dramatic shape was totally flawed because I was asking myself all the wrong questions. I was too obsessed with justifying every move, and looking too much at the small-scale stuff, the details of everything. It was just much too complicated. Plus it was my first request from a French festival, La Rochelle, and I was writing for Pierre-Yves Artaud, the Ferneyhough performer par excellence at that time; talk about pressure! My piece was a total disaster, although Artaud was very nice about it and didn't complain. He even played it again in Darmstadt right afterwards, and that's when I realized I had really screwed up. There were a few more performances, on the alto flute, by other people, then I retired the piece. The whole thing was not a great finale to my studies.

- Then you left Germany and you wrote all those pieces with German titles. Shouldn't you have stayed there, even if not in school?

Perhaps, but there was no way for me to earn a living there; just out of school, with four pieces in my catalogue, that wasn't much to show. Then there was the fact that I was getting pretty tired of the environment I was in. I felt a bit suffocated, I couldn't write music with any spontaneity anymore. That had been a bit of a dilemma all along in Freiburg, and in my third year there, I was ready to explode!

- Was that the result of Ferneyhough's teaching?

I don't think so, no. It was really just me, putting pressure on myself to do things a certain way, the only way I thought was acceptable at the time.

- What are you referring to? The "New Complexity" movement, that you were part of?

Not exactly, although that bass flute piece was certainly an attempt to match with my own means what Ferneyhough had done for the C flute in *Unity Capsule*. I don't think anybody there thought I was really part of that "movement" anyway, I was a bit on the fringes, not quite committed enough, probably. My problem was more that I tried to justify every move I was making in the composition. I thought that every decision, from small to large scale, had to be rationally made, so that everything could relate to everything else in a demonstrable manner. I was trying to control consciously as many parameters as possible. That was silly. But it wasn't anything that Ferneyhough demanded, not at all. You just have to look at his music of the time, like the Second String Quartet, to see how much spontaneity there is. I just couldn't see it myself.

- Others of his former students have voiced criticism about the way they felt they had to write music in order to gain approval.

Ferneyhough didn't exert any control of that sort on anybody. I think some students came to him because they were fascinated by his intellect and in awe of the complexity of the music. There was a kind of aura of admiration around that sort of thing. It was quite new at the time, of course, and that newness was part of the attraction, as in any period. But Ferneyhough himself didn't care whether you were writing lots of notes or not. He just wanted you to know why you were doing whatever it was you were doing. For some people that's a very hard question to answer, no matter what they're doing. So students who were there because of a kind of morbid fascination with pages full of notes couldn't find a clear reason to justify their decision to write like that. Some became quite resentful at what they thought was his pressure, but really, they were putting the pressure on themselves, and couldn't get out of it. I know that first hand, because that's just what I was doing myself. It was probably just as hard for those students who didn't want to write like that at all, because they felt excluded from the group. That's why I had to leave, not only Freiburg, but the whole scene there.

- Did you have that morbid fascination you just mentioned?

No, but honestly, I was attracted to the gestural nervousness that I saw in the music. It wasn't so much the density of events as the considerable energy the gestures liberated. It took me years to understand that this wasn't really my way of doing things, even if there's a part of me that likes a certain restlessness! The point is that, at the same time that I needed this kind of hyperactivity, I was tired of it, physically and emotionally tired. So

I left Germany and went in a different direction. That's immediately apparent if you compare the flute piece (which incidentally was reborn years later as *Par le feu recueilli*, once I finally found a way to fix it) with the beginning of *So er*. *So er* starts with just one note, for a good length of time; in that same time, the flute piece had a million of them!

- So er *is the first of the "German" pieces?*

Yes, *So er, Lichtung, Die innere Grenze* are the three pieces. They form a triptych, because they share a similar formal design.

- *In that order?*

No, that was the order of composition. The performance order is *Licht-ung, So er, Die innere Grenze*, which as a whole creates a dramatic progression toward a more and more complex formal development: *Lichtung* is for ten instruments, and is essentially linear and sequential; *So er* uses twice as many instruments and is more forcefully dramatic; *Die innere Grenze* is for smaller forces (string sextet), but compensates for this reduction in volume by being by far the most complex construction and the longest piece of the three.

- *I am curious to know how you counteracted the influence of Ferneyhough at the beginning of your studies in the United States. Since you wanted to break from your previous methods and aesthetics, to some extent, where did you look for antidotes, so to speak?*

I remember at the time of *So er* being particularly interested in Japanese philosophy, and in Japanese music, gagaku in particular. There's a section a little after the middle of *So er* with reminiscences of sho, done by the strings, and a melody in the piccolo (Example 2). So that was one thing. Another I remember now was Xenakis's *Akrata*. I liked its rawness and brutality, and I tried to translate that kind of energy in the opening section of *So er*. Finally, a major discovery of those years was the music of Claude Vivier (*So er* was dedicated to his memory—he died in 1983). I had met him in Darmstadt in 1982, which is when I heard his music for the first time. I think it is thanks to him that I started to be interested in melodic writing, although at that time, I wasn't sure how to deal with it, really. But my main preoccupation was with the particular formal design shared by the three pieces, a design that I wanted to explore in several different ways.

EXAMPLE 2: DURAND, *SO ER*, MIDDLE SECTION: *SHO*-LIKE STRINGS,
PICCOLO MELODY

- This similar formal design was also present in other pieces at the time?

Yes, there's another group of pieces from the late '80s–early '90s, a dip-
tych, *L'Exil du feu* and *Un Feu distinct*. After them I didn't revisit this
idea until *Athanor*.

EXAMPLE 2 (CONT.)

- This formal design you just mentioned: you called it formal "revelation." That sounds quite mysterious.

Actually, I had gotten the idea from Heidegger, a bit earlier. I was reading his essay on Heraclitus's *Fragment 50* at the time of the flute piece, and I became really fascinated by the idea of assembling, collecting, and storing away that he mentions in relation to the German word *lesen* (to read), whose root is *legen* (to lay down).[7] I thought it was a wonderful image, that through writing we collect and store, in a sense we protect language, we select what we harvest and we store it in a safe place. That was the image that remained of it for me, and I thought this was a great image for music as well. I tried it first in the flute piece, where I collected parts of the piece and made a last section that recalled the rest of the piece and laid down the harvest of it, so to speak.

- *But that was exactly what you had already done at the end of the String Trio, wasn't it?*

Yes, and I don't think I even remembered the similarity at the time. In the last section of the Trio, the violin solo combines one layer of a long ascending glissando with another one made up of excerpts of the previous three sections, read backwards. So that was indeed a germ of the same idea. That's probably why Heidegger's essay affected me so strongly when I read it a few years later. After the flute piece, I started to imagine forms more consciously that were based on that model. For example, in *Lichtung*, I first wrote the melody that concludes the piece. Then I extracted pitch cells from various fragments of the melody and I wrote the piece from the beginning. The idea was that progressively, as the piece is being heard, the original melody comes more and more into focus, and is finally heard clearly at the end.[8] That was the idea of "revelation." Now, it's quite clear that this only functions as an image, a metaphor in the composition. It's certainly not meant to be perceived in this way by the listener, nor is it reasonable to expect it to be.

- *Wasn't that a rather easy way to finish a piece? I mean, you didn't have to wonder how to end it, since the beginning was the end.*

Feldman once said that he was struck by a question painters were asking themselves in the '50s, when he was close to that scene: How do you know when a painting is finished?[9] In nontonal music you could ask yourself the same question, of course, because there's no longer a final cadence. Many composers have adopted various strategies to make it clear to the listener that the piece is over. One device much in favor since the beginning of the twentieth century has been the disappearing act: the music just goes away slowly in the distance, evoking departure, or death, or something of that nature. But asking oneself the question of when the composition of a piece of music is finished amounts to saying that you have no idea what the form of your piece is, that there was no formal intention to start with.[10] That's quite popular in some circles, of course, that lack of intention. And it's also a little simplistic as a compositional attitude. If you don't have any intention, sure enough, the piece will have one for you. You can't just write in a free-associative mode, and pretend that you are not aware of what is going on, of the form you're creating. Each moment a decision is made, one somehow takes into account what has been already written and, in one form or another, what is going to happen next. So saying that you don't know when a piece is finished is like saying that you weren't really paying much attention to what you were writing. Music and painting—abstract painting in particular, since that's what Feldman was referring to—are fairly similar in this respect. And I suspect that the painters who were asking that question were asking it as a provocation, in order to discover what they had lost by going abstract, and to define better what they were discovering. When there's no image to imitate, you have to rely on the shapes and colors alone, on the weight of each space of the painting, on its dialogue with the other shapes; and on problems of proportion and balance that, incidentally, are there also in figurative painting. So there was a lot of intuitive work going on to assess all that, and the question of when the painting is finished was probably an attempt at recovering some of the evidence of figurative painting.[11]

Those categories I just mentioned are exactly the same in music. We know a piece is finished not necessarily because the formal layout we have chosen indicates it's finished, but because all the weights, proportions, colors, and so on are in the right places. So working from a given layout isn't going to make the piece happen by itself. It's not going to guarantee that it will be right, and it's not going to help you if the balance is off. Just look at how many bad pieces were written in sonata form, or rondo form, or whatever; they all follow more or less the "ideal" plan, but what went wrong? So using a formal layout where the origin of the piece shows up at the end doesn't mean that what is written in between will make sense. You still have to do the work.

- Didn't you just say a little while ago that you find it difficult to know when a piece is finished?

That had nothing to do with the question Feldman related. Or if it does, it is in the sense that it's not so much about where to put the final double bar line as it is about knowing that all the moments of the piece are balanced properly in relation to each other and the whole. In fact that's probably exactly the way those painters were asking the question, not so much about where to put the final double bar line, so to speak, but whether everything was right in relation to the whole. But that question has always been on composers' minds, in that particular sense.

   - *What's the purpose of this formal idea of revelation, then?*

What I had in mind was to expose the progressive discovery inherent in the creative process. I wanted to write a piece about what happens before you write a piece.

   - *That could be really boring. If you take the example of Beethoven's sketches, you see that what happens before the piece is written is mostly discarding bad ideas!*

Indeed. I suppose if I really wanted to show what happens before I write a piece, I could just compile all my sketches chronologically, and there is the piece. No, of course that's not what I meant. I was dramatizing the creative process, enacting it, like showing life in the theater. I don't care for naturalism.

   - *Maybe you're not so self-centered after all!*

Thank you. I'm glad you finally came to that realization.

   - *So* Lichtung *ends with a melody. But there's no melody at the end of* So er.

No, that work is built on the sequence of chords that is heard at the end. *Die innere Grenze* is built on a long polyphonic passage which appears also at the end.

   - *What about* L'Exil du feu, *and* Un Feu distinct?

I had a problem with that first one. The original idea for *L'Exil du feu* was a long heterophonic passage. I mean heterophonic in the sense that each line of the texture was independent from the others, as independent as possible in fact. The model I had in mind was Ives's *Three Places in New England*, the beginning of the last movement in particular, where the strings are playing completely unrelated lines, then the winds come in with the hymn and so on. It's a typical example of heterophony, although the real definition of the term, in that sense, originated later, with Charles Seeger.

   This long passage was supposed to show up at the end of *L'Exil du feu*, but I couldn't make it fit. It didn't work at all. So I just cut off *L'Exil du*

feu, and immediately afterwards, I wrote *Un Feu distinct* so that the heterophonic section could finally appear. In fact, *Un Feu distinct* was much
more tautly constructed from the end section, so that there was really no
problem here to bring in the "revelation" (Example 3).

  - Is it right then, to play those pieces separately?

Well, *Un Feu distinct* is for five instruments whereas *L'Exil du feu* is for
twenty instruments and live computer transformations. So it's not completely practical to program them together. But then again, the best
would be to have all five pieces done together, which is even less practical. At any rate, I think each of the five pieces works fine on its own.

  *- There was quite a fashion for those kinds of cycles at one point. The most
  famous examples are Ferneyhough's* Carceri d'invenzione *and Grisey's*
  Espaces acoustiques. *Was that part of the impetus for this cycle?*

It's not really a cycle in the sense of the ones you mentioned. It's more a
group of pieces that share a specific common formal design. I think that's
why it would be interesting to hear them one after the other. Stylistically,
the three "German" works are very close together, just as the two
"French" ones are. So it's more of a three-plus-two block, if you want.

  *- That was the beginning of your period in the United States. I wonder
  how you think that new environment affected your music, beyond what
  you just said about trying a new formal design.*

I left Europe because I felt trapped in some aesthetic battles I couldn't
deal with any more. They weren't mine; I had no idea where to go from
there, aesthetically speaking—and I also needed to recover some of the
spontaneity I had not been able to use at the end of the Freiburg period.
It was good to be away from Europe just then because I thought: this is
it, there's nobody watching over my shoulder, what do I want? So in the
fall of '84, at Thanksgiving break, I just locked myself for three days in a
room without windows at school and worked there until I came up with
something usable.[12] That's how I wrote the first measures of *So er*.

  *- But you were in school again. Didn't you feel pressured by the new envi-
  ronment, by your teacher there?*

Not at all. I didn't go to Stony Brook so much to study with anybody in
particular as to get away. So I didn't put same the kind of pressure on

EXAMPLE 3: DURAND, *UN FEU DISTINCT*, HETEROPHONIC SECTION

myself that I had in Germany. It was really a period of breathing out, in that sense; work out all the stuff I had learned in Freiburg and come up with something else. Having said that, it was great to have Bülent Arel as a teacher because he was very understanding, and gave me a lot of freedom. He must have sensed that I would have blown up if he had tried to control me. I remember telling him at the beginning that I had enough of being taught and I needed to be left alone. I don't know how I would feel if a student came to me now with that sort of introduction! It must have been hard for him to hear. But he was such a generous person, I think he understood. We would just meet a few times every quarter, usually when I had advanced enough to show him something. He was quite helpful, although I think he didn't believe he was. I remember one lesson at which he kept saying, in a soft voice: "It might be better to do it this way, although I'm sure you have very good reasons for doing it the way you did." And I would just say: "Yes, it has to be this way. See here, and here. If I change it, it won't work any more." We were on different planets, really, and I was somewhat arrogant in those days. But he helped me build my confidence.

 - *You were still working for the European scene, though. Wasn't* So *er written for the Venice Biennale?*

The first version—about the first half of the piece—was written for a master class in Asolo that Ligeti was doing with the European Community Youth Orchestra. Then the final version, indeed, was requested by the Venice Biennale. The director of the Biennale had heard the premiere in Asolo and asked me immediately for something. I offered to give him the finished piece. So, although I was still connected to the European festivals, I was now writing from a different place. I was affected not by whom I was writing for, but by where I was writing. Of course I could have felt that I had to write as before, since it was for a performance in Europe; and yet, somehow, I felt safe here in the States doing other things.

 - *You didn't really break with your past, though, as much as you would like to believe. What you wrote after leaving Europe still bears many traces of your European past.*

Well, for one thing, I did finally manage to write an ensemble piece. So I had to relinquish some of my habits of writing extremely virtuosic music that I had indulged with the solo pieces. On the other hand, it's true that I wasn't going to go overboard in the other direction just in order to say that I had mended my old bad ways! I didn't think they were bad ways, and I'm not the type to do something just to react against something else.

- You just mentioned that this was your first ensemble piece. You didn't write for solo instruments for quite a while after that. Was that part of your rejection of Europe, and of the virtuosity you just referred to?

It's true that I wrote only for solo instruments in Germany, then only pieces for ensembles until 1992. The reasons were partly circumstantial. My name was starting to circulate in Europe, and I was getting commissions from ensembles. When I returned to solo writing in 1992, it was not in response to a request, it was out of a personal desire, although that first piece for solo instrument, *La Mesure de l'air*, eventually turned into a commission for Armand Angster. I like to come back regularly to writing for solo instrument because it forces me to focus on line and deal with few resources. I am glad I spent so much time on that kind of writing when I was in Freiburg. I learned a great deal about formal design by having to concentrate on single lines, and minimal changes in instrumental color. Of course, one of my favorite solutions at the time was to try to create a sense of polyphony out of a monodic instrument, so I was cheating, in relation to what I just said, by trying to add more lines. The main thing was that I had to develop formal strategies without the resource of very different instrumental colors. Writing for solo instrument is of course also the best way to learn what an instrument can do, and in Freiburg there were many students who were happy to be guinea pigs for us. It's a good thing I took advantage of those opportunities there, because once at Stony Brook all that changed completely.

- You mean there wasn't any new music at Stony Brook?

Well, there was Arthur Weisberg, who conducted the modern music group and the university orchestra. He was great, really professional and committed to new music. But usually, the few students who participated in the group were the only ones in the whole school who shared this enthusiasm. And, with one or two exceptions, they were not really aware of the kind of virtuosity that was becoming the norm in Europe. Of course, I had come from a rather privileged environment in Freiburg, where there had been a great deal of interest in new music at the time I was a student; that was quite remarkable. So going anywhere else would have been a shock, by comparison. Anyway, by the time I got to Stony Brook, I didn't need to explore the limits of virtuosity any more.

- Let's go back to your working methods. When you left Germany, you said that you needed to find some spontaneity again. How did that happen?

It took a long time. I think there's a pretty straight line of progression from the time of my departure from Europe until the Piano Concerto. The Concerto summed up many tendencies that were at work in the years before, both at the local and the global levels. Formally, a lot of my music (in fact, from the time of the String Trio) played with the dichotomy between moments created by the use of systems and such deductive kinds of procedures, and other moments of more spontaneous activity, often in reaction to the straitjacket of the other ones, so to speak. For example, in the Trio, there's the main structural idea based on the use of series of pitches, and the derivations of rhythmic phrases I mentioned before. That system of organization is then interrupted several times by inserts made up of earlier moments of the piece. That was one way to open the rigidity of the system. In other pieces, I've sometimes inserted measures of music that had nothing to do with the rest of the piece because they were invented on the spot just to be different, or were borrowed from other works of mine. I've often felt that need to insert stuff that didn't belong there, as a kind of surrealistic moment, although it never sounds gratuitous or arbitrary because it's always stylistically consistent. It's just a formal dialogue between systematic elaboration and spontaneous reactions. Metaphorically, one could say that the music gets squeezed into a small box, and tries to escape through the cracks. I enjoy opening cracks because they put the whole construction in danger. These two tendencies, the systematic and the spontaneous, were dramatically embodied in the Concerto because, for the first time, I decided to use improvisation to generate most of the piano part.

- Your own improvisation?

Yes. I recorded several sessions of myself improvising at the piano. Then I selected the parts that I liked best and transcribed them. After that I examined what I had on paper and started the actual composition of the piano part.

- You call that improvisation? It seems that there were many steps between the playing and the writing. Not exactly a typical use of improvisation. In fact it sounds more like what any eighteenth- or nineteenth-century composer would have done, except for the recording aspect!

True enough. The important point is that I wanted the piano part to have as much physicality as possible. So I decided to set aside my usual practice of writing directly on paper and sat at the piano, letting my ear and hand guide the proceedings.

   - Since you are a pianist by formation, some would say that it was a sure recipe for ending up with clichés of all sorts.

But I am a bad pianist, even after all those years of study—bad in the sense that I can't play the virtuoso music for the instrument at all. I never reached that level. So sitting at the piano to create the piano part was not about reproducing the tricks I knew, because I don't know many tricks. It had to be for a different reason. What I was looking for was ways in which my hands could create gestures that were particularly idiomatic to them, because of their size, shape, and so on. So in these improvisations, I played much faster than I could ever do if I played from a score. I didn't care about wrong notes or such things. I was just using my body, not just my hands, to bring out something that I hadn't discovered yet. Then I cleaned up the "wrong" notes during the transcriptions, selecting by ear what I wanted to use. In a way the improvisations themselves were garbage. They just provided raw material for decent recycling. But I was very careful to keep as much as possible of the gestural quality of the original.

   - Schoenberg once called composition "slowed-down improvisation."

Because ideas come so fast that the pen can't keep up with them, exactly; but Schoenberg was referring to music writing, not playing. That's always a problem when writing music, that you can't write down everything that comes to mind because the hand is too slow. In the case of this piano part, the tape recorder could keep up with the speed; after that the pencil had more time to think.

   - What about the orchestral part?

That's where I staged the dichotomy between the two tendencies I mentioned before. The orchestral part was much more systematically written. But because I needed to leave room for the orchestra to interact with the piano, I came up with the idea of creating a compositional "environment" which enabled me to make local decisions spontaneously while providing enough constraints to maintain cohesiveness; so I could decide at any moment whether, for example, the orchestra would be going on its own independently or would interact more clearly with the piano. By bringing that dichotomy to a much larger-scale level, piano in charge of the spontaneous level and orchestra of the more systematic one, I actually didn't need to "mess up" the system, in the way I was indicating earlier.

- We'll come back to this subject of environment in a moment, if you don't mind. You later extracted the solo piano part of the Concerto, which became the piano piece, Le Chemin.

Yes. The image I had in mind was drawn from the emotional relationship between the Concerto and my days in Freiburg, when I would wander for hours in the forest. I sometimes drew sketches of particularly remarkable places on the path along which I was walking in the forest, places which seemed to have a kind of magical power, a mysterious presence. I was hoping to find a way to transform those sequences of trees or bushes, or the alternation of light and darkness, into musical forms. That's what I was drawing, really, succession of moments that had remarkable forms over the time of the wandering. That became the guiding image when I was writing the concerto. When I extracted the piano part, I had an image of the forest in mind, and that the piano in the Concerto was indeed something of a path (the *Chemin* of the title) and the orchestra the various surroundings for the path.

- That's the second time you've referred to the habit of walking: once with your idea of going on foot to offer your Trio to your teacher, and now a piece derived from walks in the woods. What is so attractive about walking?

It's not just the walking that is attractive. I like the idea of journey, of going through places, from an origin to a goal. More specifically, I have a fondness for the forest, particularly in the mountains, because there's such a variety of perspectives. You can be in the middle of a dense area of trees, and suddenly there's a clearing, light everywhere, the temperature changes, the ground is drier; and then again back into the trees for a while; then, above the tree line, it's more continuous, drier again, but you see all that variety below. I'm not a fanatic about hiking, backpacking and so on, and I don't need to walk in order to think or find inspiration; but walking, particularly in the forest, exerts a considerable attraction on me.

Then, starting with the Piano Concerto, I became more and more conscious of the power of writing, and listening to music as a kind of journey of discovery. The Concerto was that kind of experience for me, traveling through different densities, different intensities of light and darkness, seeing far then looking closely at details. I managed it better than in any previous piece, I think, although I had been trying at least since *Lichtung* ("clearing," in German, by the way).

  - And the last word of Thomas Bernhard's Correction.

Yes indeed; as I said before, that book had made a very profound impression on me from the time I first read it, in '79 or '80 I believe. That was the first novel I ever read by Bernhard, and it is still the one I like best. I had had the idea at the time of reproducing in music the typical dense and completely continuous prose he uses in *Correction* and a few other books. That's what happened at the beginning of the Trio.

  - All the large-scale works you wrote between 1984 and 1991 were based on the idea of formal revelation that we discussed a moment ago. After Un Feu distinct, *in 1991, the next large piece is the Piano Concerto: did it also make use of that idea?*

Yes and no. When I started to work with this kind of formal design, at the time of *So er*, I was thinking that the long-term goal was eventually to manage to write a piece in which the ending would somehow write itself, so that it would be possible to extract the essence of the piece. So I decided to prepare myself consciously for several years through the type of organization that the formal revelation required, so that someday, perhaps, I would be able to write an ending that arrived through a revelation of what the piece was about. When I wrote the five pieces I mentioned earlier, I deliberately decided what the ending would be, before starting to write the pieces themselves. By doing this, I was progressively preparing myself to be able to write a piece in which the ending would appear as the collecting–selecting (to re-use the image from Heidegger) of the rest of the piece. I was hoping that it would be possible to train myself over the years to realize such an ending spontaneously, without the preplanning that went into those five pieces. The real test would then be to find out if the process of revelation could work spontaneously, for me, rather than being staged just for the listener to experience. In that sense, it was a little like the idea I mentioned earlier, to rewrite the same piece over and over (here, using the same formal design over and over), until its real origin would be revealed to me.

  With the Piano Concerto, I decided to jump into the pool and see if I could write the piece without having planned its ending beforehand, while still using the same formal idea. What I discovered was that there was no organized entity that could appear in this way (such as a melody or a set of chords); that probably shouldn't have been a surprise to me, because it wasn't planned that way, of course. What I could then have done was to construct an ending by reading through the piece and selecting elements to make up such a construct, but that would have been forced, and not along the lines of what I was trying to achieve with this project. Something, however, did emerge, of a different nature: it was a sonority, the sound of the third, which had been so prevalent throughout the piece. It seemed to encompass all the figures that contained it. Once I realized that, it became possible to use the source of this sound image to conclude the Concerto: the piano reaching into the highest register, with chords based predominantly on thirds.

The other important aspect of this ending is the fact that it played a role of reconciliation between the two main forces that interact in a conflictual manner for most of the piece: the linear and the vertical writing. There are many instances in the piece of heavy vertical sonorities trying to annihilate melodic lines. This is often heard as a conflict between the orchestra and the piano, but basically the whole piece was constructed on that dichotomy: horizontal lines opposed to, or becoming, vertical sonorities. This was realized either through the classic isomorphism of melodic and harmonic intervals, or by a more abstract derivation of rhythmic lines (time) into vertical intervals (spaces).[13] That aspect of the Concerto was very consciously worked out, as opposed to the process of the revealed ending I referred to before. The vertical/horizontal opposition was supposed to parallel the two opposite identities already in place: on the one hand the individual, constantly trying to express its identity; and on the other hand, the mass, here constituted by the orchestra sitting behind the pianist. That idea was of course outside the realm of pure music, moving instead into the abstraction of symbolic representation and, more generally, into the oppositions of internal/external representations of the world. I wanted to reflect (on) the fact that what we refer to as the "outside" world is just as much a part of ourselves as the supposedly inner one. So that was one aspect of the piece. The other main dimension I explored through the revelation of the ending was, on the other hand, realized purely in musical terms, as I just explained before. I think that the whole formal process gained a decisive richness from the fact that these two dimensions, the symbolic and the musical, join in the end to support each other, while remaining conceptually independent. Symbolically, again, the opposition individual/group, or inside/outside, is somewhat reconciled by the concluding piano sonority: in the higher register, the piano sounds can be heard both as harmony and as individual tones (much more so than in the lower register). So the typical massive and somewhat undifferentiated sounds of the heavy chords played by the orchestra, particularly in the first half of the piece, where this vertical/horizontal opposition is most clearly and outwardly enacted, become at the end much more differentiated because of the register and the specific intervals used. This is precisely the way in which both dimensions, the symbolic and the musical, become unified, expressing at the same time the reconciliation and unification of the oppositions.

> *- You mentioned in the program notes to the Piano Concerto the social dimension inherent in the idea of confrontation between the individual and the ensemble. Is that the symbolic dimension you were just referring to?*

Yes, I was quite involved with that kind of idea at the time, probably because I was trying to define more clearly to myself my social role, as composer and teacher, as well as, more generally, human being. I felt quite at odds with the "group," whatever that might represent, the "others," the "world," and so forth. So writing the piece was a way to work that out, to discover how real the problem was, and what I could do about it.

It is clear that this particular type of social conflict experienced by the composer as a confrontation probably started around the time of Beethoven, when the composer's relationship to society began to change markedly from what it had been in preceding centuries. At that time the social "relevance" of the composer was brought into question, in the sense that he couldn't be integrated into the social fabric as smoothly as before (the masculine pronoun here is crucial, because the situation was rather different for female composers, who had practically no role in the professional musical world of the time); he had to justify his own relevance to society by becoming an entertainer. The composer became progressively less integrated into a specific group (the court of noblemen) and more and more nomadic. He had to survive on the fringes of society. By and large the twentieth century created new opportunities for the composer, by institutionalizing the teaching of music in organized schools. This circumstance is of course most prevalent in the United States—but, ironically, it has led to another kind of alienation for the composer from the rest of society, because there are practically no public resources devoted to music outside the schools and universities. That is really dramatic, culturally speaking, as far as the integration of art in the consciousness of the society is concerned.

So that image of the isolated individual who has to justify his or her (we can now use both genders) choice of career, in general in opposition to what the rest of society feels is useful and marketable, is more real now than ever. I personally experienced this isolation for many years, in my own family. To stay on the personal level a little longer, I can now see that in most of my music until the Piano Concerto, the oppositions of organizations I referred to earlier act as a sort of psychological working through of those tensions. Oftentimes, the systematic type of organization is being subverted by alien elements, the bits that try to escape through the cracks that I mentioned earlier. This image certainly makes sense on the personal level as well as the more general, social one, which I experienced deeply for years. I simply generalized it, or brought it out of myself —ex-pressed it—in the Piano Concerto, because that medium offered a more obvious potential to realize it musically.

It's easy to see that all these "social" considerations came to a head in the course of the twentieth century, as is reflected in many artistic forms at the time. Think, for example, of the number of writers (Beckett, Musil, Walser, and later the French existentialists and the Nouveau Roman novelists, among others) who tried to describe their alienated condition, their feeling of separateness from what they perceived as the outside "world": the opposition between the self and the world and—eventually—the questioning of the very notion of self. So the sense of conflict that I used as a starting point for the Piano Concerto, between the inner and the outer worlds, the inner self (insofar as it can be conscious of itself as autonomous) and the world is nothing new; all these ideas have been at work for a long time in our civilization. They originate from the fact that we have developed a very strong and marvelous capacity to analyze the world, to separate all its components into isolated little bits, in order to examine them rigorously. The problem is that we've lost the ability we used to have to see the world as a whole, in the old mystical way. So we end up with that general feeling that everything is isolated, alienated from us. I believe, however, that we can bring a sense of reconciliation, by turning ourselves inward again in order to observe, in qualitative terms, rather than only quantitative ones, how the world inhabits us and how we shape it ourselves, and not necessarily always for the worse. We can get to the next step without losing what we've gained so far. It's not a question of denying everything and rejecting what we've discovered already.

- But that sense of alienation is rather pervasive in our culture. It's been documented by many artists.

Yes, of course, that's what I was referring to, that total infusion of our culture with a sense of alienation. It is curious how this has progressively developed into a sort of fascination for the alienated conditions in themselves, wherever and in whichever form they have appeared. Nowadays, it's quite similar to the lure of the "exotic" that was so pervasive in the

nineteenth century, of whatever was outside the dominant culture, spatially speaking: foreign places, foreign cultures, and so on. Now that
everybody travels a lot more, what used to be exotic has become more
commonplace; and of course the attitude of looking at other cultures as
less developed, quaint, and so on has been so much criticized as cultural
misunderstanding and colonialism that we've learned to look at them
differently. What hasn't gone away, though, is the tendency to believe
that we're too "normal," too much like our neighbor; so whatever can
distinguish us from others is interesting, and the more extreme the better. The more we don't understand, the less we try, because it's easier to
put it in the "genius" or "deranged" box. There it's inaccessible, there's
no discussion needed; and of course, the more inaccessible it is, the
more it fascinates. Examples abound here: Nietzsche, Schumann,
Walser—not that these people didn't create great things while their
minds were clear, but when they start to wander off, we cannot judge
them in the same way (in the case of Nietzsche, obviously, creative activity simply stopped altogether).

> *- You seem to exhibit a somewhat moralizing attitude toward those who
> are fascinated by the "margins" of society, who try to discover original life
> there, but isn't your obsession with rules and that "music trying to escape
> through the cracks" reflective of your own difficulty with this issue?*

I'm not moralizing, I'm just saying that being in psychological difficulty
is not a guarantee of great creative potential. But, yes, it's true that I was
fascinated by this myself for a long time. It's so prevalent in many layers
of the intellectual landscape of our day that it's ridiculous to pretend that
it doesn't have any influence. The temptation toward the "chaotic" in
general, toward that which destroys order, has been a constant force in
my work, from the Trio on. In fact, it's even more complicated than that
because I think that there is already a sort of perverse pleasure in the
establishment of constraints, of severe rules in order to limit oneself, to
test one's limits. I realize that every time I start a piece: there is often a
period during which I hesitate to engage in extremely constraining systems, built on arbitrary rules.[14] I go back and forth for a while, unsure as
to whether I should lock myself up, so to speak, or let doors open. These
constraints exert a sort of fascination because they offer a sense of
unknown challenge, of uncertainty (will I manage to live with them and
write something after all, or is it all going to fall apart?), while at the same
time they repel because of their limitations. There's a level of violence
exerted upon oneself as soon as the first ideas are formed. Then there's
the other violence, the one that reacts against the rules, once they've

been chosen. That's almost a revenge. So, then, it's a matter of finding a course that can be steered between the two extremes, rather than yield to one side only.

- These two tendencies were pretty fundamental to the composition of the string sextet (Die innere Grenze), *weren't they?*

That's right. I already explained how they first arose in the Trio. Another example is *Lichtung*, where I inserted in a few places a kind of small "chorale," very slow, that stops the flow of the music (Example 4). It was a way of creating a little zone of reflection, in the middle of the action, as well as bringing in something completely foreign to the rest of the piece. It's been different in each piece where I've done that.

EXAMPLE 4: DURAND, *LICHTUNG*, "CHORALE" SECTION

- Are there other, purely musical purposes for these inserts?

I have already mentioned that they offered a chance to bring a spontaneous element into a constraining system—so, early on, I did this primarily
for subversion, out of an urge to rebel against the rules that I set in the
first place, to undermine order. Now my purposes are not so negative any
more, and I still use the idea occasionally. I did it again in the more
recent *La Terre et le feu*, with short passages that come straight out of my
organ piece, *Les Raisons des forces mouvantes*. I do it when I find that it
adds something to the general context, a depth of perspective. There can
be other reasons: curiosity about the unknown, for what is beyond the
context of the world circumscribed in the piece; the need for escape
hatches from the confines of the systems, the need to create a distance
from which to reflect on the order and "logic" created by the systems.
The inserts then seem to ask the question "Why?" without attempting to
answer it.

There's a painting by Pollock, *Blue Poles*, that fascinated me some years
ago, in which we can see the conflicts between two different types of elements. The general texture is typical Pollock dripping, very dense, and
then there are these long blue lines that cut across, from bottom to top
(or top to bottom). They seem to take on a foreground role but I find it
interesting that they interact with the background in a very dynamic way.
They don't just stand there in the front because the background doesn't
let them, it's so rich and alive, it can't stay back there passively. In fact the
poles look like extensions of the smaller straight lines that are found
throughout the background. At the same time, the poles themselves are
crossed and messed up by blobs and curves, which reflect some shapes of
the background. So there's a great dynamism between the levels, they
clash with and confront each other. Now, compared to techniques such
as collages, my inserts might seem a bit timid, shall we say. That's because
I'm not interested in violent stylistic contrasts. I am more interested in
the fine line that defines coherence: when do you perceive something as
not belonging to the context, and how does the perception adapt and
makes sense of it, or not?

- Is that what you tried to do in the sextet?

Yes. Chronologically speaking, though, I think I first saw *Blue Poles* after
I had written the sextet, so that wasn't the impetus for it. I was just men-
tioning it to indicate that particular type of relationship between formal
elements in the painting, one that bears some similarity to my piece. In
Die innere Grenze, for the first time, I made a conscious effort at devising

two unrelated systems of organization. I mentioned earlier the long polyphonic passage that ends the piece: I derived from it a number of segments that I used in various ways to form the main sections of the sextet. That was the first level of organization, which had to do again with the idea of formal revelation. But the other thing that I wanted to do in there was to expand considerably on the idea of the inserts, as these cracks that put the construction in danger. This time, they had to be on a much larger scale than what I had done before. So to make up those inserts, I came up with the idea of using my String Trio. Since the score of the Trio was written with two music systems per page, I had twice a string trio on each page, made up of two violins, two violas, and two cellos. So I took a scissors, cut each page of the Trio into several bits, and then shuffled all the cuttings. After they were all out of order, I simply rewrote the resulting music, in the order in which the fragments had fallen, and that gave me a new sextet that I could incorporate into the other one. The Trio had become a *found object.*

- This is getting more serious: a stylistic suicide?

A structural one, maybe, but the image of the suicide seems a bit excessive in this case, don't you think?

- Well, it brings us back to Bernhard's final correction. Do you prefer to call it recycling?

Either way, my purpose was to test the limits of structural coherence, and to do that, I worked the resulting Trio music into the flow of the sextet so that, at times, the Trio music was very clearly interrupting the sextet, usually because it is heard as violent outbursts—whereas, at other times, it was completely seamlessly blended. The very beginning of the piece shows an example of blending. The first five measures are from the sextet construction, then the Trio enters apparently in the middle of the phrase without any break or change in texture. The Trio is easy to recognize at that point, though, because it happens to be the beginning of that piece that is used in three of the voices. I wanted to see what kind of energy would come out if one mixed together two systems that hadn't been conceived together (Examples 5A and 5B).

- You could have actually conceived two different systems, couldn't you?

Yes of course, but it was very tempting to use the Trio because of the similarity of layout on the score I mentioned, and because it gave me a

EXAMPLE 5A: STRING TRIO CUTTINGS

chance to play with the element of historical/personal time in a constructive manner, so to speak: the fact that the Trio had been written so much
earlier meant that I would have enough distance from it to make that
kind of play possible.

> *- To go back again to Bernhard, was that another way of "correcting" the
> Trio, as you had dreamed years earlier?*

I don't think so. The correction in Bernhard concerns the reduction of a
text to its most essential form, which is not what I did in this case because
I used the whole piece, albeit in a new ordering of its fragments. Maybe it
was a way of forgetting the Trio, or rather of putting it behind me for
good. Just before the sextet, I had used the same kind of string writing in
Lichtung, so it was time to move on. The main point is that this way of

EXAMPLE 5B: DURAND, *DIE INNERE GRENZE*, PAGE 2 OF SCORE

working was the largest-scale enacting of oppositions I had realized so far. The Piano Concerto was another way to achieve that dichotomy, but with the two different types of organization being superimposed on each other, rather than generally juxtaposed, as in the sextet.

III.

- From our vantage point now, the line appears to be more or less continuous from as far back as the String Trio all the way up to the Concerto. If that piece was the end of the progression, what happened after that?

A bit of a slump, I'm afraid. I didn't write much music between 1995 and '97, just a small piece for electronic carillon, and the organ piece, *Les Raisons des forces mouvantes*, which took me a long time because I was trying to break away from old habits that had accumulated up until the Concerto. I think what happened was that I had been writing music with many conflicts and oppositions, such as those I mentioned earlier in the Piano Concerto between improvised and strict layers, or more generally between constrictive systems and spontaneous gestures—and then suddenly, after having experimented with the idea of environment in the Concerto, I had no more reason to build up such obvious conflicts in the formal designs. The environment allowed me to introduce these oppositions between systems and spontaneity, strict organization at some level and the possibility of unpredictable reactions at another, on a different level, psychologically and technically. They could now interact in more subtle, less directly conflictual ways. But I didn't realize that at the time. All I knew was that I was very tired of these types of conflicts, and couldn't find a way to make them work any more—I didn't know why. It wasn't until *Athanor* that I really understood the power of the idea of compositional environment, for me in any case. I stress that personal aspect because it really originated from a very personal idea of musical drama, which up until then I had conceived of as made up of staged conflicts between different types of approaches to writing music. In spite of the need to break certain habits, I know that there were already seeds in my music before the Concerto for what came afterwards. That's what finally allowed me to move on.

- Strict, free organizations. This dichotomy calls to mind Barraqué's Piano Sonata, on which you spent quite a lot of time during your studies in Germany.

Indeed, the Barraqué Sonata has been at the back of my mind ever since I started to analyze it, around my first year in Freiburg. Somehow it's been a catalyst for many ideas I've had over the years: the opposition between strictly organized techniques and the less controlled results of spontaneous writing; but also the basic formal layout in two parts, where the first part is generally fast, and the second one slow, also characteristic of the Piano Concerto. I like that layout because it has something unfinished about it, it denies the return of the fast part typical of a lot of previous music in history. In contrast to the typical three-part form (based on the *ABA* scheme), it seems to project the music beyond itself, to open the space after the end of the slow part. In Barraqué's piece, the second part of course is, emotionally speaking at least, a disintegration of the

musical discourse, as it had been elaborated in the first half. The return of
the passages from the first half, now in retrograde in the second half, is a
little rigid in terms of formal momentum, but it has an interesting metaphorical value. More remarkable, I think, are the various ways in which
the musical lines toward the end refuse to go forward: the sequences of
trills, and especially the use of the chords in the last few pages. That led
me to think of vertical sonorities in terms of their potential for violence
and aggressive negation of the lines. That's a kind of gesture that is quite
common in my music up until the Concerto. It had a lot of resonance for
me, after I heard it in Barraqué's Sonata. Finally, I realized much later
that the Barraqué piece, in the way it ends with the original form of the
row, is somewhat similar to my idea of formal "revelation" that we discussed earlier.[15] The Sonata is one of the pieces that has had the most
lasting influence on me, although I don't listen to it much any more. I
don't care so much for its systematic working out of rigid serial processes
and the way it inhabits time, its proportions and so on. But its image, its
aura, is still with me in some way.

  - Are there any other pieces that have been important to you?

Well, most of Berg's music, as I said earlier, and in particular *Lulu* and
the *Lyric Suite*. Other than that, I am interested in many types of music,
Western or not, and I often find bits and pieces in many different places
that seem to respond to particular questions I have at any given time. For
example, toward the end of my studies at Stony Brook, I spent quite a bit
of time with Stockhausen's *Inori*. That was when I was starting to discover in other composers precedents for my own interest in structural
hierarchies. I was looking for examples of music which had overcome the
kind of amorphous quality of the serial music of the '50s, and
Stockhausen seemed to embody that more than any other composer at
the time, among those who had been on that path at any rate. During the
last few years, I've looked quite a bit into Scelsi's music because I sense
there's something in it that I can explore.

  - The spectral aspect?

No, not at all. The opposite in fact: the line. But we'll talk about that
when I'm done with it, if you don't mind.

  *- You just evoked the layout of Barraqué's Sonata as very significant for
  your approach to formal design. Can you share your thoughts about musical form?*

I would say that what used to be traditionally referred to as form, which was really just the basic layout—first theme, second theme, and so on—is only one small aspect of the form, even in tonal music where those categories are still broadly used and relatively easy to see. The form is constituted essentially and exhaustively by the interaction of moments, by the way in which the moments liberate energy and momentum through the time of the piece, the way in which they radiate outside of and beyond themselves— project themselves ahead—and the way in which, at times, they attract attention to themselves, or recede at other times. It's about processes generating other processes, concepts growing out of one another, rather than static elements interacting with each other.

- Isn't that a very teleological way of looking at form?

Not necessarily. There's no denying that music fundamentally progresses through time, and time goes in a forward direction, in spite of and concurrently with the fact that our consciousness doesn't always function linearly. Nevertheless, what hits our senses is chronological. It's the consciousness of the events that can then take different temporal paths. In fact, this difference between physical time, so to speak, and perceptual time is precisely what makes us aware that we constantly establish a hierarchy between the events we perceive. And ultimately, in our consciousness, we can achieve simultaneity of presence. That's the highest form of consciousness. So the question of teleology is rather minor when you consider the bigger picture.

Another thing that I find fascinating, on the subject of perceptual time, is that I see two fundamental and very different ways of listening to music. The first one is based on direct experience, either listening to live music or a recording, or playing an instrument. In that situation, the listener is living in the stream of time, even if the experience is somewhat discontinuous because of the various recalls and expectations that the discourse constantly offers. The second type of listening is retrospective listening, which occurs when one tries to recall a piece of music from memory, either with all its details or just as a sort of afterimage. That listening can be much more elastic. You can slow down or speed up at will, depending on what you want to pay attention to, or how well you remember singular moments, because of the amount of presence those singular moments happen to have in your mind. It's actually quite remarkable how different this kind of presence can be from the presence of the live listening experience: it's much more capricious, much more unpredictable. You can slow down the time of inner listening at a passage that you don't remember so well, or on which you want to dwell more attentively. You can also distort what you remember; I often have those short-circuit types of memory lapses, when I'm singing a piece I know in my head and it suddenly branches out into another one, or into something that doesn't exist yet. That kind of distorted retrospective listening is quite fascinating because it can become entirely fictional.[16]

In fact, it often works with my own music, in the way a piece might generate seeds for another. In the last few years, for example, there have been at least two obvious instances of pieces that kept coming back in my head in a distorted manner after I had written them, and both came from my *Au-delà, Cinq Etudes pour Piccolo*. The first example is the second Etude, which for some reason started to sound in my head like a peasant dance, after I'd finished the piccolo version. It was slightly distorted, and without quarter tones, with a heavy string sound. That's how I started to write the *Five Musical Tales*, with the idea of the peasant dance that became the first of the *Tales*. It's funny to compare them and to realize how the undulating and light figures of the piccolo piece become the heavy and dark tune of the dance. The dance had originated from a distorted memory of the piccolo line (Examples 6A and 6B).

The second example is the fourth of the piccolo pieces: for weeks after I had finished it, I kept hearing the first couple of measures on the oboe. I don't know why, but that particular gesture, the repeated note and the downward inflection that follows, kept coming back in my mind with an oboe sound. It wasn't anything specific about the piccolo piece, it was just the memory of this gesture, the kind of expressivity it recalled, that seemed well suited to the oboe. Eventually, when I started to write the oboe concerto, *La Terre et le feu*, I devised a large-scale plan to integrate the whole piccolo piece into the oboe part. In that case, I didn't work exactly from an imprecise memory, as I was suggesting before, but from the original image itself, and that became the basis of a specific type of reading of the piccolo piece by which its semantic content became totally transformed in the oboe part of *La Terre et le feu*.

So, to come back to this idea of how we establish a hierarchy in the perception of music, what we're really looking at here are basic entities, moments of the musical discourse, or textures—at this point it doesn't really matter what one calls them—acting as individual centers in a kind of force-field, to borrow a term from Adorno.

- Because of their potential to take specific directions?

Not exactly. The idea of something having a certain potential is too general. Everything has *a* potential to become something else; everything changes all the time. As soon as something enters the realm of time, it is

EXAMPLE 6A: DURAND, *AU-DELÀ*, II

bound to *become* something else. So the idea of field doesn't define a potential so much as what is already there; and that has more to do with

EXAMPLE 6B: DURAND, *FIVE MUSICAL TALES*, I

how important that something is felt to be at a particular time. One extreme case that might be easy to represent is when the moment has certain connotations built in: connotation in the sense of what one hears, how one relates it to what is already known or has already been experienced, how it reminds one of something else heard before, in another context. To refer to Adorno again, that's part of what defines musical "material": its historical accretion. The image of connotation is only used here as an example of how a moment can draw attention onto itself. It doesn't have so much to do with where it's trying to go at a particular time, although inevitably that's part of it, as with how much importance one attaches to the particular moment, how much it stands out from the rest for certain reasons. This importance creates an immediate hierarchy in the listening, whether we want it or not. It also creates a certain distance from the event, because the affective engagement is different from what happens with something one does not know at all: the connoted moment becomes more of an "object," in the sense that it is immediately clear that, in itself, it doesn't represent the subject/composer (the subject is then experienced in the context in which the object is placed). This context works at specific as well as general levels: a single chord, for example, that is particularly reminiscent of other music(s), or a timbral sonority, even a global gesture spread over many bars (a constantly rising line, for example, usually has connotations of trying to reach somewhere). There are a number of such connotations that create a fairly similar response at any given time, so it's obviously important to be aware of what they are, of how generally shared they are at any given time, to become aware of the fact that they have become "objectified."

So, in general terms, the idea of center inside a field, or rather of center generating a field, is usually a musical idea chosen by the composer for specific, personal reasons, which generates enough of an aura around itself to be perceived as particularly active within its surroundings, active in the sense of creating a certain impetus, a movement forward, or a certain affective resonance which can have to do with memory, in a personal or historical sense. We could call that its degree of presence at that particular moment. These resonating moments are sometimes difficult to control because they can easily take over on their own and it is then very hard to "stitch" them back to the rest of the piece. We've seen that numerous times with the technique of musical collage, where pieces keep being pulled in all kinds of directions without ever recovering their own identity, so to speak. But that's the specific problem of historical resonance. For example, in a piece like Zimmermann's *Photoptosis*, which is one of the most successful works among those that involve quotations, the sudden irruption of the quotations has a very literary meaning; they function insofar as one has to *think* about the reason for their presence in the context. But in purely musical terms, the quotations have an unbearable amount of presence that damages what's near them. Another well-known example of collage, the third movement of Berio's *Sinfonia*, is less jarring because everything is borrowed, so there is no strong shift in the levels of presence between the various elements. There is no level perceived as the "composer's level" as opposed to the borrowed levels that try to converse with the main one. In the Berio example, the "main" level is already a quotation (from Mahler), and so are all the other levels. It's all fake, so to speak, and one doesn't hear, in one place, The Composer, and in the others the quotations. That doesn't make it a better or worse piece of music; the conflicts of presence are just not as noticeable, that's all.

   - So these centers you mentioned before are not necessarily recognizable upon listening?

Not always, although most of the time they have to be, otherwise they can't generate any momentum. But indeed there are cases where they are not perceived at first as decisive moments, consciously, although they are nevertheless sensed as important (it's up to the composer to create those opportunities). In that case their formal power is noticed only afterwards, when they take on a more foreground role, or after repeated listenings. This often happens when one hears a piece for the first time, even in older music. You can't take in everything, you just try to keep actively involved, in particular when it seems that, at a specific moment, something of importance is happening.

   In the early atonal music of Schoenberg and Webern, it's often very hard to figure out immediately what is more important and what is less so. It sounds as if everything is essential, until you become quite familiar with it, through analysis. In Schoenberg's music, for example, motives heard in the background of an accompaniment become a main theme later on, and vice versa. So the question of centers can be quite elusive. A center can be defined quite clearly as a main theme, for example, in which case everybody can agree on the fact that it's a center in the piece, but it can also be defined, so to speak, by what it is able to generate in the rest of the piece; in that case, it's harder to say exactly what it is, or to be more specific, one can only find how it becomes elevated to the rank of center by analyzing carefully how its various constituents radiate throughout the piece. The interesting point is that we as listeners must constantly re-evaluate how we perceive centers, because one idea can be heard as an important center at a particular moment, and then recede into the background when other centers appear that turn out to be more important in the unfolding of the form.

   - And that leads to the idea of field. That comes from physics, right?[17]

Exactly, although we find it already in Adorno's writings (as *force-field*). The field is then the area in which a particular center is active, be it in the foreground or the background, its space of resonance, so to speak, either at the moment of occurrence or in relation to the changes occurring to the center across large time spans. Fields are related within the piece through their being occupied by their centers, either because the centers are clearly present, or because they somehow radiate their presence, even though they can be separated by vast intervals of time.

- Why are these notions of center and field more relevant than the old categories of motif, theme, and the like?

A center isn't necessarily a theme or a motif, or a "figure," in Ferneyhough's sense of the term, for that matter.[18] It can be, if that's the way the music is constructed, but it's also possible to imagine a moment of music that has a high degree of presence but is not at all "figural" in the sense usually meant by such terms as motif and theme. Even a single pitch can take on this kind of strong formal role. For example, the whole first section of *Athanor* is built on that principle. There's very little figural activity for almost 100 measures, yet a lot of things are happening on the local as well as global level.

As I was saying before, a center is more generally defined as a moment of particular resonance within the piece, or the movement. It's a moment filled with a particularly relevant activity, defined as relevant either in the moment of its occurrence or retrospectively—sometimes much later. The point is that, because of this resonance, it projects dynamically, either forward or backward. So it is part of a momentum which activates strands of the music. That's the main thing: it is dynamic, it pushes the attention of the listener in specific directions. That's also why the image of field is particularly evocative, because embedded in it is the idea of a physical space, of a continuity because of the coherence and similarity of what constitutes it. This relation to the physical space is a rather static image, but added to it is the more dynamic aspect of tension and pushing/pulling that exists in the language of physics, as well as in anything evolving in time.

The other thing about the question of centers and fields is that centers are heavily dependent on each other. You can't imagine a music with just one such center. There's the implicit notion that the whole thing is based on hierarchies, where some centers are more important than others because they have more "presence," either because they take more room in the whole or because they are simply more striking. This distinction is important, incidentally, because it points to the difficult differentiation between quantity and quality. A center that comes back many times, even in different guises, is easy to recognize and identify as such (think of some of Beethoven's themes). But a center that relies only on its striking quality and doesn't come back much, if at all, is more ambiguous. Centers of this type usually have a less immediately dynamic role in the form, in fact they can seem at first to stop everything, to call attention on themselves at the expense of what came before. But their aura can project over the whole thing, and give it a particular tone, an atmosphere that permeates the rest of the piece. A particularly striking and unusual modulation, for example, can do that in some tonal pieces of the past. More recently, in some of Messiaen's music, the objects have to be very striking because they don't develop much, just come back once or twice; among the many instances of this kind of technique in his music, the first movement of *Chronochromie*, for example, plays precisely with the interaction of sections that are repeated, with variations, and sections that occur only once. So the hierarchy between them is really established on a qualitative level: Which of these passages are more striking than the others, and why are they more striking? This can work within a particular movement, as in the case of *Chronochromie*, but also on a more general level, if a passage is, for example, extremely different from the usual manner of the composer, or really completely original by comparison to any other work of music.

Another approach to the idea of center can be seen in Webern's music, before it becomes strictly serial. There's a sense that these pieces, in part because of their brevity, in part because of the actions of centers, expand beyond their actual duration. One can't always perceive any direct relation between a center and its "radiations," but each of them is active even if it's not heard clearly. Often that's because the relations are not necessarily of pitch or rhythm, and are not necessarily perceptible. A similar length, or a similar occupation of a metric unit, can be enough to create a field in which a center radiates in different ways. There's a wonderful such example in his Op. 6 no. 3, where the individual durations of the initial melody in the viola are found again in several other places, but with different rhythms to inhabit them (in the middle section, the little ostinato in the flutes and horn, for example). So in this case, the durations create a certain type of relation (temporal) between the centers, and in consequence define a field. In fact this whole piece is an extraordinary study in exchanges between meter, duration, and rhythmic patterns, and how they constitute the form itself. At the same time, this viola melody, echoed in the trumpet in the last measures, is active as a center of a completely different field: the beginning of the initial viola line and the trumpet melody at the end share similar intervallic content and contour. This property creates another type of relationship inside that field, which in this case is more easily perceived. In fact, this audible connection is reinforced by the similarity of timbres because the trumpet color of the end was already used for the chords under the viola melody at the beginning of the piece. Similarly, the string sound of the viola is echoed faintly by the repeated note in the harp, at the end. So there we have a center (the viola melody) which connects with other centers in different ways, each of them generating its own field.

This multi-directional activity, where a center is projected forward, leads to Christopher Alexander's idea of a "vector field," because that sort of field encompasses not only the quality of presence of a particular moment but also its direction, a fundamental aspect of music, since it works in time. That's also where the idea of center differs from Ferney-hough's figure, because a center can remain completely unused in the piece, except for the one moment of its occurrence (as in the Messiaen example I mentioned before). Because of its presence, the center projects itself, even in spite of its subsequent physical absence, over a much larger scale. It changes some, or all, of the perspective by having appeared just once. In fact, this points to another kind of center to which I was allud-ing earlier, the one that is not to be found concretely in other places of the piece, but is defined more by a certain similarity in its fields. In this case, the fields point to the center, which might not be "present" at all.

- That again seems to correspond to these inserts we were discussing earlier. Is there a relation to this idea of the cracks, where you could introduce alien material?

Certainly, although I wasn't very aware of this idea of presence at the time. But I realized clearly that these inserts could project an aura beyond themselves within a piece. In that sense, they create fields of activity which relate to each other. The center of such a field cannot be perceived, though, because it's not explicitly presented in the piece. For example, in the case of the Trio being inserted in *Die innere Grenze*, the moments that could be perceived as centers in the Trio can no longer be perceived as such in the sextet, because their presentations are frag-mented, and sometimes even assimilated into the sextet itself. But it doesn't mean that they are not active any more; their quality of presence has changed, which make them act differently inside the sextet. As I said before, I'm curious about testing the limits of the coherence I create with the use of systems, and the effect of their subversion. So the image of subversion is not necessarily negative, because I end up with a new qual-ity of presence.

- You use the word "presence" a lot.

Yes, because that term brings attention to a specific quality of observation. You can't analyze everything in music just by observing discrete elements. The presence of a thing, or of an event, is the way in which one senses the present in it—as opposed to its past, which is the concept of it, its abstraction. Sensing the presence of a thing or an event is experiencing its immediacy, either before one develops a sense of it as a concept, or by separating oneself from its conceptual aspect. So it is not an intellectual experience; nor is it a sensorial one. It is about experiencing the thing speaking itself, rather than perceiving what it says—an intuitive realization. In music, presence is that particular quality of certain moments of a work that are immediately recognized as more important than the others, although one can't always define exactly what makes them more important. It has to do with their specific constitution, the formal weight they acquire from a particular structural importance; but it can also be due to a singular originality, to the fact that they don't sound like anything else in the piece, or more generally like nothing else in other music; in other words, the way they draw attention to themselves, by whatever means. And again, by drawing attention to themselves, in the moment of their unfolding, they immediately open up a large perceptual space, because they just grab you by the neck and tell you: "Hey look here, look through this window, it's important!" That's the special quality that can define a strong center: it has more presence than other moments. So it's a term that is useful to point to something whose behavior needs to be observed closely, even if, from a normal analytical point of view, all one can say about it is that it has a major third and a couple of minor seconds in it. Oftentimes its more specific qualities are its "tone," its character, its inflection. Those are what make up its unique character. But of course, every moment in music has a certain quality of presence. So the idea is to try to observe the amount of presence, qualitatively speaking. The greater the presence, the more important the center will seem.

- How does that work in your music?

What we're really talking about here is form again: when you try to see how those basic "elements" are transformed and how processes generate each other, you realize that cataloguing intervals, or sets, or rhythmic patterns only tells you how similar or different the structures are; it doesn't tell you which ones are drawing more attention than others. That's because this quality has nothing to do with statistics.

The fact is, when you're composing, you're not aware of the relations between all the bits and pieces. You know the ones you're trying to set up, but more often than not you just end up with a lot of connections because all that is working in the back of your mind, without you being really conscious of it. What you do know, though, is: "Yes, that's right in this place, it feels like it's working." Then you leave it. And that is precisely because what you've assessed is that it has the right presence, at this particular moment in the piece. You've actually experienced the degree of presence of that center, assessed more or less subconsciously its field (in constituents and directions), and drawn from that source. Later you might be able to analyze what you've done and find hidden relationships. There's the story of Schoenberg wanting to rewrite the second theme of his *Kammersymphonie* because he thought it didn't have any relation to the first theme. Well, many years later, he did find that there was some relationship, even though it was a rather obscure one; but it was sufficient to satisfy him.

So, in the composition, I don't feel that I'm working so much with musical "objects" as with something that has this or that degree of presence, or a certain quality of moving forward, or not. And I use the feeling I have about that quality to expand it or cut it short, whatever is necessary for the whole. That work involves to some extent thinking of and hearing the connections created by the intervals, rhythmic patterns, instrumental colors, and so on, but not only these; the more elusive part of the work is in deciding how to present the whole thing, how to give it the right "tone," the right character at every moment, how to create the momentum needed. One needs to stay connected to the source from which the first impetus came, and to keep pulling at it—to maintain concentration and focus, really, in order to remain open. The rest doesn't need to be all that conscious. But the more experience you acquire with this kind of concentration, the more you can be conscious of it and control what you take from it and where you put it. It's not just improving the craft, really, it's about developing, digging inside yourself to find where your source is.

- *It sounds a little mystical, that sense of openness, doesn't it?*

Yes, of course. In fact the whole idea of "revelation," that I mentioned earlier in relation to the form, although derived from my reading of Heidegger, also draws on that realm of spiritual resonance. I was quite conscious of it at the time, without really knowing where it would take me. It was only later that I very progressively realized the possibility of a spiritual context for music. At the time of the formal revelation, I was just cautiously opening the door, staying alert and ready either to go through it or to close it altogether.

Another aspect of this idea of openness is the way in which I prepare the ground, establish the boundaries of what I want to explore, open a space in which I can exist as a composer, for the time of a specific piece. It's like meditation: you can daydream all day, thinking you're meditating. But you're getting nowhere. That is why, in the traditions that have developed meditation techniques for centuries, there are very strict rules for preparing oneself, physically and mentally. The same goes for creative preparation. Of course, you need to train your hand continuously, so to speak; one can always improve the basic technical craft. But then comes the question of how to prepare oneself for a particular piece, for the particular kind of expression one is after at that particular moment in life. That's what I call the "environment" of the piece. Is this a good time now to approach that subject?

- Certainly.

The environment is conceived to allow for the possibility of spontaneous choice at every moment of the composition, without losing sight of the whole. It allows one to keep in mind the relation between local and global levels. The limits offered by the environment (a set of pitches, or of harmonic colors, a temporal frame, and so forth) provide the *possibility* for discovery, at the moment of writing the notes on paper. Ideally, they offer the opportunity to be completely open to the intuitions that arise, because the boundaries as they are defined beforehand allow one to know the context in which the work is going to emerge. The making of the environment is the first step in defining the world the work is going to inhabit: the composer discovers and defines this world first in general terms, with the consciousness that its definition is what is going to make the expression of the work possible. It is an open and closed space at the same time: open so that the composer can become the medium of the work's occurrence, and closed to keep the mind focused and aware of the thread it is pulling. Its closedness is what allows its openness.

To go back more concretely to the idea of environment within a particular piece of music, the environment can be, for example, a temporal grid, associated with pitch sets or harmonic colors. What it does is provide boundaries, create spaces that the composer can inhabit in the moment of writing. One example that comes to mind is Cage's early music. In the 1940s, Cage would establish cycles of measures, according to seemingly arbitrary numerical rules, then fill them up with particular gestures, sound or silence. It's fascinating to try to "learn time" like that, to try to sense beforehand how long the blocks will take, in the experience of the listening, and what to put in them, depending on how fast or how slow one wants the time to go by when they're heard. The elaboration of the environment is the first step in the process of sensing the presence of the various moments of the piece. It develops the capacity of the mind to project itself into what it is trying to create. The environment is defined before one can take one's place in it, before one can inhabit it through the act of composing.

- *That sounds like the idea of precompositional schemes so dear to certain compositional schools.*

That can be an aspect of environment. In any case, it's hard to imagine music with no planning whatsoever, be it psychological or material. Even with people like Pollock, the celebrated exponent of improvisation, there was some kind of preparation, of mental projection, so that the particular gestural need could be realized to its fullest extent. It was not about doing whatever, during the dripping period in particular, not just throwing paint in any old way. The same goes for a composer like Feldman, who modeled himself to a great extent after those painters. He spoke of letting the sound guide him, and it's possible that this is the way Pollock worked as well, letting the brush guide him. In either case, there's at the same time a strong need for a specific kind of space/time activity and a great opening of mind so that nothing gets in the way, so to speak.

- *Can one really have such a physical relation to music?*

I think so, yes. This idea of gestural need is very similar in music, for me in any case. When I start a piece, what arises first in general is that vague feeling for a gesture across space, and time, as it were, which is really the "expression" of the piece. Sometimes it's more specific, with intervals, pitches, rhythms, colors, and so forth, but fundamentally, it's a feeling of how to occupy space and time with a musical line, its general speed and density. I think that's essentially what we call "expression," that way of reaching out through space, to others.

- *We were talking about precompositional planning.*

Right. What I referred to as environment has some relation to that, except that we're not talking about logical, rational working out of abstract schemes, which is often the case when this is mentioned. It's not either about having the whole piece in your head before you take up your pencil or turn on your computer, though, because as much as I like to feel a piece as far as I can before I start, I am ultimately more interested in that kind of spontaneous dialogue between constraints and local desires that can only happen if you have some boundaries to play against. Intuition functions best in a defined space. Even if it can look abstract from the outside, what I am referring to is a type of approach that allows me to sense the boundaries, temporal and gestural, of what is going to happen as I write. So it doesn't have to be all that specific in terms of generative power, it doesn't need to produce strings of pitches or anything else like that, which are then copied down in the score. It creates little (or large, depending on the scale) spaces that can be felt ahead of time, as far as their weight and character are concerned. Obviously if I want to build a specific pitch structure throughout the piece, I can already inform those spaces accordingly. For example, the orchestral part of my Piano Concerto has a temporal layer (a rhythmic phrase, if you want) running in the background throughout the whole piece, that delineates "windows" in which a particular chord, or a set of pitches, is used. That allows me to control the large-scale harmonic rhythm, to borrow a term from tonal theory. I've used that again in other pieces, in different ways. In *Athanor*, the temporal frame controls the duration of specific single pitches, instead of the chords of the Concerto. So in the first third of the piece, for example, there's a main note associated with each window of measures. The notes are colored in different ways every time they come back, but since each one is active for one to three measures, altogether they create a kind of large-scale melody in the space of over 100 measures. The grid is active throughout the whole piece in other ways, to control transpositions of the basic notes and their harmonies.

- *The centers again?*

No, that's a different kind of "center." These "main" notes of the first section I was referring to are simply heard more prominently than other notes. It's essentially a quantitative matter. The centers I was speaking of earlier are based more on the qualitative value of their presence. That's a fundamental difference.

Having said that, it's interesting to observe how a single note can actually become a real center, both because it is used more often than others, therefore is brought to a higher level of the quantitative hierarchy, and also because, in the way it is used locally, it acquires a formal weight that is higher than other events. That's what happens to the F♯ at the beginning of *Athanor*, for example, and later to the D. Of course, the pitch itself can only acquire that value because of the way it is emphasized, through the musical gestures associated with it (the instrumental colors, and so on). This sounds a bit like the tonic in tonal music, because I'm emphasizing the structural aspect, but the fact is that the traditional tonic is not really a center in the more generalized meaning of center I'm referring to here. The tonic can participate in a center—and often does, of course—but it doesn't have such a structural role because, in tonal music, composers were focusing on completely different compositional resources to create centers (themes, in particular). In our time, though, the individual pitch can be elevated to this level, if there is nothing more "present" to compete with it within a given moment (think of Scelsi's music, for example).

So this idea of compositional environment is important to me because it allows a great deal of freedom in the local decision-making, while at the same time guaranteeing a high level of meaningfulness to these decisions. As I said before, in the Piano Concerto the environment gave me a sense of the harmonic rhythm in the orchestral part, at the large-scale level, so that the local figural aspect could then be more spontaneously related to the piano part if and when needed. Thanks to this preparation, both systems, the large-scale and the local one, were able to interact quite freely. In *Athanor*, the purpose of the environment was different because, as I explained earlier, the idea was for me to "learn" time, so to speak, by establishing a temporal space which was being revisited cyclically. The cycles of measures imposed an artificial regularity, which was constantly varied by the different types of events that filled the measures.

- You seem to call environment two rather different things: on the one hand, a kind of training that one undergoes to be prepared to create (that was your allusion to meditation, or your mention of Pollock's prepared spontaneity); and on the other hand, something very concrete, essentially unique to each piece, that has to do with which pitch you can use, and where, or which duration, and so on. Aren't these too different to be grouped under the same terminology?

These two seem to be different, but in fact they are the same thing. Each one depends on, or informs, the other one. In terms of the actual experience of composing, they are the same thing. They stem from the same need to create inner boundaries. That's why I see these two aspects as one. Creating specific environments for specific pieces *is* working on oneself, at a more general level. It's an attitude, as well as a technical approach. For example, in *Athanor*, I just mentioned that the temporal cycles were useful for two reasons: first, to have a global phrase rhythm (the large melody formed by the individual notes), and second, to "learn" time. That describes both aspects you just mentioned.

Now, it's entirely possible to look at this from the opposite perspective and say that, when working with time, one can achieve the proper relation to temporal proportions only by letting time speak for itself, letting it dictate how long each particular moment needs to be (depending on its resultant presence). That experience of time is expressed very well by the Russian filmmaker Andrei Tarkovsky as the "pressure of time":

> The distinctive time running through the shots makes the rhythm of the picture; and rhythm is determined not by the length of the edited pieces, but by the pressure of the time that runs through them. Editing cannot determine rhythm (in this respect it can only be a feature of style); indeed, time courses through the picture despite editing rather than because of it. The course of time, recorded in the frame, is what the director has to catch in the pieces laid out on the editing table.[19]

That's a great definition of musical rhythm as well, and it's not contradictory with what I described as environment, as far as time is concerned. One cannot avoid the experience of the pressure of time, and the idea of environment is not meant to alleviate or avoid it. Working with a particular temporal grid, for example, forces one to work from both angles at the same time, and the question then becomes: How does one "fill in" those blocks of time (as in the Cage example I mentioned earlier) so that each moment is imbued with life and is afforded the right amount of presence within the given time and in relation to the general flow? I find it a remarkable challenge to try to experience this pressure of time, to understand how time runs through the piece *despite* the temporal organization, while the musical events are being set in the temporal frame. Presence has a role to play in this idea of pressure of time because its quality informs the way in which we react to the passing of time: the pressure of time is to a certain extent a function of the quality of presence.

I just mentioned the process of "learning" time, which can be realized by putting oneself in what could be seen as a rigid situation. That goes back to what I was describing earlier, the fact that one can progress in knowledge through imposed discipline, because that experience can in turn allow oneself to develop a more acute intuition. This way of training the feeling for time through the dialogue between abstract (outside-of-time) organization and in-time realization is, again, a way to develop that particular type of concentration which leads to the openness I was describing earlier. Ligeti mentions this in another way when he says that: "The primary conception of new pieces contains the imprint of the working processes used in the development of previous pieces."[20]

What Ligeti is alluding to here is that one actually always "prepares" oneself over time by using working processes which impose a particular type of discipline, so that they become, so to speak, "built into" the mind. If we consider Schoenberg for example, in the years of Opp. 11, 15, and 16, it seems that most of these works were written very quickly; we can assume that there was probably not a whole lot of planning. To work so fast, Schoenberg had to rely essentially on intuition; but the point is that he had imposed on himself a very strict and traditional training in the years before this period. His Op. 9, for example, was highly organized, and consciously so in the tradition of the symphonic forms that preceded it. It is formally forceful, it converses consciously with History. With Op. 16, on the other hand, Schoenberg lets loose, so to speak. He has to imagine everything from scratch—form, use of pitches, instrumentation—and he has to rely on his intuition more than anything conscious to make it work. But the constructive skills had been prepared for years; the composer had created enough automatisms to allow himself to stop thinking about them. The elaboration of his personal compositional tools had been so internalized that he couldn't help using them even without complete consciousness. This is very clear in his use of motives that completely saturate the textures. I have already given the example of the second theme of his first *Kammersymphonie*, and I'm sure that he didn't really analyze what he did in most of Op. 16 as he was writing it (or in *Erwartung*, for that matter!).

The same process is evident in Berg's and Webern's music of the same period, in spite of their different types of complexity. Berg's *Altenberg Lieder*, Op. 4, for example, are remarkable in this respect: in the fourth song, there is hardly an element in the vocal line which cannot be related in some way to its other parts and to those played by the orchestra, yet the form of the piece is highly elusive, precisely because of the complexity of the motivic relationships (it is hard to speak about motives in this case, actually)—something that Berg could not have managed if he hadn't trained himself thoroughly, in a conscious way, to work with motivic construction. What I'm talking about here is partly musical craft of course, but not only that. It's something that cannot be achieved without the highest level of craft, but it requires far more. The environment, in the larger sense, allows the composer to reach inside him/ herself in greater freedom. It's clear that every composer goes through a kind of alternation, and at different levels: at one time needing to be very strict and controlled, at other times free rolling, so to speak, with the momentum his own discipline has gathered internally. What makes the results different in quality, from composer to composer, is the intensity of both kinds of involvement.

IV.

- After the Piano Concerto, how would you characterize what you've been doing? You seem to have expanded expressively in a different direction— less tortured, perhaps, if I may say so?

That's an amusing way of putting it. Certainly the quality of expression is more direct, more relaxed maybe, and that must be because the structural conflicts I was talking about earlier aren't so prominent now. Starting with the piccolo pieces (*Au-delà*), my music became less about confrontations of systems or of gestures. That's probably why I was able then to revise the flute piece (*Par le feu recueilli*) I had written in my last year in Freiburg, and to be satisfied with it.

- It's interesting that after so many years, you were able to revisit the one piece closest to the "New Complexity" that you had ever written. Did that indicate a new involvement with that aesthetic, which had by that time spread to various corners of the world?

Not really. I had never lost my interest in the works of the composers who follow that aesthetic. What happened is that I had originally spent a whole year of hard work on the flute piece, then tried to fix it at least once a year for about five or six years after its composition; so I couldn't admit that it was a failure. This was a big investment, and not just in time, so I felt really sorry that I couldn't make it work after all these efforts; it had stayed in the back of my mind all that time, unresolved. Then in the summer of 1997, I suddenly saw what had to be done to make it work. I fixed a number of details, pitches mainly, to improve the lines, and I rewrote a whole section in the middle that had been completely unfocused in the first version. It was interesting to tackle that sort of language again, but all it did in terms of getting me involved in that kind of writing was to make me interested again in nested odd-number rhythmic patterns. The quintuplet-inside-triplet and triplet-inside-triplet rhythmic patterns from the flute piece became the impetus for the fourth of the piccolo pieces, and soon afterwards, for the whole system of tempo and rhythm relationships that govern *La Terre et le feu*. Most of this oboe concerto is based on the constant re-use of these patterns, associated with metric modulations based on the same proportions. But those are hardly examples of "New Complexity," especially since by then this style had been taken to far greater extremes.

- It is significant that you mentioned the piccolo pieces, because they seem to have triggered more than just a renewed interest in nested odd-number rhythms. There is a different tone in your music, starting with them.

Yes, that's what I was alluding to when I was saying that all these structural conflicts weren't interesting me so much any more. That happened sometime after writing the organ piece. I wrote those little piccolo pieces quite spontaneously, and for no particular occasion. I wanted to try something with no planning, no preconceived organization, and the small scale favored that approach.

- Improvisation again, as in the Piano Concerto?

Yes, but with a different purpose. It was not for the gestural quality here of course, since I don't play the instrument. I was in a slump after the organ piece, again, as I had been a couple of years before, and looking for a way out. I was tired of all my systems, so working freely seemed like a good break.

- And a very fertile one.

Yes. These piccolo pieces engendered several works: three of the *Five Musical Tales* were derived from three of these piccolo pieces, *La Terre et le feu* came from the fourth one, and *La Mesure de la terre et du feu* was a new interpretation of *La Terre et le feu*. I think I'm done with them now!

- Was that a form of recycling, along the lines of what you had done with the String Trio in Die innere Grenze*?*

Not exactly, because I wasn't trying to destroy anything to create something else. After I wrote the piccolo pieces, some of them kept coming back in my head in different ways. I had not consciously decided to use them again, like the Trio in the sextet, it was not forced, it just came to me. I have already mentioned how the second piccolo piece became transformed in my head into the peasant dance of the *Five Musical Tales*. Besides that, the fifth piccolo piece had a luminous quality in the original that really seemed to call for more light, so it became the fifth *Musical Tale*, "The Song of the Light." The transformation of the fourth one into the oboe part of *La Terre et le feu* was a little more elaborate. As I said before, the opening measures of the piccolo piece got somehow transformed into an oboe sound. But the generation of the oboe part itself took more preparation.

In 1998 I discovered a way to adapt a technique used in poetry by the American poet Jackson Mac Low, the diastic reading.[21] The basis of diastic reading is to read through a text (chronologically) and, for each letter of each word of the original text, to find a word that contains that letter further down in the original. Mac Low has complex rules for using the technique, but in 1998, I applied a simplified version of it to read through a Shakespeare sonnet (no.109) in order to create the text for a solo baritone piece, *She or not*. In my reading of the sonnet, I simply used each letter of the original poem to identify a corresponding word that started with the same letter; that word was then used to create the new text. Going through the whole poem in this fashion, I ended up with a kaleidoscope-like text, in which one can "read" the original poem by selecting only the first letters of all the words. Here are the first four lines of the Shakespeare sonnet:

O, never say that I was false of heart,
Though absence seem'd my flame to qualify.
As easy might I from myself depart
As from my soul, which in thy breast doth lie:

And here is what happens to the first two words, after applying the diastic reading:

*O **never** easy* (v) exchanged reign(ed)

The first letter of each word read the words "O never" from the original line: "n" is the first letter of "never "; "easy" is the first word of the Sonnet that starts with "e"; there is no word beginning with "v" in the Sonnet, so that letter remains isolated; "exchanged" is the next word in the Sonnet, after "easy," that starts with "e" (line 7, not shown here); "reigned" is the next word that starts with "r," if one keeps reading in the Sonnet after the word reached so far, "exchanged" (line 9). The process is quite systematic at the beginning, reading through the whole text cyclically. After the fifth line, "That is my home of love," I avoided using the first four lines when scanning, and I privileged the later part of the original text as far as possible, in order to create a greater frequency of the words coming from that part. Shortly after that point, I started to choose the words to use throughout the whole text, rather than being systematically cyclical. That allowed me to create some meaningful bits of phrases which, while they don't actually exist, did relate to the context. That way, the process created quite random juxtapositions at the beginning (while reading the first four lines of the sonnet), then progressively started to make more semantic sense (Examples 7A and 7B).

She or not (1998)

O never easy (v) exchanged reign(ed)

Say ? absence (y)
        That (h) absence to
              I was absence (seemed)
                   false absence like
Of flame   *so easy*
Heart easy as ranged That,
Though (h)
O universe good home
Absence
        breast so easy not
           could easy *Seemed*
              easy exchanged
                  myself easy depart
      My (y) *flame* lie
          again myself easy *to*
Of qualify universe
Art lie is frailties (y)!

As soul, Easy as soul (y)
Might I good heart to
I *From ranged of my*
Myself (y) soul exchanged leave for
Depart exchanged (p) all rose though,

As soul   From   *ranged of my*   My (y)
Soul of universe lie, Which home I could
               heart In not;
            Thy home
            (y?)
        Breast ranged, exchanged all, so time
Doth of that heart, Lie if exchanged.

           That is my home of love.

If from I have again (v) easy ranged, again,
Never good easy depart,

Like I (k) exchanged, him, in myself;
That him again, time travels
Reigned again (v), easy love stained;
I return exchanged that universe, rose not,
Again again, good again in nothing,

Just universe save thou
To, O the heart exchanged, time I myself exchanged

EXAMPLE 7A: DURAND, TEXT FOR *SHE OR NOT*, BEGINNING

After I had finished rewriting the text, I applied a similar technique to create the musical setting. I first wrote a little song on the Shakespeare text, a bit in the style of Dowland (with some quirks), with one note per syllable. I then used the diastically read poem, with each word attached

Sonnet 109

O never say that I was false of heart,
Though absence seemed my flame to qualify —
As easy might I from myself depart
As from my soul, which in thy breast doth lie.
That is my home of love. If I have ranged,
Like him that travels I return again,
Just to the time, not with the time exchanged,
So that myself bring water for my stain.
Never believe, though in my nature reigned
All frailties that besiege all kinds of blood,
That it could so preposterously be stained
To leave for nothing all thy sum of good;
    For nothing this wide universe I call
    Save thou my rose; in it thou art my all.

Shakespeare
(1609)

EXAMPLE 7B: SHAKESPEARE, SONNET NO. 109

to a note (or several, for the words with more than one syllable). That formed the basis of the melodic line attached to the "new" text, which was subsequently transformed through transpositions and other simple manipulations. What I was trying to achieve through this approach was, first, a very consistent method of creating text and music, and second, a particularly chaotic type of musical expression which mirrored the chaotic rendition of the text.

Once I had done this successfully with the baritone piece, I decided to expand the technique in the oboe-ensemble piece. To that effect, I used the fourth piccolo piece to create the oboe part of *La Terre et le feu*, a bit in the same way that I had derived the music for *She or not* from my pseudo-Dowland song.[22] I then adapted the result of the diastic musical reading in order to recover some control of this automatic type of derivation: I didn't just read the string of notes resulting from the diastic segmentation to form the oboe part. Instead, I often used the new line as a reservoir of pitches, with or without their original contours and rhythms. That way, I could bring bits of the original piccolo line to the foreground if I needed, by keeping contours and rhythmic patterns intact, or transform them into completely different phrases by changing their rhythms, for example, or transposing the pitches. This allowed me to elaborate the form of the oboe part by creating a large spectrum of melodic relationships. In the ensemble, the parts for the instruments were based on scales made up of symmetrical or non-symmetrical arrangements of half and whole steps (something I had already explored in the organ piece). But the fact that this arrangement of intervals and the basic rhythmic pattern were actually derived from the first few notes of the fourth piccolo piece as well insured that the relations between oboe and instruments would be far closer than those of the Piano Concerto, and, as a consequence, gave the whole piece a generally less conflictual type of expression. So the expressive and the structural aspects supported each other, just as in the Piano Concerto they had opposed each other.

- *And that piece found a new life in the duo* La Mesure de la terre et du feu.

That's right. The relation between the oboe-ensemble piece and the oboe/viola duo resulted from another idea. When I planned *La Terre et le feu* I already knew that it would be followed by a version for oboe and viola, to become the third part of the group *La Mesure des choses*.[23] So I wrote the string parts of *La Terre et le feu*, and in particular the part of the first viola with the projected transcription to the duo in mind. But when it came time to write the duo, I was bored at the prospect of just transcribing the concerto the way it was. I thought it would be interesting to try something different: I decided to reconstruct the oboe part in a different way from the original by changing the order of the sections. What I had in mind there was to see if it was possible to create a new form, to reorder the original "story" to create a new narrative that would still work, dramatically speaking. I tried several different orderings of the sections of *La Terre et le feu*, and chose the one that seemed the most successful. Maybe there are other possible solutions to explore, but I chose the one that seemed most different from the original and that also had an interesting dramatic form. As we know, the idea of a literary narrative being exposed in a non-chronological and purposefully confusing fashion was an important technique for some authors in the Nouveau Roman movement of French literature of the 1960s (Robbe-Grillet in particular).[24]

Of course, since music is not language based on meaning in the way literature is, the kind of reordering I applied to write the oboe/viola duo doesn't create the linguistic difficulties that it would in literature. But the categories I mentioned earlier when I was trying to define musical form are the ones that made that enterprise challenging and worthwhile: since each section had a specific momentum in the original and each moment in each section has a specific weight in relation to the whole in the oboe concerto, I wanted to see how changes of contexts could generate a new dramatic form. In a way, it wasn't that far from my earlier rewriting of the String Trio inside *Die innere Grenze*, or the idea of formal revelation I explained earlier. In all these cases, the formal ambiguities can't be experienced as they could in literature.

- It wasn't quite as destructive, either.

That's right. It was more playful.

- Speaking of destruction, there seems to be a lot of fire in your titles.

Almost in spite of myself, really. I don't want to analyze that too much, although it's hard to avoid because, as a subject of reflection, it's over 2500 years old, so there's a lot of writing about it—some of which I have read (I particularly like Heraclitus, one of the earliest writers on the subject). I like to keep it as a kind of mysterious need. I find that I keep coming back to the resonance the idea of fire has in me. It started with the group of pieces *La Mesure des choses*, where I set out to examine each of the traditional elements of mythology one after the other: air, water, fire, and earth.

- Not true; there was already fire in the two pieces L'Exil du feu *and* Un Feu distinct!

Yes, you're right. It was a bit different, though. Those two belong together and, as I said before, the second one was written in order to make the original idea of the first one come out in the open. The title *L'Exil du feu* simply referred to the fact that the original "fire," the original sequence on which the piece is based, had not been presented, had been exiled; so here the idea of fire was not very positive, and the title was an expression of that absence. But you are right, that's when the image started to appear.

- There's also some fire in the organ piece.[25]

Yes, that was another work that had to do with the four elements. I started to think of fire in more positive terms too; no more exile. The feeling I was trying to convey in this one was the creative fire, the inexhaustible fire that constantly renews its energy.

- *Were you being illustrative?*

Illustrative only in the sense of the kinds of emotions the image evokes in me. I think all music is illustrative at that level. I don't think there's much direct illustration in the lines themselves. It was the most elaborate contrapuntal texture I had written to that point, so I guess it had more to do with the idea of having fun with technique, as an illustration of creation. There's no drama in the piece, no climax, it's just a run of constantly renewed figures, in a kind of joy of creation.

- *Sounds like Bach.*

Yes. In fact it was modeled after one of the numbers of the *Orgelbüchlein*, the "In dulci jubilo" (Examples 8 and 9).

- Athanor *is another of your pieces that has to do with fire. Isn't the athanor the alchemical furnace?*

That's right. The concept of the four elements has inevitable connections with alchemy. Alchemy is quite a fascinating subject, in its spiritual aspect: the transformation of the human being from a sack of matter into a higher spiritual entity.

- *A very unfashionable and, shall we say, pre-modern conception of the human being?*

Unmodern, perhaps, in the Nietzschean sense of the term (as in: *Unzeitgemässe Betrachtungen*). But that "unmodernity" is inherent to the whole idea of alchemy, in the sense that the processes involved in alchemical transformation are just as relevant to our time as they were to the Middle Ages: the separation of matter into discrete elements for analytical purposes, the purification of the elements, and the putting back together of the whole (the *opus contra naturam*). In our time, we are very good at separating everything and analyzing; we talked about that earlier. We're not so good at purifying, and we have little idea how to put the elements back together to get a new sense of the whole! We just look at the pieces, unable to find the processes that can put them back together. That's because we don't understand how we perceive the world, how we filter everything we perceive, and we don't see the universal laws. It's very

EXAMPLE 8: J.S. BACH, "IN DULCI JUBILO," FROM THE
ORGELBÜCHLEIN

hard to do nowadays, but that doesn't mean it's impossible. There are people who work specifically in that direction, trying to find methods to reach that kind of knowledge, while using the results of the analytical ways of research as stepping stones. Again, as I said before, we can't just

EXAMPLE 9: DURAND, *LES RAISONS DES FORCES MOUVANTES*, IV

deny or refuse the results of that analytical way of examining the world.
It's a necessary step. We just need to keep going from there. So yes, the
idea of alchemy is inextricably linked to the making of art, in my mind.

To come back to the idea of the athanor, the formal processes in *Athanor* are supported by a layout based on the actual construction of the ath-

anor: three parts, each part sustaining the one inside it so that the temperature remains as stable as possible in the central one. In that central one is where matter is finally transmuted. But if you look at it metaphorically, the athanor is the human body, in which the transformations need to take place so that the spiritual nature can be revealed. So that spiritual nature is there from the beginning; it's just not seen until one has gone through the process.

 - Of purification?

Yes, and through that, of reaching higher consciousness. As I said, the spiritual dimension is always there. It needs to be revealed.

 - We're back to the idea of revelation.

Exactly. In fact, it's no coincidence that, again, the melody on which the whole piece is based appears clearly only at the very end, as in the groups of pieces from the 1980s that we were discussing earlier. But in *Athanor* the formal process leading to it is very different from the ones I had used years before.

V.

 - You just mentioned the importance of the melody in Athanor, *which brought us back to the series of works from the mid-'80s (*Lichtung *was also based on a melody). So is the next piece based on a sequence of chords, or a polyphonic section?*

No, I'm working more and more with the idea of melody now, to which the harmonic dimension is much more integrated than it was in my earlier work. So I can concentrate more specifically on the melodic dimension, attempting to answer the question: How is it possible to use melody to generate a form, to use its structural potential as well as its immediacy of presence?

 - What is the difference between melody and line?

Presence, again. A line is a general movement, and is characterized by a global contour, a direction of activity. It's usually perceived in a kind of statistical way: it goes up, down, has a beautiful arch, and so on. A melody is imbued with a specific affect; the stronger its presence, the more memorable it is. It doesn't necessarily have to do with length; a melody can even be quite long, and be present with varying degrees of presence throughout. So I see the melody as a structure-bearing unit that has enough of a singular character to acquire strong presence in its individuality.

There's also the question of focus. There can be many lines governing the movement of a piece, and one doesn't need to be all that aware of them. For example, in Carter's music, there is often a rich polyphony, but few of the lines stand out at any given time, unless they suddenly come in focus, for example the piccolo at the end of the slow section of the *Double Concerto*, at which point the line can acquire the quality of melody. A melody is in the foreground, there's no ambiguity.

- Does the emphasis you put on melodic writing imply a sort of return to tonal harmony? After all, the heyday of melody in the past was in large part made possible by the great number of common structural elements between melody and harmony. How is it possible nowadays to bring the melodic element to the foreground without reverting to the kind of hierarchy active in tonal music?

That is indeed one of the fundamental questions I am asking myself at the moment. In *Athanor* I dealt with this problem by assigning to each note of the melody a particular harmonic color, which can be varied as the notes reappear. It's a bit similar to the approach to colored notes that Messiaen followed in his *Mode de valeurs et d'intensités*. I have always found it very odd that this piece by Messiaen triggered the idea of integral serialism, when what he was really doing there was to create another level of modal music, where each note is not just a pitch, but a complex of pitch, attack, register, and rhythm. These parameters are completely fixed for each note, and Messiaen then simply writes a three-part counterpoint with those fixed sounds. It's very similar to playing a keyboard on which each key would have a specific timbre (defined by its pitch/attack/register) and duration, and on which the composer would basically be improvising. In *Mode de valeurs et d'intensités*, this "keyboard" of colors is the basis for a type of music that is vaguely motivic, but really not organized in any strict fashion. It's true that there is a little bit of numerical manipulation in the ordering of the "complexes" which have led some to think that this was a serial work, but there is really no implication of permutation between the parameters, in any case, as opposed to the way it was understood by the early integral serialists. I think it's much more interesting, as an idea, than integral serialism, because if you extend it a bit you can think of an orchestral "keyboard" in which individual notes are colored by instrumental groups. That leads to a new approach to the role of harmony, which is basically dependent on the melodic dimension, rather than the opposite, as in tonal music.

- *How is that idea of melody relevant to our time?*

It's just as relevant as representational art is to our time, in spite of the enormous importance abstract art has taken in the foreground of the art scene throughout the twentieth century. Indeed, the difficulty with using melody is close to the difficulty of exposing recognizable shapes in visual art. In a way, representational art has now to deal with the fact that if objects can be identified, they acquire a presence that is often overwhelming, considering how much our perception has been conditioned by the subtleties and difficulties of interpretation of abstract art. So the most successful examples of representational art nowadays are the ones in which the figures are suggested, or partially hidden, transformed, so that they can act both ways: as identifiable objects, or as subjects—but with a layer of uncertainty as to their purpose. The difference between representational art and abstract art is that in representational art, the painter makes it clear to the viewer what the elements of the painting are. It's easy to see that the object is a pear, or a face. In a sense, that's not what the painting is about, because that aspect is a given, it's not ambiguous. In abstract art, everything is subject to interpretation if one cares to apply it; there is no transmitted meaning at the level of what those shapes are. The painter might not have known what the shapes were (or even cared what they were), so it's up to viewers to decide if they want to give them a specific meaning.

One also needs to differentiate the question of representation from the question of narrativity, as the surrealists did, among others. It's not because there is representation that there is a particular narrative, or that the narrative is clear and linear. Pollock's late paintings, for example, certainly demonstrate that the figures we can recognize (more or less, as the case may be) don't necessarily interact with each other to create a "story" of any sort, or even a continuity, as in the case of *Easter and the Totem* or *Portrait and a Dream*. In the latter painting, the representational parts act as an enigma: they anchor the painting in a specific imaginary world, they indicate that something familiar (recognizable) is being shown, but don't give any context for it; in fact, the context is being denied. This happens also in some of Malevich's late paintings, the ones of people without faces. The expressive power of these images, where something is there, but refused at the same time, is extraordinary.

- But we know what the Pollock painting was about in Portrait and a Dream. *He even said it himself: it was a self-portrait while drunk.*

But that's just one side of the painting. The other side is not figurative, and that's where the critics like to interpret all kinds of things. That's the "dream" side.

- Don't you think Pollock was conscious of what those abstract shapes represented?

Well, maybe it was along the same lines as the drunkenness of the face: distorted images that he experienced while being drunk. But I find it more interesting not to know that there's a possible story behind it. I like the total discontinuity between the two parts, which happens on a purely graphic level. That's more powerful than to try to relate the two parts through some kind of narrative.

- Do you prefer abstract art then? I thought you leaned toward the side of representational art.

It's not so much that I prefer one over the other. I prefer what has the greatest poetic suggestion. And that often happens when the image is at the limit between both, as in the paintings by Kandinsky when he began to try abstraction. Or more recently, in Francis Bacon's paintings, although I'm not so interested any more when the imagery becomes too obvious, as it is in some of the triptychs. And again in some Pollock's early or late paintings, and in late Malevich, where the images are more obvious but missing fundamental elements (the missing faces I spoke of just now). In connection with narrativity, I can also mention Tarkovsky again, or Werner Herzog, who are really extraordinary in this respect, because of the way the narrative threads are often hidden or disturbed by a kind of temporal elasticity, in order to create a larger space of narration. I have already mentioned Jean-Luc Godard, whose fractured narrativity is more directly related to the Nouveau Roman techniques of the 1960s.

- You were talking about this in relation to melody?

Yes, that's also what it is possible to do with melody, and that's also why I just mentioned two seemingly different topics, representation itself and narrativity. We have the same situation in music, with the melody as an object of definite presence—it's right there, clearly in your face, or it can be, at any rate—and it can be integrated into, or can become the support for, an obvious narrative structure. As you can imagine, I'm not talking about melody in the sense of pretty bits of music that can be sung back easily. The difficulty with melody is its almost excessive presence, just like the image in a representational painting; yet the presence melody can acquire in music is also its main strength, and is quite different from complex motivic transformations or purely statistical, global sound images. The challenge lies in finding ways to introduce the melody in always varying perspectives: structurally by exploiting its structural qualities to infuse the temporal frame in many different ways, as well as purely sonically by giving it different degrees of presence (a structural as well as gestural and purely instrumental problem).[26] It's quite similar to what I was saying about painting, really. I don't want the image to be too obvious, at least not all the time, yet I want to use it for its enormous structural potential of continuity and directness. It can have a very stabilizing function, so to speak, structurally and emotionally.

That's one of the main things I tried to achieve in *Athanor*. There is a basic melody which is heard throughout the first third of the piece, as I mentioned earlier. Each note of the melody lasts for several measures. It's impossible to perceive it as a melody because the time frame is much too vast for a conscious perception. The perspective is beyond human ability. In the second part of the piece, the melody is not heard any more, but it serves to structure the pitch content because its notes form a kind of modal frame on which the lines are based; the general "pitch color" of the original melody is present (with transpositions) but the figural result is entirely different. One could say that the melody has here taken on a more distanced role. In the third part, the melody regains a more direct presence, as bits of it start to appear on a more perceptible time scale. By the end of the piece, the durations of the notes of the same melody are reduced to their smallest scale, and the melodic line is quite clear, on the foreground. So by the time it's finally heard, this melody has structured most of the linear activity of the whole piece, but without being presented explicitly as a melody. This shift in perspective creates in fact a semantic displacement because the notes with long durations at the beginning have a completely different role in the formal deployment from the notes with short durations at the end. And in the middle of the piece, they have yet another role, structurally speaking. This whole process creates a shift in the experience of the tones themselves. At the beginning, it's hard to perceive anything but isolated events, which are constituted mainly of the repetitions of the main notes and their associated colors (harmonic and instrumental, as well as the "distortions" of colors caused by other tones set in close contact with them); in other words, there is little sense of a higher organization, of a continuity that links those events (it's there but, as I said, on a scale that makes it very hard to perceive). By the end, the same notes come back, but what is heard then are the relations between them, the movement that links them to each other: their continuity. The smaller scale now allows this perception, and the relations between notes (the intervals, the sound between the notes) come to the foreground. So it's a global movement from isolation to relation.

> *- In your mention of a kind of superhuman perception, are there overtones of a spiritual nature again? Is that a cosmic image? I am reminded of Stockhausen's handling of the extremes of temporal duration.*

Which came from Messiaen, of course. The relation to a spiritual dimension is certainly relevant, and I like the idea of a temporal scale that is not perceptible to humans, but does communicate something else, on a more subconscious plane.

> *- This is getting a bit fuzzy, isn't it?*

Necessarily so, because, again, as when we were talking about presence, we're leaving the realm of what everybody can measure and relate to on the physical plane. That's a basic problem when you leave the usual materialistic approach to things. Most people, if they don't flatly refuse to talk about the subject of spirituality in music, just look at you as though you've lost your mind, they don't recognize you any more. Or, possibly worse, there's a whole group that just agrees with whatever you're saying as long as it sounds against the dominant materialistic ideology. The fact is, I'm not opposed to the materialistic understanding of the world, or rather I should say that I'm not opposed to the view of the world brought to us by natural science, based on empirical observation of nature. It's not very enlightened to deny all the knowledge that this approach has brought us in the last 300 years, even in spite of the staggering excesses of its applications. But it's equally important to explore what we've lost by focusing so much on that sort of observation.

The same goes for music. There's the obvious, unavoidable fact that there is something physical about it; it's made of waves, vibrations in the air that we can measure and therefore reproduce artificially. But it's also made up of something that has an effect on our feelings, and that hasn't been examined much because there isn't much to measure, not with our machines anyway. And yet it clearly affects us, and it's also true that some of these hard-to-assess elements of music seem to generate fairly generally similar responses; think of the major/minor modes, an obvious example.

- When we were discussing the Piano Concerto, you alluded to the idea that the composer, while reacting to the social environment he is involved in, would be able to generate changes in the social fabric. Is that a moral statement about music-making?

I think that what a composer puts on paper has a moral effect, somewhere, somehow. After all, the same is true for any of our thoughts which are followed by actions with resonance in the world once they're out, just as, for example, a weapon is the result of somebody thinking about killing other people. With the thinking comes the function, then the action to make that become reality. So why would it be different with other things we do? It's a bit naïve to assume that actions don't have any consequences, in one form or another; irresponsible, even, if we pretend to ignore the outcomes. Of course that's a generalized sentiment these days, that not all our actions have consequences—wishful thinking.

But I like to imagine that with music (as with the other arts, of course), we can have a beneficial effect on others, we can actually help people. Jonathan Harvey expresses a bit of the same thing when he says that music is here to relieve suffering. If you look at it in that way, you realize what a great responsibility we have in the world, as soon as what we're doing can reach beyond the composer's studio. Of course that extends well beyond writing music, but since I invest so much of my life in that activity, I have to look at it from that perspective. You can just not think about it, and deny all the consequences, but that doesn't make them go away; or you can try to use your imagination to visualize what the sounds you're bringing out might do out there, and act accordingly. As a composer, one needs to develop a kind of sensitivity to sound and musical "language" that affords this visualization. It's hard to talk about those things because there's no "scientific" basis for them, and they can sound completely off the wall, or utopian—but at this point, they are one of the main guiding forces for me. Of course there is also, maybe foremost, the sheer pleasure of living in sounds; that will never go away, fortunately. I suppose that if it weren't for that, I would have to try to accomplish these goals by other means. But music it is.

- This sounds a bit old-fashioned in our time, doesn't it?

Either old-fashioned or permanently true. I defend the value of art as a privileged way of experiencing and rendering manifest a deep understanding of the world, beyond facts and material knowledge. Art has a duty to offer that to others, and those who want to make art need to work on themselves to get there before they show it to others.

- A dangerous statement, to be sure, when nowadays we're aware that everyone can create, and one can't really look down upon anyone else's accomplishments.

Yes, of course; everyone can create, and that's an essential part of the development of civilization at the present time because it corresponds to the general movement toward self-identity, as opposed to the group identity that was still prevalent a few centuries ago. But what I am saying is that, whatever you do, you need to be as conscious as you possibly can of the consequences it might have. Look at the gigantic movie and TV industry. If the people responsible for putting most of these products out on the market really thought through to the end about the consequences of revealing their thoughts to others, that whole industry would simply collapse. I'm not talking about technique, which is often totally dazzling. (That's only the most materialistic aspect of it, but it's usually all that is talked about—and understandably so, because it's easier to communicate on that level at the moment.) I'm talking about what those people think daily, the kinds of opinions they have of others: it all comes out so clearly. There is a remarkable contempt and hatred of the human race expressed by most of the products that come out of TV and film studios, and not just in the United States. And it is all swallowed by audiences, as if this were the normal way of looking at others. I can't imagine that it has no practical consequence in the world.

- It's easy to attack the art of cinema because of its realistic or naturalist nature. Music can't have the same effect, can it?

Realism and naturalism are not the same thing, of course. Some people argue that the only way to apply realism in cinema is by making documentaries, because that really describes reality. Naturalism, on the other hand, would be trying to reproduce life as faithfully as possible, in a fictional context. In either case, everything we do is a trace of what we think, so it's always about reality, in one form or another, about how we understand the world. But there are other ways of making movies. For example, Tarkovsky, one of my favorite directors, was constantly looking for another dimension in describing life: is that not reality? I think Tarkovsky was a great artist because he found original ways to convey his remarkable understanding of people and great sense of wonder for nature. Every frame is infused with a kind of respect for the outside world that is extremely rare to see. Another aspect that I find fascinating is that his movies are so mysterious, beyond the narrative of the stories. You don't always know what he's saying, why things are happening the way they are, you can just sense it; it affects you beyond words, it's always right and moving, you just don't know exactly why. And that's what music does too; it affects you beyond words. Composers, obviously, tend to be sensitive to that quality, so they need to be oversensitive to the effects. That's where the moral dimension comes in. The only way to control that is by knowing yourself, your shortcomings, and so on. Adorno said that music is not just pure expression, but rather a mode of cognition for understanding the world. Although I don't completely agree with this view, it is true that whatever you know and feel as a composer is all you can put in a piece of music. Then the listener can participate actively in this discovery.

- Music pointing to a higher dimension?

Yes, I would tend to think that music has the capacity to point toward the spiritual dimension of life, and in that sense it goes beyond pure cognition, and enters into the realm of revelation. Again, as I just said in relation to the consequences of our actions, it reveals something of the spiritual life of the artist whether he/she wants it to or not. Insofar as what composers do concerns their entire being, they disclose their most intimate relation to the world, including their relation to the spiritual dimension. It's there no matter what, just as it's the case with any action performed by a human being in any context. If the spiritual dimension is highly developed in the creator, music, like art in general, has the ability to reveal it in the world by creating strong emotions that point toward it. It doesn't have to be the vehicle for religious text or obvious religious associations or images to achieve this. In that sense music is not a tool of knowledge; it doesn't explain how to understand life, but it offers a chance to experience its spiritual dimension through emotional response.

- If composing music reveals so much of the nature of the composer, is a musical work a kind of self-portrait?

Is music fictional?

- I don't know about music, but the question of fictionality in the self-portrait is of course quite interesting, not the least because of the delicate border between intentionality and innocence.

Indeed, a painter can paint a self-portrait either to invent him/herself, or to document some kind of reality as best as possible; the same goes for the writer's autobiography. In both cases, the intention itself can be either in large part fictional, or not, in which case it is nevertheless somewhat fictional. (There's no such thing as an objective documentary, because there's always an intention that shines through.)

- Or both can decide to make a portrait of someone else; in other words, painters (or graphic artists in general: photographers, sculptors, and so forth) and writers have a choice. But can a composer write someone else's music? Or, to put it differently: What is the meaning of a "musical self-portrait"? Can a composer talk about somebody else but him/herself in a composition? Is it thinkable?

Probably not. So then, what is being represented in a musical composition?

- Another question? Aren't you the one in front of the mirror?

Indulge me. What is represented in music?

- Nothing, I suppose. Music does not represent.

Yet it expresses something; is that something outside the composer? Then, who is the *I* of the composition? Isn't it the composer? The composition cannot represent the composer, who is nevertheless the only subject being represented.

- I see: the subject is and is not represented.

The music represents the subject but the subject is not representing him/herself in the composing. Something of the subject is being represented, in spite of itself. The subject tries to represent itself, because there's nothing else to represent, and in the process of doing so, ends up with something that is beyond its representation. The subject loses itself, disappears, regardless of, beyond the representation and in so doing is afforded a chance to reveal something much bigger than itself, to transcend itself.

- Is this the meaning of self-portrait?

In the case of this one, I would say that it is, in the sense that many things I think are things I don't know yet, not fully. They are things toward which I tend and don't yet own. They become real in the process of thinking them, and of expressing them, and through this they become known. So we could say that this is a speculative self-portrait.

- But if you are saying things you don't know—yet—is this entirely fictional?

The fact is that the ideas I am expressing here have a certain resonance in me; whether they are true, in this particular presentation, is less relevant than the fact that they point toward something not yet expressed: this is where the truth lies, in that pointing forward. That might become music, some day, and the music will reflect this search.

- Are you trying to avoid the question?

Well, you're the one writing the text, I'm just answering the questions.

- If you continue on this path, I am going to have to turn the lights up again.

A threat? But I promise I didn't lie anywhere. If I invented something, it was true nevertheless.

- Yes, of course, you retreat into subjectivity. . . . But in painting as well as in literature, where it would seem that the topic of self-portrait—or autobiography for that matter—is more obvious and direct than in music, one can ask the question: What is the relationship between the "objectivity" of specific descriptions and the author's "subjectivity"? Furthermore, is it possible in music composition to reach objectivity, or, maybe better stated, to start from objectivity?

Well, one could argue that the purpose of descriptions of the outer world in painting as well as in literature, in the context of a self-portrait, is to make us aware of some kind of emotional relation we experience between the subject (and ourselves, by identification) and the objects around the portrait, which can be natural or man-made. So in that sense, music as composition starts with those "objects," those "materials" in the sense of Adorno, and a dialogue is then established inside a musical work between those objects and the author's subjectivity, which is the way in which the composer transforms them. It's the same thing with everything that is manipulated by a subject, be it a musical composition, a painting, or, indeed, any kind of self-portrait.

- We are almost saying that everything created is in a sense a self-portrait, because it portrays the relation of the author to the objects he/she chooses to use. That seems too general, because in painting, as in literature, there can be the I, right there in front of everything, which is different from a "thing," or another subject, even if the thing is being immediately

interpreted by the I. *The* I *of the painter, or author, is not the same as the he/she/it of the subject in general, is it?*

What is the author trying to do when realizing a self-portrait, or an auto-biography? He is trying to step outside himself and invent a character that he hopes will be close to what is perceived as the real *I*—as perceived by the author, of course. We don't need to play endless mirror games to realize that this is at best just one possible image of that *I*. The whole enterprise, if the author manages to avoid the dangers of self-indulgence, is a construction of identity. I think music writing is also an attempt at self-construction. At that level, it's always a self-portrait.

- Or an autobiography.

There is an important difference between self-portrait and autobiogra-phy, and it has to do with time: the autobiography is an attempt at recon-structing an identity through time that has gone by, by recollecting the past. A self-portrait is more like a slice of the present, of what the author interprets of herself in the moment: what her image of herself is right now, as opposed to trying to reconstitute what she thought at a particu-lar moment in the past (a painter doing a self-portrait at an earlier age— or older—would be an example of autobiography, rather than self-portrait). So music probably tends more toward the category of the self-portrait; the past is always assimilated in the present of the act of compos-ing. By the way, this idea of the *I* being represented through the self-portrait only partially, as only one possible image among many, does not mean that the *I* cannot reconstitute itself, that it doesn't exist fundamen-tally as a "one." That is certainly not an automatic implication. The *I* is obviously made up of these many possible images; and saying this only means that it may be difficult to gather all these images and bring them together to get a global picture of the *I*; but it doesn't mean that it's impossible to find it, that it doesn't exist anywhere.

- Well, there are already two of us here!

VI. Coda

- Earlier on I alluded to the need to keep moving on all the time that seemed to drive you until fairly recently. At that point you didn't want to respond to the question. You haven't been tempted to go away again in recent years?

The practical reason is that I have a somewhat stable job now, so it becomes increasingly harder simply to leave and start over. When you're a student, there are ways to find support, financial support, so that you can go to another school and survive for a while. Obviously, if the need to keep moving were still very strong, I would have to find ways to satisfy it. I'm sure I would take the chance, find something else to do. So that's not the reason why I've stopped. The allusion you were making, though, was not just spatial. It was in response to my confessed decisions to leave a place twice because I couldn't deal with it any longer. In that sense, going somewhere, leaving a place where I had formed a community of some sort, could be seen as a sort of escapism. It was a reaction to the social environment. When I was younger, I used to find it very hard be involved in any community on a long-term basis. Do you see what I mean?

- I see that you've exiled yourself farther and farther away from Europe, while maintaining ties with it as much as you can. Is there a conflict here?

Probably. That question of exile was very sensitive particularly at the time I was in New York, as you know. I had started to make professional connections in Europe, and when I left I had to start from scratch in the United States. As a student, it was quite difficult to gain recognition, whereas in Europe I was already starting to be seen as a professional. So I was in a strange situation, far from all my friends and contacts. On top of that, new music performance opportunities in the States come up far less frequently than in Europe, so if it hadn't been for the need to discover a different relation to making music, I would have returned pretty quickly. All in all, it's really a dynamic situation, because of the conflicts that come with it: I want to be in Europe and at the same time I need to be in the States, for different reasons.

- Can we come back to this idea of escapism?

Well, I've already mentioned how I got into music partly to escape the situation I was in at the time, because I had this idea of forming my own world, outside the social realm. That has worked in my life at many different levels: it's an inherent part of my personality.

- Yet you don't need to go away any more?

It has to do with the way I've progressively realized the moral dimension of art. That came through reading the Austrian philosopher Rudolf Steiner. He brought me to realize what the extent of our responsibility is, in this life, as members of the human community. That has given me a greater sense of the social responsibilities that come with being alive, in the sense that there is something you need to do, and it's your responsibility to find out what it is, and how to do it. So in that sense, I wasn't escaping at all. I was just looking for the place I needed to be in.

- Have you settled for good?

No, I didn't say that. The place I need to be now is indeed where I am at the moment. I had to come here to do exactly what I'm doing, to become what I am now. As well as to write the music I am writing now. I've always been very conscious of the fact that, if I hadn't left Europe, my music wouldn't be what it is now. It sounds pretty trivial, but if you think about it carefully, that's not necessarily so obvious. I could very well have been afraid of leaving Paris, or I could have stayed in Freiburg, doing copying work or other work of that sort in order to survive there, in order to stay in the same intellectual environment. Leaving Europe was not very easy, believe me. But if I had stayed in one of those places, I would have missed the boat, so to speak. It doesn't mean that it won't change, that this is the place I will stay in until I die. That, I don't know at this point. I still think it would be great to live again in Europe and participate more actively in that intellectual community, but it will come if it needs to.

- That's assuming what you're doing now is better than what could have been.

There's no doubt about that in my mind: I was right to leave, for my personal development in any case. I know that if I had stayed in Paris or in Freiburg, I would have been too influenced by the environment I was in to find the courage to look away. Or it would have taken a lot longer. And there's an odd image associated with that, because, from Paris, I moved in a kind of centrifugal fashion, spatially speaking: first to the east, then to the west, then farther again to the west. And at the same time as this geographical centrifugal force was taking me farther and farther from my origins, there was a centripetal force that has brought me closer to myself all the time: the spatial exile has created a greater closeness. So it's not so much that I think what I'm doing is better than what is being done there, it's only that I am sure that it is closer to what I need to be doing. It's a pretty big distinction.

- Isn't that a bit fatalistic? You didn't do what you didn't do, therefore you're doing what you're doing because there was no other choice?

Not at all. You're always free to follow what your impulses tell you, or not. The only difficulty is to know yourself enough so that you can recognize who's talking to you at any specific time.

- Who is asking the questions, in other words?

That's right. Me or you?

- Know thyself?

Bas les masques!

January 29, 2004

NOTES

1. The students' revolt in Paris, which took place for the most part during May 1968.

2. Pierre Boulez, *Penser la musique aujourd'hui* (Geneva: Gonthier, 1963); *Boulez on Music Today*, translated by Susan Bradshaw and Richard Rodney Bennett (Cambridge: Harvard University Press, 1971).

3. Bachelor of Music Education.

4. Pierre Boulez, "Possibly . . . ," in *Stocktakings from an Apprenticeship*, collected and presented by Paule Thévenin, translated by Stephen Walsh (Oxford: Clarendon Press, 1991), 111–40.

5. "Row-engineer": an allusion to Adorno's sarcastic comment about some of the composers who adopted integral serialism in the 1950s.

6. Werner Herzog, *Vom Gehen im Eis: München–Paris 23.11 bis 14.12.1974* (Munich: Hanser, 1978); *Of Walking on Ice: Munich–Paris 11/23 to 12/14, 1974*, translated by Martje Herzog and Alan Greenberg (New York: Tanam Press, 1980).

7. Martin Heidegger, "Logos," in *Essais et conférences* (Paris: Gallimard, 1958), 249–78.

8. There is actually an older example of this, which I looked into at the time: Obrecht's *Missa super Maria zart*, in which the cantus firmus is heard complete only in the Agnus Dei, after having been presented in various fragments in all the previous sections of the mass (see Gustave Reese, *Music in the Renaissance* (New York: Norton, 1959), 193). Although this is not exactly the same procedure as mine, the idea of having the melody of the whole piece appearing only at the end is similar.

9. For an account of the influence of such ideas on Feldman, see Jonathan W. Bernard, "Feldman's Painters," in *The New York Schools of Music and Visual Arts: John Cage, Morton Feldman, Edgard Varèse Willem De Kooning, Jasper Johns, Robert Rauschenberg*, edited by Steven Johnson (New York: Routledge, 2002), 173–215.

10. It might be worth noting that the idea of "open form," in which a piece is intentionally left "open," is not contradictory to what is stated here. In the context of open form, the composer is not wondering "when" the piece is finished, as a composition; what is unde-

cided in this case is indeed where the double bar will be, but that's a question for the performer, not for the composer, who by then has finished the work.

11. Of course, one can ask the same question in regard to the reproduction of an object: Do you stop when the object is clearly recognizable? When you've expressed the feeling you have about the object? How do you assess that for sure? Either way, you only know intuitively that you're there. In this connection, it's interesting to read the interviews of Francis Bacon with David Sylvester; they are great examples of a painter talking about figurative art. (See David Sylvester, *The Brutality of Fact: Interviews with Francis Bacon*, 3d ed. (New York: Thames and Hudson, 1987).)

12. At the State University of New York at Stony Brook, where I was pursuing a Ph.D. in composition.

13. For further details, see Durand, "On Some Aspects of the Piano Concerto," elsewhere in this volume.

14. I am not discounting here the fact that constraining rules, even very limiting ones, can support and enter into dialogue with the musical ideas themselves—indeed, can become part of the musical ideas themselves. The notion of "arbitrary rules" is necessarily a relative one.

15. In Barraqué's Sonata, as in my approach to the idea of revelation, the appearance of the row at the very end is not a revelation to perception. It's more a formal "gesture."

16. Reading a score would probably fall somewhere between these two types of relation to time: one can read in "real time," or slow down or speed up at will, while never diverging very far from the text.

17. The concepts of center and field, as approached here, are very similar to ideas developed by the architect Christopher Alexander. In a note to Volume One, Part One, Chapter 4, Alexander mentions the notion of field in physics: "A field is a system of variables whose values vary in some systematic fashion throughout space." See Alexander, *The Nature of Order: An Essay on the Art of Building and the Nature of the Universe* (Berkeley: Center for Environmental Structure, 2002), 141n.

18. Brian Ferneyhough, "Form—Figure—Style: An Intermediate Assessment" and "Il Tempo della Figura," in Ferneyhough, *Collected Writings*, edited by James Boros and Richard Toop (Amsterdam: Harwood, 1995), 21–8, 33–41.

19. Andrei Tarkovsky, *Sculpting in Time: Reflections on the Cinema*, translated by Kitty Hunter-Blair (Austin: University of Texas Press, 1986), 117.

20. György Ligeti, "Fragen und Antworten von mir selbst" (1971), translated by Geoffrey Skelton in *Ligeti in Conversation* (London: Eulenberg, 1983), 126.

21. The diastic technique is explained in Jackson Mac Low, *Words nd Ends from Ez* (Bolinas, Calif.: Avenue B, 1989), Afterword (89–93).

22. See "Melody—Three Situations," elsewhere in this volume, for further details concerning the derivation of melodies in this piece.

23. *La Mesure des choses* is a cycle of four pieces, of which three have been completed to date: *I. La Mesure de l'air*, for clarinet (1992); *II. La Mesure de la mer*, for piano (1993); and *III. La Mesure de la terre et du feu*, for oboe and viola (1999). Still to come is *La Mesure des choses IV. La Mesure du temps*, for percussion.

24. It has become quite fashionable in cinema lately, too, although Jean-Luc Godard, for one, has been using the technique for a long time.

25. *Les Raisons des forces mouvantes*, in which each movement is related to one of the elements: I: water; II: earth; III: air; IV: fire.

26. Not to mention, of course, the more recent awareness of the structure of sound itself (its spectral components) that has developed over the last thirty years. Thus the structural qualities of a melody, as I just mentioned them, include not only the relations between the sounds, but also the qualities of the individual sounds themselves.

MELODY—THREE SITUATIONS: UN FEU DISTINCT, LA TERRE ET LE FEU, ATHANOR (2004)

JOËL-FRANÇOIS DURAND

Melodies are born spontaneously within collective groups or in a stylistic frame when all the "parameters" of music are at peace, and start "singing" together.

—Luciano Berio[1]

WHILE IT MIGHT SEEM a bit anachronistic to discuss the topic of melody in these early years of the twenty-first century, long after the demise of the harmonic functions that supported tonal music, and also a good while after the violent rejection of melodic writing in the middle of the past century, it is still a fact that the need for linear organization of the musical discourse stubbornly survives, even if in radically new forms (such as in Ferneyhough's *figure*, for example). The German musicologist Carl Dahlhaus warns of such anachronism in his *Theory of*

Melody: "A theory of melody appearing in 1972, in the era of sound composition, of electronic and aleatoric music, cannot provide instruction in the composition of melodies (this falls within the realm of manufacturing hit songs), but merely directions for analyzing them."[2] Fortunately, the state of composition has largely changed since the early 1970s, and it is now again quite relevant to approach the subject without recourse to past compositional techniques and aesthetics.

I. Identification and Function of Melodic Lines

Any melodic element has the potential to bear structural weight, whether in a concealed manner or through clear exposition. A melodic line can exist in the background as support for more prominent activity in the foreground; it can be part of a global, even statistical, texture in which it exists on equal terms with other elements (horizontal or vertical); or it can acquire structural weight by progressively developing importance in the course of the work, even if it seemed to have little or none in its first presentation.

In all these cases, the melodic line can be presented either as having direct—or indirect but nevertheless real—relations to other dimensions of the work, or as being deliberately contrasted, even isolated from its surroundings. In other words, it can be of structural relevance inside the whole, or remain outside, incidental. The emphasis on "organic" forms since the nineteenth century has led to a sense of greater value assigned to lines or melodic fragments that show significant relationships with the whole, as a parallel to organic processes found in nature.[3] A new approach to musical analysis, set theory, has been devised for the purpose of exposing hidden relationships beyond the syntactic level in post-tonal music—in music, that is, which at times expressly denies any thematic connections.[4]

The traditional categories of theme and motif (cellular relationships) constitute an attempt at classifying melodic lines according to their function in the whole, beyond their local presentation. These categories are most useful for analytical purposes. The composer, on the other hand, is often confronted with situations where the structural elements cannot all be kept under strict control. In fact, one of the most important dimensions of composition resides in the never-ending interaction between the elements (figures, gestures, and so on) which appear as the result of rational control and the ones that result from more spontaneous decisions: the control of the mind and the intuitive reactions that these processes created by the mind inspire, *au fil de la plume.*[5] This is hardly a modern phenomenon:

In art, strict organization is confronted with a material that is incommensurate with this structuring process and more or less evades it. The inevitable contradiction between the inherent value and dynamic force of historically defined material on the one hand, and rational processing on the other, is a precondition for any sort of artistic production. This state of affairs is not entirely new, even as far as music is concerned. Throughout various periods in history, composers have had to tackle the basic contradiction between expressive detail and the structure as a whole. This contradiction appears in the works of Ludwig van Beethoven as the relationship between theme and form. On the one hand, the sonata principle is incompatible with simple statements of themes: it attempts to dynamicize the themes and to integrate them into the structural process. On the other hand, the themes themselves have a propensity towards "cantabile," or even to become melody. Either the theme is self-sufficient and evades processing because it requires none (e.g., Schubert's "Unfinished"), or it is subjected to this processing, thereby sacrificing its own unmistakable quality to being a function within the thematic process, where it is merely a "cog" (e.g., Beethoven's Piano Sonata, Op. 31 No. 2).[6]

GENERAL CONSIDERATIONS

The melody is the main element of musical discourse in the horizontal dimension. In order to scrutinize it more closely, let us examine:

First, the categories of organization that provide identity to a melodic line, so that the composer can control the quality of presence it needs in any specific situation, and so that the listener is in a position to recognize it when it comes back, either unchanged or significantly altered.

Second, the formal contexts in which melodic materials can be found. Contexts fundamentally affect the ways in which melodic materials are used and the ways in which our perception can assess their formal identity (in other words, their *role*, syntactic and semantic, inside the work). For example, traditional musical forms, insofar as they constituted formal archetypes at the time they were used, created specific contexts within which melodic materials were to be used. Composers were constantly engaged in interaction with them, and designed their melodic materials accordingly. In spite of the influence of tradition—indeed, even by reaction against it—this situation necessarily was and remains a dynamic one, because a context needs to be created so that a musical element can exist through the time in which it is heard; conversely, the very recurrence of an element, transformed or not, gives meaning to the context in which it is presented. This double movement between the small scale and the large establishes the very basis of musical form.

CATEGORIES THAT DEFINE A MELODIC IDENTITY

Interval. A very strong parameter as far as the *emotional* content of the melody is concerned, it is not always the most important one for ensuring the identity of a melodic line and its possible recognition. Structurally speaking, intervals can play a major role in ensuring the cohesion of a piece in the way they inform specific levels of organization (surface, depth, in the melodic or harmonic dimensions), but, as far as the individual melody is concerned, and insofar as a melodic line can be separated from its context, intervals constitute only one possible agent of recognition. A classic example of such a situation, taken from a work by Schoenberg, will be shown below.

Rhythm. The role of rhythm, on the one hand, is fairly similar to that of interval because a given rhythmic pattern can be used in order to guarantee a stabilizing role and constitute a central point of reference for perception, as for instance with a particular set of intervals; conversely, vast distortions of a rhythmic pattern can prevent any possible recognition just as, again, would be the case with intervals. On the other hand, a fundamental difference in perception emerges between the two domains when they are examined in conjunction: if a rhythmic pattern is repeated with little change, the relation between the original and the transformed one is easy to establish, regardless of whether or not the other categories of organization have been modified. Not so with intervals: if an intervallic pattern is repeated with extreme changes in its rhythmic presentation (for example from short values to very long ones, or from regular to extremely irregular), it is much harder to establish a relation in aural terms. Here, analysis is often necessary to decipher those similarities. There is no isomorphism in the psychoacoustic reality of these parameters, and this of course constituted the principal thrust of the criticism voiced against the idea of integral serialism in the 1950s (although it was expressed in a slightly different form).

Register. Register is a strong component of the sound imprint because it imposes a timbral presence to perception. Strictly speaking, register works in close conjunction with instrumentation (also a timbral constituent of sound), another strong element in fixing presence. Register is the most immediate component in the perception of the general "color" of a melodic phrase. On the other hand, it is hardly a very significant agent of recognition: two melodies with different intervallic and rhythmic contents will not be perceived as related simply because they are in the same register (and the same can be said for instrumentation). Thus register is useful in maintaining a certain quality of presence to a melodic line, but it does not necessarily have a significant role within the formal framework in which the melodic line is exposed.

General and local contour. When the intervallic content is unstable or extremely variable, one tends to rely more heavily on the local or global contour the line is following, because it allows a more generalized (less detailed) type of perception. It is therefore an important category of organization.[7] An important aspect of this category is the rate of change: a phrase with many changes of direction is less easily memorized than one with a limited number. (This is of course somewhat relative: attention to global contour might preempt the local if the latter is too unstable, or if its rate of change exceeds a certain speed of enunciation.[8] In general, the two types of contour constantly interact with one another.) Obviously, the degree to which rate of change in direction affects perception is dependent as well on the number of different types of interval in the melodic line: a melody with a large number of changes of direction but containing only one or two types will appear less complicated than one with a wide variety of types.

EXAMPLE 1A: SCHOENBERG, *DREI KLAVIERSTÜCKE*,
OP. 11 NO. 1, MEASURES 1–3 (RIGHT HAND ONLY)

The importance of contour in defining the identity of a melodic line is readily apparent in an example from Schoenberg's *Drei Klavierstücke*, Op. 11 no. 1 (see Example 1). The melodic line exposed in the right hand of measures 1–3 returns several times throughout this piece, sometimes with drastically altered intervallic content. In fact, its first recurrence, at measures 9–11, demonstrates the fact that its identity is perfectly maintained in spite of considerable pitch and intervallic differences: at measure 9, the line starts on F♯ instead of the original first pitch,

B, and all the following intervals are different, at first through a somewhat consistent augmentation (minor third becoming major third, minor second becoming major second), this tendency being immediately contradicted by two much larger expansions (G–A becoming C–G♯, and A–F becoming G♯–A). The final interval remains a minor second but represents a modification in contour (now ascending, rather than descending). In spite of all these transformations, there can be little doubt that the melodic line from the opening measures does indeed return at measure 9. As is clear in this case, contour combined with rhythm has come to replace the traditional use of intervals as the main factor of identity, and therefore recognition.

EXAMPLE 1B: SCHOENBERG, *DREI KLAVIERSTÜCKE*,
OP. 11 NO. 1, MEASURES 9–11(RIGHT HAND ONLY)

Dynamics. This category is of relatively low importance in defining the identity of a melodic line. It can certainly be used to great effect to articulate small- or large-scale formal processes (beyond its obvious affective, emotional, or dramatic role), but as was the case with register and instrumentation, it seems unrealistic to expect relations of real correspondence to become established merely on the basis of melodic lines that are presented with similar dynamic profiles.

Tempo. The tempo, or speed of presentation, of a melodic line can have an impact on the recognition of its recurrence mainly in a negative sense: a very different speed (significantly faster, slower or with large and constant variations) might hinder or even prevent such recognition. Speed is of course also bound up with rhythmic variation (such as rhythmic augmentation or diminution).[9]

Length. The length of a melodic line has a direct relation to the ease with which it can be perceived as a whole, rather than as an assemblage of smaller parts of varying importance. It is interesting that one of the favorite means of establishing melodic continuity in late Romantic music (Wagner and Liszt in particular) was the sequence, which with its shorter units considerably aided the recognition and memorization of long melodic lines. Indeed, the idea of "endless melody" has nothing to do with an unformed melodic line of limitless length. As Dahlhaus explains: "An inherent postulate of the idea of 'endless melody' is that throughout the course of a piece of music each instant will possess a 'significance' equal to that of every other instant. This resulted in the shrinking of the thematic period . . . to the short, as it were 'prose-like,' shape of the individual musical idea."[10] In contrast to such structures, one can imagine a melodic line of great length in which few, if any, of its constitutive elements would be reducible to small, repeated units. Without motivic elements to rely upon for support, such a melodic construct would have a very different formal role from that of a traditional melody. Examples of such melodic lines will be shown in the second part of this essay.

FORMAL CONTEXTS

Keeping in mind that for present purposes it will be of little use to separate historical consciousness (and knowledge) from compositional intentions, in this section I will attempt a brief outline of the different formal contexts in which melodic lines can be found. Much has been written on the subject by music historians, which needs no recapitulation here, since the object of this study is not to review the most elaborate definitions of musical terminology but rather to survey the situation in terms of its relevance to contemporary practice. Moving from smaller to larger scale, then, let us examine the basic formal uses of melodic lines.

Motif. It might seem redundant in our time to mention this formal category (and theme, below), since they have been talked about so much over the past two hundred years. Yet, even though they are less useful to composers nowadays, they continue to influence the way music is written, even if not directly. This is doubtless due to the fact that they have proven their usefulness as tools in helping to control the degree of cohesion in the musical construction, particularly in the domain of instrumental music. The first of these two most famous formal categories, the motif, is actually more ambiguous than it seems at first sight. Indeed, the difficulty in defining theme and motif is readily apparent in most of the texts that use these terms, which often show little effort to provide any actual differentiation of them.[11] In order to fulfill its role in ensuring cohesion, the motif must be able to undergo fundamental transformations of its structure in any of the dimensions of interval, rhythm, and contour (local or global). While some of these dimensions are altered, it is essential for the identity of the motif that at least one of them remain unchanged; for example, an interval set can return in a completely different rhythmic and agogic context, or a rhythmic pattern can be found carrying unrelated intervallic sets, to name two of the most traditional situations. Because of this inherent flexibility, the motif can inform the musical texture, even saturate it, by appearing in many different (dis)guises. The motif's role is not only to weave a network of relationships at many levels of the musical discourse, but also to guarantee cohesion by establishing a form of musical logic in which motivic units can be understood as consequences of previous ones. This has been the archetype of development since the Romantic era, in which melodic cells drawn from larger thematic units are worked out through sequencing, transpositions, and other technical means of transformation, as if they had been logically deduced from their original matrix (which already points toward specific types of relationship between motif and theme in which the motif is a subunit of the theme). Schoenberg's, Berg's, and Webern's works of the atonal period pushed this technique one step farther, in that their music of that time relies only on motivic weaving, excluding altogether the previous category of theme: "athematic" works such as Berg's *Altenberg Lieder* Op. 4, Webern's *Sechs Stücke für Orchester* Op. 6, or Schoenberg's *Erwartung*, among others of the same period, are particularly remarkable examples of this approach. These works contain numerous examples of just these types of transformations, in which the musical space is saturated with small motivic cells (related to each other by intervals, contours, rhythms, even combinations of rhythmic and metrical patterns) that can be found everywhere in the texture.[12]

Theme. As opposed to the motif, the melodic object built for thematic purposes cannot undergo extensive transformations, particularly in the domains of interval, rhythm, and contour, because a theme must always be clearly recognizable in order to fulfill its semantic and formal potential. Here the combined dimensions of interval and rhythm acquire the highest status in the hierarchy, as they work in tandem to ensure the original identity of the theme. Themes are not as a rule simply repeated over and over, of course; they constitute the main subject of developments or variations (although in non-developmental forms such as the rondo they are usually repeated almost unchanged), by being subjected to transpositions, elongations, liquidations, and so on. In cases where the theme is affected by more fundamental alterations, for example when some of its constituent parts are separated through fragmentation or any other form of individualization, the theme itself actually disappears, temporarily metamorphosed into smaller motivic units. Those motives can have the power of recalling the theme *in absentia*, a confirmation that reinforces its central role in spite of its material absence. What differentiates themes from motives, then, is the way in which they are treated in the course of the piece: a theme needs to retain a strong similarity of identity throughout, whereas motives are smaller units that can be parts of a theme, or are entirely separate, and can be subjected to more radical dissociation of their parameters. It is clear that themes have been the subject of much attention on the part of composers of tonal music, at first in the field of instrumental music, with Beethoven holding the central place in shifting the emphasis toward motivic deconstruction of the thematic materials. (Indeed, it was probably in Beethoven's music that the line between theme and motif began to be blurred in the formal construction—even sometimes as early as in the very first presentation of the melodic materials.)[13]

Gestures, figures, and textures. The first two terms are not equivalent, nor are they directly related to the notions of theme or motif. The figure, as defined by Brian Ferneyhough,[14] is essentially a dynamic and unstable nexus of parameters whose actualization can take many different forms, depending on the purpose that is assigned to them in the perspective of the whole work; in other words, it is a *potentiality* defined by the lines of force which give it its essential movement (see the image of the wave in the poem by Ashbery quoted by Ferneyhough in the opening of his text, *Il Tempo della Figura*). This concept of musical figure was initially introduced by Ferneyhough in an attempt to draw the analytical (and compositional) attention away from the inherently more static, iconic idea of gesture, because *gesture* is usually overloaded with affective connotations, and therefore blocks the kind of formal projection that the figure possesses. In an interview he gave in 1990, Ferneyhough complemented this duality with a third member, texture, in order to qualify a "global form of activity characterized by some recognizable consistency."[15] In this manner, he identified three clear levels of observation (for the listener), and of action (for the composer): the global (texture), the emotional (gesture) and the relational (figure).[16]

A melodic line can represent **a subjective expression of the passage of time**, without being tied to the larger functional role that characterizes the traditional use of themes and motives. In this capacity, the melody does not need to be repeated—or, if it is, it can only reappear untransformed, or nearly so (in other words, it cannot undergo any sort of development, such as a thematic process). This manner of using melodies has usually been considered "inferior" to traditional usage because it is less structural in terms of the relation of the parts to the whole (the ideal of the organic, again).[17] It also encompasses the more traditional use of the term *melody*, connoting "cantabile" or "pure expressivity." Although this presentation of melodic objects is typically associated with nineteenth-century Italian opera, and is then often justified by dramaturgy and text rather than by overarching structural considerations, its possibilities are by no means exhausted by such usages.[18] For example, this type of melodic approach can be particularly desirable for exhibiting a specific relation to time inside a work, in which the music neither projects toward its future nor reflects upon its past; as an exceptional moment in an otherwise "organically" conceived work, it can be used to bring a sense of non-coherence or non-unity, which points to the "outside" of the work.[19] Indeed, this interpretation can suggest an understanding of the function of those *con espressione e semplice* passages in the first movement of Beethoven's Op. 31 No. 2 mentioned above (see Example 2). This type of approach can also lead to a completely different formal process, as will be shown below in the context of my work for orchestra, *Athanor*. In this case, the melody functions both lyrically—as an essential expression of "cantabile"—and as a fundamental agent in the structuring of the whole piece. Here, melody can become a locus of reconciliation between the structural and the expressive, between the object and the subject.

EXAMPLE 2: BEETHOVEN, PIANO SONATA IN D MINOR, OP. 31 NO. 2, FIRST MOVEMENT, MEASURES 137–58

Another possibility for the use of melodic lines is based on their inter-pretation as **spatial curves**. In this situation, a melodic line is considered simply as a continuous curve in space, with imaginary lines drawn between its individual notes. By applying a new rhythmic profile to the original line, one can obtain an entirely different intervallic content, while the original contour is maintained. This category presents analytical challenges in that the resulting musical objects share no traditional common features with each other. The structural potential of the original line is not exploited, indeed is actually denied because none of its further transformations relates to it in the traditional sense. Yet it is possible to base formal processes on this type of transformation because the results share elements of both the idea of repetition and of continual mutation. As will be shown in the first work examined below (*Un Feu distinct*), the potential for the original line to be recognized in its further presentations rests mainly on a subtle mixture of contour similarity and rhythmic proximity.

Klangfarbenmelodie. It would be more than a mere oversight to close this short survey on melodic usage without a reference to the "melody of timbres." In this context, the mention of this category relies essentially on the few historical examples of lines created with minimum pitch movement and mainly through timbral changes. Although the mention of Schoenberg's name in this relation seems unavoidable, examples of this type of melody are found more explicitly in music such as Scelsi's orchestral works from the 1960s, insofar as one can admit the metaphor of a timbral change creating a line in space (or in time). Whether or not there is any psychoacoustical reality behind this metaphor, the parameter of timbre has lately acquired great structural power. But the very limitations of Scelsi's works in the melodic domain suggest that there is no evidence to date that timbre has acquired an independent *melodic* dimension. Beyond this observation lies the question of what exactly in his music creates momentum, and a sense of forward movement, if it is not a line. Pushing this idea a bit further, if we consider timbre, not as a separate parameter, but as the nexus of a complex made up of pitches (single or simultaneous), instrumental colors, and dynamics, it is then entirely appropriate to imagine a kind of "thick" line moving through space and time, in which pitches play, if not a secondary role, then at least a role no more important than that of the other parameters, timbre and dynamics, with which they form the global color, the timbre. It is then possible to conceive of a form in which the quality of the line (warmth, coldness, and other color qualities, such as its varied thickness) is the focus of variations and transformations. What exactly can constitute this quality is hinted at in the presentation of the third work below, and will be part of the future of melodic presentation.[20]

II. Three Examples

In the three situations to be described below, one can observe a progressive shift of the use and role of melodic lines in three works I wrote over a period of a decade. In the first example (*Un Feu distinct*, 1991), the melodic lines are interpreted as continuous contours in space which can be read in a variety of ways, depending on the temporal points that are selected for the readings. In the second example (*La Terre et le feu*, 1999), I took the opposite approach, working from the small parts to the whole: the original melodic line is cut into syntactic units which are meant to simulate the use of words in spoken language, and these units are reassembled in constantly varying ways. In the final example (*Athanor*, 2001), a melodic line is projected throughout large sections of a piece by alteration of its temporal proportions: in the process, the melody acquires a unique formal function.

UN FEU DISTINCT: MELODY IN SPACE

In 1989–91, I wrote two works based on a particular type of reading melodic lines as if they were spatial curves: *L'Exil du feu*, for sixteen instruments and live electronics, realized at IRCAM during 1989–91, was premiered in Paris in May 1991; *Un Feu distinct*, for five instruments (1991), was written a few weeks after this premiere, and took the same approach, but without the use of live electronics. In both works, I used a computer environment designed at IRCAM (based on MAX™) to create derivations from an original melodic line. In *L'Exil du feu*, some of these derivations were realized live by the computer, while in *Un Feu distinct* the program was used only to assist the composition.

Let us examine this process of derivations as it is applied to the beginning of the melodic line found in the violin part at measure 167 of *Un Feu distinct* (see Example 3). If one reads this line with the sparse rhythm shown in Example 4a, the new line contains only a few of the original pitches (Example 4b). The relation between the original line and this new reading depends on the importance that was given in the original to the notes that remain in the new version (if these notes had been at first clearly isolated, for example by being set two octaves lower than the other pitches, the relation between original and derived version would be much more obvious). Using a rhythmic phrase that includes more attack points, we see that the original contour can be now more readily recognized (Example 4c). This constitutes the basic procedure employed in *Un Feu distinct* to derive the violin, flute, and clarinet parts from the melodic lines that they play at the end.[21] Before examining the way in which this line is actually presented at the beginning of the work, I need to introduce three techniques that were developed in order to give more flexibility and variety to this procedure.

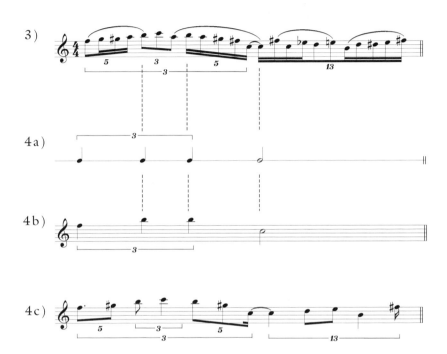

EXAMPLES 3 AND 4: DURAND, *UN FEU DISTINCT,*
MEASURE 167, VIOLIN

    First, the attack points of the rhythmic patterns used for the readings were at times allowed to fall between pitches of the original line (as opposed to what is shown above). To that effect, lines were drawn between the consecutive points represented by the original pitches, producing new pitches (see below).

    Second, all the resulting pitches were "forced" to fall into one of two different scales (Examples 5a and 5b). These scales, which are simply pitch collections without any tonal or hierarchical function, were used in order to gain a level of control over the "structural distance" between the original line and the derived result: if the scale used contains at least all the notes of the original, the rhythmic pattern has most of the responsibility for keeping as many as possible of the original pitches, thereby ensuring a closely related pitch structure. If the scale contains only a few of the pitches of the original, the structural distance between original and new readings will be necessarily increased. Notice, for instance, that some of the pitches of the original melodic line (F♯, G♯, A: pitches that are used repeatedly in the first part of the original) do not even appear in Scale 2.

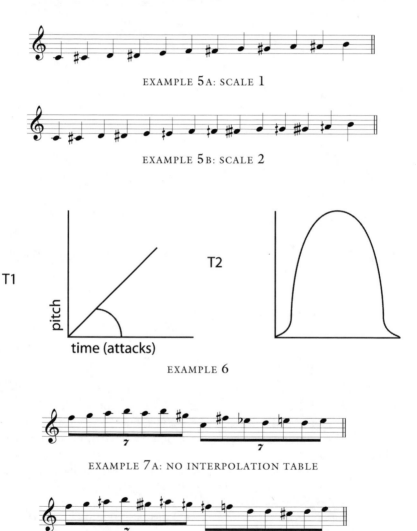

EXAMPLE 5A: SCALE 1

EXAMPLE 5B: SCALE 2

EXAMPLE 6

EXAMPLE 7A: NO INTERPOLATION TABLE

EXAMPLE 7B: INTERPOLATION TABLE T2, SCALE 2

Third, in order to obtain even more possibilities of variation in the readings, I used two "interpolation tables." An interpolation table is a curve that "interprets" the distance between two points by drawing an imaginary line between them, obtained with a mathematical equation. Two such examples of curve are shown in Example 6. The first curve, T1, is a straight 45° ascending line, whereas the second one, T2, is a bell-shaped curve. Example 7 shows how such a table can influence the reading of the original melodic line: the first part of this example (Example 7a) is a reading of Example 3 with two continuous septuplet patterns, without using any interpolation table (which means that when an attack point falls between two pitches of the original line, the reading is of the closest pitch; in other words, all the pitches of the new reading belong to the original); the second part of the example (Example 7b) shows the use of T2 combined with Scale 2. The resulting line, affected now by two quantitative levels of distancing (the interpolation table plus a scale with a number of pitches that do not belong to the original line), is much farther removed from the original. Its degree of recognition, its closeness to the original in qualitative terms, is relative to the similarity between the two contours, which in turn depends on the quantitative difference between their attack points: the more attack points are used in the new reading, the more similar the contours will be.

One can now see that this method offers great flexibility in controlling the quantitative as well as the qualitative aspects of melodic repetition (and recognition). Because this approach creates a sort of "pseudo-thematic" organization, the ear can find common elements between the various readings, in spite of the sometimes completely different pitch and rhythmic structures. The formal potential is quite remarkable, because it makes possible the realization of a continuum of structuring—from extreme closeness of relations to complete separation—throughout a work, which involves simultaneously, and in a relationship of intimate dependence, both pitch and rhythmic organization. *Un Feu distinct* is based in great part on this potential.

Example 8 demonstrates the same procedure applied to the clarinet part. The original line is found in measure 168 (in reality, one octave lower than shown in Example 8a). It is first read through a rhythmic pattern of quintuplet eighth notes, with no interpolation table and filtered through Scale 1 (Example 8b); with T1 and Scale 2 (Example 8c); and through a pattern of septuplets, with no interpolation table, in Scale 1 (Example 8d). A combination of two of these readings is found in *Un Feu distinct*, measure 3 (Example 9), where the resulting line jumps from the quintuplet patterns of Examples 8b and 8c to the septuplet pattern of Example 8d in the second half of the measure (transposed one octave

EXAMPLE 8A: DURAND, *UN FEU DISTINCT*, MEASURE 168, CLARINET

EXAMPLE 8B: NO INTERPOLATION TABLE, SCALE 1

EXAMPLE 8C: INTERPOLATION TABLE T1, SCALE 2

EXAMPLE 8D: NO INTERPOLATION TABLE, SCALE 1

EXAMPLE 9: DURAND, *UN FEU DISTINCT*, MEASURES 3–5

higher, with a slight rhythmic change: a quarter note replaces the two eighth notes). As can be seen, the structural potential of the original line is not subjected to any traditional derivations or developments. Nevertheless, we notice here that the melodic identity of the original is maintained; coherence is achieved in spite of the structural distortions. This type of relationship between original version and derivations can infuse the musical form much as thematicism once did: through memory and contextual associations.

LA TERRE ET LE FEU: MELODY AND MUSICAL SYNTAX

The use of melodic elements in the second work to be introduced here, *La Terre et le feu*, for oboe and ensemble, demonstrates a different approach to formal organization. Here, the part of the soloist was realized with the help of a technique for reinterpreting a melodic line that was borrowed from the American poet Jackson Mac Low, the "diastic" reading.[22]

The melodic line at the origin of the oboe part of *La Terre et le feu* is the fourth of my set of piccolo pieces, *Au-delà, Cinq Etudes pour Piccolo* (see Example 10). Proceeding more or less intuitively, with the aim of providing some variety and interesting potential, I cut the melodic line into small units (indicated by the brackets in the score) and then interpreted each of these units as a musical "word."[23] Then, following a technique similar to the one I used with Shakespeare's Sonnet No. 109 to create the text of *She or not*,[24] I "read through" the piccolo piece: as each pitch of a word was read in turn, the melodic line of the piccolo piece was scanned until another word starting with that pitch was found. That new word was then extracted, and the resulting new line became a chain made up of these isolated figures of the piccolo piece, now in a new order. This can be seen in Example 11, which reproduces the process of generation for the beginning of the oboe part from *La Terre et le feu*. After the initial two Es, the second word in this example is the descending line E–D–D♭–C–B♭–E–D♭. Scanning through the piccolo piece, we find a word that starts with D at measure 9: D–C–B–B♭–A♭–A♮ (the initial E starts the word itself, so is not used for scanning). D♭ is the next pitch of the second word, and scanning reveals it as the first pitch of a word in measures 14–5 (C♯). Then comes C, found at the beginning of a word in measure 15, and so on.

Now, it is obvious that if there is only one word in the whole piccolo piece that starts with the pitch C, for example, that word will be used each time the C appears in another word. Conversely, one can see in the first page of the piccolo piece that many words start with the pitch E, yielding a greater number of possible figures for that pitch.

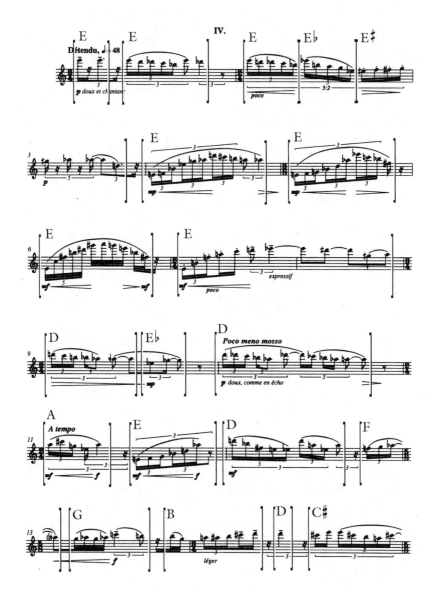

EXAMPLE 10: DURAND, *AU-DELÀ, CINQ ÉTUDES POUR PICCOLO*, IV

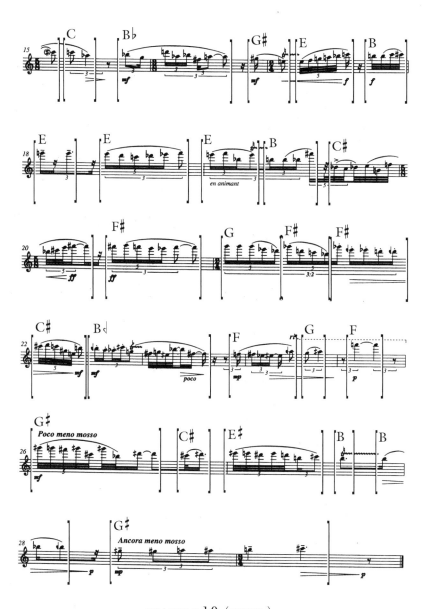

EXAMPLE 10 (CONT.)

m. 1 from *Au-delà* IV

EXAMPLE 11: DURAND, *LA TERRE ET LE FEU, MEASURES* 1–8, OBOE

In general, the scanning is done chronologically, but there is a tendency to use words from the first half of the original melodic line at the beginning, then move to words of the second half as the oboe part progresses. One such example will be shown below, in the case of the C♯.

This simple diastic reading technique was applied to generate the whole oboe solo part from the piccolo piece, at first fairly literally, as shown in Example 11 where the rhythmic patterns, registers, and contours from the original figures are preserved; later, the readings were subjected to somewhat freer interpretations. Example 12 displays the application of the technique to a passage which starts at measure 129 in *La Terre et le feu*. We see here that the resulting line has been rewritten with new rhythmic patterns and registral displacements, as well as some further repetition of notes designed to intensify the focus on certain pitches.

The next example follows the use of the words that start with C♯, a pitch that is found at the beginning of three words in the piccolo piece (at measures 14–5, 22, and 26). The first of these is always referred to whenever a C♯ is needed, until these measures themselves are reached in the progressive reading of the piccolo piece (so, roughly, when using the first half of the piccolo piece to generate the oboe part). Its presentations are constantly varied through transformations of its rhythmic pattern, registral displacement of some of its pitches (resulting in new contours), and transposition, giving it always varied syntactic and semantic functions (see Example 13). After the point where measures 14–5 have been reached in the generation of the oboe part, every time a C♯ is found, it will trigger one of the other two words starting with C♯ (measure 22 or 26). Because of this circumstance (which occurs with other pitches as well), there is a global reflection of the melodic chronology of the piccolo piece in the oboe part. The small scale of the original melodic line is reproduced in a statistical way at the much larger scale of the oboe part.

Such outcomes might invite a comparison of this approach to "thematic" process, as can be seen most clearly in the use of the C♯ word from measures 14–5 in Example 13. But, although there is indeed a sense of evolution in the transformations of this particular word—especially at the syntactic level, since the new figures are progressively more and more integrated in larger phrase units—one cannot really speak of process here. The words are neither developed nor reduced to their constituent motivic elements; they simply appear and disappear at the will of the diastic reading, and their original syntactic function is then reinterpreted in their new context. This also means that, whatever internal structure the original piccolo piece had, its revelation (and further exploitation) is not the focus of the transformations the line undergoes in *La Terre et le feu*. In other words, "The 'meaning' of the music is [not] determined solely

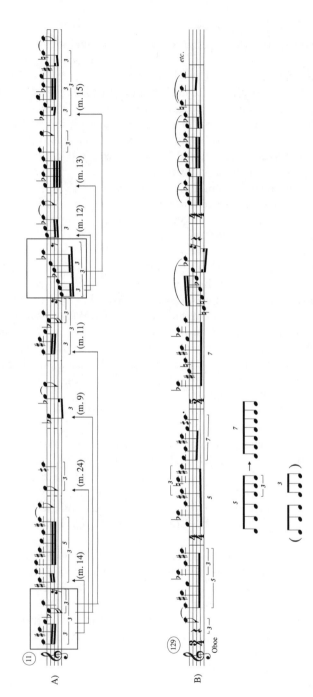

EXAMPLE 12: DURAND, (A) *AU-DELÀ*, IV, (B) *LA TERRE ET LE FEU*, MEASURES 129–32, OBOE

EXAMPLE 13A: DURAND, *AU-DELÀ*, IV, MEASURES 14–5: C♯ "WORD"

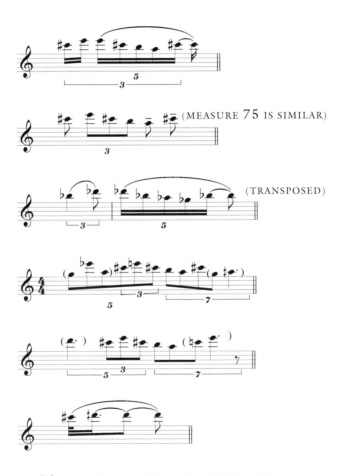

EXAMPLE 13B: DURAND, *LA TERRE ET LE FEU*, OBOE,
MEASURE 11; MEASURE 73; MEASURES 117–8;
MEASURE 130; MEASURE 152; MEASURE 350

by its inner relationships," to misquote Adorno.[25] The original melodic line of the piccolo piece provides a reservoir from which new contexts—as opposed to new melodic materials—appear constantly. Indeed, the relationship between material and context constitutes the most significant aspect of this construction, and points toward a shift in understanding the role of material in music that is further explored in *Athanor*.[26]

In this orchestral work (2001), I approached melody in yet another way, in terms of both pitch and time dimensions. Here, instead of being distorted (as in *Un Feu distinct*) or fragmented (as in *La Terre et le feu*), the melodic line is used to structure large spans of the temporal scale, a phenomenon that has profound syntactic and semantic consequences. In response to the quotation given at the beginning of this essay, *Athanor* constitutes an attempt at creating a space within which a melody can be heard both as a "cantabile" moment and as the main structuring constituent of the whole work.

THE TIME DIMENSION

The time structure of *Athanor* resulted from a desire to gain a different, more global type of control over the temporal construction of phrases and their proportions in relation to each other. To that effect, I devised a large-scale temporal frame, the first part of which (Part I) corresponds to the first third of *Athanor* (measures 12–110), and is shown in Example 14. There are nine cycles of eleven measures each, with each cycle subdivided into segments three, two, one, two, and three measures in length, always in that order. As can also be seen on this scheme, specific pitches (written in the blocks) are associated with each group of measures so that, together, they create a kind of large-scale melody spanning a period of over a hundred measures. For example, F♯, found in the first block of the temporal scheme, is the first note of the melody and is in measures 12–4; the next pitches E and, again, F♯ (measures 15–6); G♯ is the main note of measures 18–9, followed by F♯ returning in measures 20–2; A follows in measures 23–5; and so on. The one-measure blocks at the center of each cycle (measures 17, 28, and so forth) contain no pitches; they are resting points. Finally, it must be noted here that these main pitches are not actually exposed as explicitly as Example 14 might suggest: they are colored/harmonized in different ways every time they recur (more on this below).

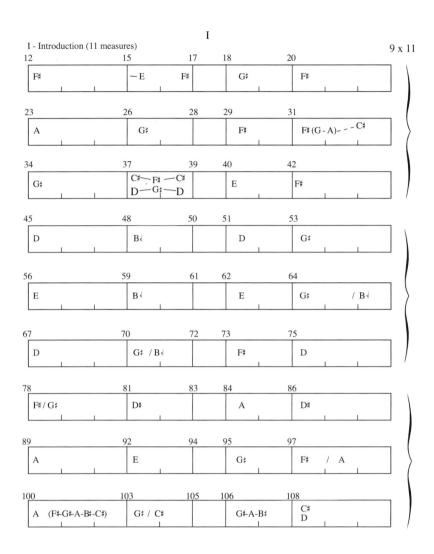

EXAMPLE 14: DURAND, *ATHANOR*, PART I,
PLAN OF DURATIONAL CYCLES

In the second main part of the piece (Part II, measures 111–209), there are eleven cycles of nine measures each, and the segments within each cycle are differently ordered each time (2–3–3–1, 4–3–2, 2–3–2–2, etc.; see Example 15). This constantly changing periodicity, as opposed to the regular periodicity of the first part, affects large-scale rhythmic activity, as if the breathing of the piece were becoming irregular, under the shock of an emotion.

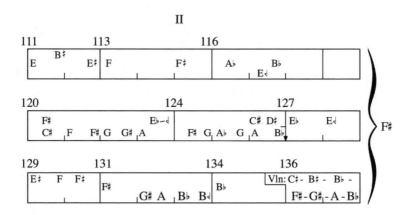

EXAMPLE 15: DURAND, *ATHANOR*, PART II,
EXCERPT FROM PLAN OF DURATIONAL CYCLES

It is in this image of emotion that we find a first relationship to the basic conception alluded to in the title: the athanor was an alchemical furnace, and was built in three nested parts in order to maintain an absolutely constant temperature for the alchemical transformation to take place in the center. But the athanor was also a symbolic representation of the human body, which needed to be purified in order to gain its full spiritual dimension. So each of the three parts of the athanor, in that sense, can be seen as a particular dimension of the human mind: intellectual, emotional and spiritual. These three levels are reflected in the construction of *Athanor*. Part I (intellectual) is dominated by a system of numbers ordered in constant periodicities, Part II by deviations of this regularity because of the "temporal emotion" just mentioned, while in Part III (measures 210–308) aspects of I and II are combined: the nine cycles of eleven measures return, but the order of the segments of one, two, and three measures follows a different system of organization, more concealed than in I. This brings about the revelation of the origin of the whole piece, at several levels. The most obvious aspect of this revelation is the appearance of the melody that forms the basis of the entire piece, starting at measure 276 (Example 16, pages 51–2 of the score). Notice

that the pitches of the melody are precisely the pitches that were used in
the block of measures in I. This portion of the melody first appeared in
measure 123, particularly in the brass (Example 17, pages 3–5 of the
score), but set in a much larger time frame.

EXAMPLE 16: DURAND, *ATHANOR*, MEASURES 276–81, FIRST
VIOLINS, LOW STRINGS, AND PERCUSSION OMITTED

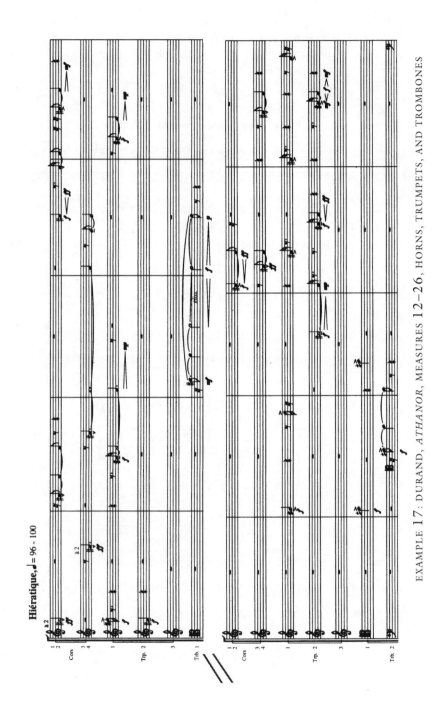

EXAMPLE 17 : DURAND, *ATHANOR*, MEASURES 12–26, HORNS, TRUMPETS, AND TROMBONES

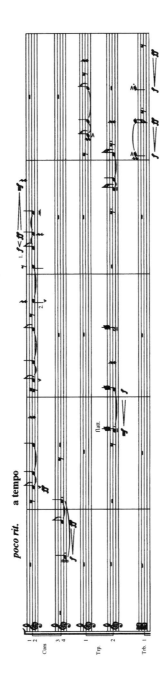

EXAMPLE 17 (CONT.)

THE PITCH DIMENSION

The melody mentioned above uses pitches found in a specific region of the spectrum of a fundamental pitch: the natural overtones 8 through 17 of a low D (see Example 18). Each of these main notes is colored (through harmony and instrumentation) in a different way each time it comes back in the first part of *Athanor.* Example 19 displays all the harmonizations of the first pitch of the melody, F♯ (the numbers at the beginning of each measure refer to the measures in which the F♯ occurs). The chords use pitches that correspond to the higher overtones of the low D (thirty-second partial and above), and we can see in that example that, in most cases, the construction of the chords ensures that the main note is always clearly present (in particular through doublings at the octave, affected or not by quarter-tone deviations). In this way, each block of measures becomes a kind of temporal resonant space for the pitches: together they create a large-scale melody whose pitches are colored and characterized by constantly varying harmonization, instrumentation, density, gesture, and dynamics. (Recall my earlier reference to a "thick" melody in which the main notes are identifiable by their general colors.) But during this first part of the piece, this melody is hardly perceptible because of the temporal scale on which it is exposed.[27]

EXAMPLE 18

The fundamental D is active throughout Part I as a kind of tonal center, from which all the other pitches are derived. The D itself, however, when it appears as main note in a block, is more concealed than any of the other pitches of the melody in Part I, either because its color is rendered quite diffuse by the complexity of its harmonization, as in measure 45 (Example 20), or because it is presented in competition with other prominent pitches of the melody that are allowed to remain active outside of their own respective blocks. (For example, in measure 51, the F♯ is also present; in measure 67 it is the C♯, and so on.) In other words, the

EXAMPLE 19: DURAND, *ATHANOR*: HARMONIZATIONS OF FIRST PITCH
OF MELODY (F♯)

D completely ("fundamentally") colors this whole first section, without itself being exposed clearly, but only through the use of its overtones: its structure is displayed before it emerges in reality. Its real presence will be revealed at the very end of the piece, displaying another level at which the origin of the work appears only in the closing moments.

EXAMPLE 20: DURAND, *ATHANOR*: HARMONIZATION OF MELODY
PITCH D

In summary, we observe in this first section two different levels in the hierarchy of pitches:

First level: The notes of the melody, which are based on overtones 8 through 17 of D, are the most prominent pitches used in the melody.

Second level: The colors that accompany harmonically each of these notes are taken from much higher regions of the spectrum (thirty-second overtone and up); they are more in the background, and color the main notes in the same way that overtones color the fundamental.

FUNDAMENTAL PITCHES: LARGE-SCALE ORGANIZATION

After Part I, in which D is the only fundamental used, the identity of fundamental begins to migrate, following a system of "modulation" similar in principle—although not in application—to the tonal technique of "common-tone modulation": a pitch in one series of overtones is found again in another series, allowing a change from one fundamental to the other. The table in Example 21 shows all the fundamentals used in the piece (the numbers above the table are measure numbers): the D spectrum colors measures 12–110; the F♯ spectrum, measures 111–37; the F, measures 138–95; and so on. It is easy to see here that the rate of changes of the fundamentals accelerates as the piece progresses, which creates a sense of large-scale increasing tension. This acceleration is at its highest point at the beginning of Part III (measure 210), where the fundamental is E♭. The next pitches on the table show a symmetrical ordering of the fundamentals, which brings back the overtone complex of the original D at the end; this return corresponds to the moment when the melody is finally exposed (as was shown in Example 16). This symmetrical ordering of the fundamentals is then what allows the two main structuring agents of the piece to appear fully and perceptibly at the end: the pitch D and the melody on which it rests. Through its temporal and large-scale pitch conception, *Athanor* reflects the unveiling of not only the melody upon which it is entirely constructed, but also of the one tone on which this melody is based, D, which had remained hidden.

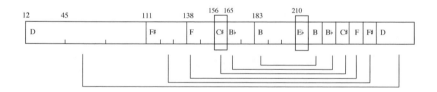

EXAMPLE 21: DURAND, *ATHANOR*: TABLE OF FUNDAMENTALS

It is in this final image of unveiling that the deepest relation to the idea of the athanor is expressed. As the work progresses, the perspective is slowly modified: at the beginning, the most perceptible elements are the timbral and harmonic colors, in the very moment where each pitch occurs, as if each note were an independent entity. Little by little, melodic relations become established, which signal a movement toward the notion of dependence, of *relation* between the elements. This movement can only be revealed through the temporal dimension: from a large, superhuman scale to a smaller one in which this relational perception is rendered possible. This process parallels a movement of the consciousness which, starting from an analytical perception of the material details comprised by each moment, evolves toward a perception of the relations between them, more global and holistic.

CONCLUSION

All three examples shown above have, as common feature, a basic melodic line that either stands outside the work (*La Terre et le feu*), or appears at the end (*Un Feu distinct, Athanor*) as a self-sufficient musical object, and is sometimes of considerable length. As I stated earlier, it is possible to realize a musical form based on a melodic line of great length in which few, if any, of its constitutive elements are reducible to small, repeated units. Such a line, however, without motivic elements to support it, must play a formal role very different from that of a traditional melody. In all these examples, the melodic construct is at once a self-reliant unit and the basis for the whole work's existence. It is not exploited in any motivic or thematic manner, nor is it allowed to become a figure, either in its entirety (very likely an impossibility) or through fragmentation. Even in *La Terre et le feu*, where the initial melodic line is reduced to a number of smaller units which are subjected to some modifications, there is no attempt to transform or "develop" these units: they are merely repeated, albeit often in constellations that are not immediately perceptible in relation to the original.

It would therefore appear that, looking back at the array of possible formal contexts exposed in the first part of this essay, the three examples of melodic lines offered above are closest to the category of "subjective expression of the passage of time," which epitomized melody in nineteenth-century Franco-Italian opera. But the techniques outlined above in the three works demonstrate that these melodies have been given a structural role never previously assigned to melody. They qualify as melodies because of their self-reliance; in addition, they acquire an essential role in the structure in that entire works are derived from them. Here, it has become possible to combine the purely expressive and the structural, the subject and the object, without reducing the object to a collection of fragmented constellations, in search of a long-lost wholeness.

APPENDIX A

It is curious that the two most traditional formal contexts for melodic use, the theme and the motif, are also the ones most often confused by composers and musicologists alike. Although it is beyond the scope of this essay to engage in a historical overview of their analyses, the notions of theme and motive deserve closer scrutiny and tighter definitions than are usually found in the musical literature, where they are often used in an indiscriminate and interchangeable fashion.

In his lectures at the Collège de France, published in *Jalons (pour une décennie)*, Pierre Boulez devotes a whole chapter to *L'Enjeu thématique*.[28] In the first part, he explores "the notion of theme and its evolution," where one would expect a clear definition of what a theme is. Yet Boulez is remarkably vague in his choice of words:

> In Berg, the thematic conception of the music in relation to its dramatic content is quite explicit as early as the Altenberg songs. He changed the name for this: instead of leitmotiv, he preferred to speak of "remembrance motif" (*Erinnerungsmotiv*). But its function in relation to memory is obviously the same. Motif is connected to a dramatic character, a feeling, a situation. . . . Motifs are of greater or lesser scope: there are general motifs that circulate throughout the entire work and local motifs that are connected only to a specific situation. Some of them undergo development; others function only as signals. One could call them *variant*, like the themes of the sonata, the rondo, the adagio, and *invariant*, motifs that are quoted with their surrounding context or apart from it.[29]

We see here a strange mixture of terminology, including the new categories of *variant* and *invariant*, which all seem to fall under the general idea of "thematic conception." The use of the term "motif" in relation to a character in a play, a feeling, or a situation is in fact particularly maladapted, as can been seen in Boulez's words himself. He writes earlier in this same text:

> But this word "theme" is also a synonym for illustration. In this way, a director who wants to specify a bit of stage music can speak of the theme of anguish, the theme of joy, of pride. . . . In this legacy of the Wagnerian leitmotiv we find the word "theme" tied to description of a character, a type, or a concept.[30]

As Boulez explains that the notion of theme is also used to describe relations to emotions and feelings, he switches immediately to the Wagnerian *leitmotiv*, which he qualified indirectly in the previously quoted passage as "motif."[31] All this is indicative of a basic confusion (certainly amplified by commentators on Wagner's music when they adopted the term "leitmotiv," which would have been more aptly named "leit-thema,"[32] even if it is a rather poor vocable).

Schoenberg saw the motif as the smallest unit of musical discourse, from which logical development follows. It is indeed in Schoenberg's statements that one can find the closest approach to an understanding of the role of the motif:

> Schoenberg himself defined the [motif] more clearly than the [basic shape]. In essence, the motive is smaller than the basic shape, it is the "smallest common multiple," the "greatest common factor," which "generally appears in a characteristic and impressive manner at the beginning of a piece" and whose "features . . . are intervals and rhythms, combined to produce a memorable shape or contour." . . . It is a "unit which contains one or more features of interval and rhythm," . . . and it seems clear that Schoenberg was willing to abstract a single interval class or interval type from a more varied line in order to propose an underlying generative motive of a single interval.[33]

We see in this discussion the appearance of yet another category for melodic materials, the "basic shape," which leaves the notion of theme out of any precise terminology. The basic shape seems to be a more general term than theme, since its main role lies in the fact that it contains any number of motives—the motives themselves being the essential elements in generating development and ensuring coherence—and does not have the "affective" role that the theme carries.

While Dahlhaus also falls at times into terminological traps (see note 18, for example), he introduces an interesting new category in his book on Beethoven, under the idea of "subthematicism." This category, according to Dahlhaus, constituted a solution for Beethoven in his search to integrate lyricism inside constraining forms, by offering a greater flexibility of treatment than thematic and motivic techniques: "The lyricism that is confined to an enclave in the classical sonata became the predominant structural principle, causing a crisis for the idea of thematic process."[34] As Dahlhaus observes in the A-minor Quartet, Op. 132, the subthematic idea is "an 'abstract' configuration of two (rising and falling) semitone steps with a variable interval between them."[35] Any such configuration where the intervallic content is variable, a phenomenon that appears in this quartet as well as in a number of Beethoven's other late string quartets, can be grouped under this category. Whether this category deserves the new name of "subthematicism," or whether this technique could be construed as a generalization of the motivic technique, is a question beyond the scope of this study. An argument for including it under the heading of "motif" is discussed briefly in Appendix B.

In summary, the theme is a self-contained melodic unit, which has both a constructive and an affective role: constructive in that it must remain clearly recognizable, even while undergoing some modifications; affective because it serves as signpost to indicate a moment of specific affect in the piece and to project an emotional aura around itself. The motif, on the other hand, has first and foremost a constructive role in ensuring cohesion of the formal organization. It must therefore be able to permeate the discourse at very diverse levels, in the foreground or the background, in the pitch, intervallic (melodic or harmonic), rhythmic, instrumental, and other dimensions;[36] and as a combined set of parameters (or categories of organization), it must be able to undergo significant alterations. Length is also a category in which the motif and the theme are often quite different: themes can have all kinds of length, whereas a motif is preferably of short duration so as to allow for maximum flexibility and "stealthiness."[37]

Appendix B

Here I introduce the idea of "center"—a point from which various parametric threads are extended—in the context of an analysis of motivic technique in Webern's *Sechs Stücke für Orchester*, Op. 6 no. 3 (see Example 22).[38]

III.

EXAMPLE 22: WEBERN, *SECHS STÜCKE FÜR ORCHESTER*, OP. 6 NO. 3

EXAMPLE 22 (CONT.)

The piece opens with a phrase in the viola that contains several remark-able elements. These can be examined in three different domains: rhythmic/metric, intervallic/contour, and timbral. First, with regard to the temporal aspect, the introductory viola line, while set in $\frac{4}{4}$ meter, is syncopated in such a way that it implies a ternary meter. If we disregard the barline, the rhythm is as shown in Example 23. Until the last eighth note, the pattern could be read in 6/8—although not heard as such, because of the syncopation, of course. This interplay between binary and ternary meters, in their relations to the rhythmic patterns that express or contradict them, is one of the most pervasive features of this piece. It can be found in many places, but one example, in which the rhythmic pattern is elevated to the level of a consistent motif, will serve to demonstrate this interplay clearly. The first three notes of the viola line project the pattern of durations (in eighth notes) 3–3–2. This rhythmic motif is found again in measures 5–6, across the barlines of a 6/8 meter followed by a 3/4, in flute 1, French horn 1, and glockenspiel: two three-note groups in 6/8, one two-note group in 3/4. In this situation, however, the speed of these eighth notes changes as the barline is crossed: in the 6/8 the eighth notes are equivalent to a speed of triplets in relation to the initial tempo, whereas in measure 6 the eighth notes return to their speed in the first measure. In fact, another version of this same pattern has already been heard in the clarinet line at measure 3 (with the first eighth note missing, replaced by a rest), continuing its descent into the low register in the solo contrabass: in this case, too, the triplet feel of the clarinet is followed by the "normal" eighth-note durations of the contrabass. The same rhythmic motif is found again in the bassoon, measures 7–8: now the first group of three notes is set in 6/8, whereas the rest of the pattern, in which the group of two eighth notes has been rotated with the group of three (3–2–3) in the bassoon line, is heard in the following 4/4. Notice here that the overlapping descending line of the solo violin in measure 8 fills in the last group of three eighth notes. (An amusing musical "pun" is found at the end of this measure 8, in the French horn playing a quarter note inside a triplet: here the ternary feel is imposed inside a binary meter, recalling the exchanges already mentioned across barlines.) The descending eighth-note figure of the clarinet at measure 3, a 6/8 bar, is recalled in the glockenspiel of measure 9, now in sixteenth notes inside a 2/4 bar: here again, the ternary division of the first figure is found again with a binary rhythmic subdivision. In the last two measures, it is only the syncopated aspect that recalls the original rhythm; the durations have been changed, and can only be found again by stretching the reading to integrate the rests (see Example 24). Example 24 shows the agogic ambiguity of the rhythmic pattern in either a 3/4 or 6/8 meter (the use of 3/4 instead of the opening 4/4 is also indicative of this metric/rhythmic system of variations, since 3/4 and 6/8 provide measures of identical lengths). Finally, the 3–3–2 pattern is reproduced again at a larger scale, in the final three measures, whose lengths follow the pattern, in augmentation: 2/4 (♩ = ♪♪), 3/4 (♩. =

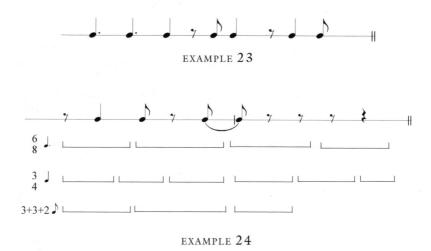

EXAMPLE 23

EXAMPLE 24

♩♩♪). Thus the use of the term "motif" to describe this rhythmic pattern is justified in that the pattern undergoes many different readings and takes on very different roles, from the first measures to the last. On a more abstract level, the metrical layout of the piece shows an elaborate system of symmetrical correspondences, confirming at the large-scale level this interaction between binary and ternary divisions:

[measures 1–4]	$\frac{4}{4}$	$\frac{4}{4}$	$\frac{6}{8}$ (= ternary $\frac{2}{4}$)	$\frac{3}{4}$
[measures 5–7]	$\frac{6}{8}$	$\frac{3}{4}$		$\frac{6}{8}$
[measures 8–11]	$\frac{4}{4}$	$\frac{2}{4}$ (= binary $\frac{6}{8}$)	$\frac{3}{4}$	$\frac{3}{4}$

As for contour, this quality of the melodic lines in the piece confirms the symmetry laid out in the rhythmic dimension: the opening melodic line in the viola comprises two members, each of them following a similarly ascending-descending arch contour, with three pitches in measure 1, then four pitches in measure 2. This arch shape appears again at measures 7–8 in the bassoon and at measures 10–1 in the trumpet. Viewing these four locations as a progression of steps, one notices this basic contour following a progression toward increasing tension, as the intervals, starting from a major second in measure 1, grow larger until measure 8, when the ascending line in the bassoon jumps higher into the overlapping violin entrance, and finally decrease in the last measures, to a minor second. The second basic contour to be found in the piece is the descending line heard in the clarinet and contrabass at measures 3–4; as noted above, it is found again in the glockenspiel in measure 9. The only other descending line, played by the solo violin at measure 8 and situated roughly between the two just mentioned, acts as mediator between the arch and the descending shapes in that it is juxtaposed with the arch-like line of the bassoon, increasing further the highest point of the arch (the first A in the violin can be heard as a continuation of the ascent in bassoon), while at the same time recalling the clarinet descent of measure 3. The last basic melodic contour heard in the piece is more static: the wavy shape of the small "ostinato" of measures 5–6, which can be also interpreted as a variation on the ascending-descending arch contour.

Intervallic relationships play a less foreground role in this work, confirming Webern's intention to avoid any thematic connection (see note 3 above). The first important intervallic constellation to be found is again in the opening viola line: it is the pentachord (01236), an all-interval set. Interestingly, the chord in the trumpets that accompanies this line is one of the two all-interval tetrachords, (0146). A few subsets of these two "Ur-sets" are of particular interest in that they inform a number of melodic lines, without participating in any of the gestural relations noticed above in the discussion of rhythm: set (0123), which is particularly noticeable because it is heard in the opening viola line—if one disregards the highest pitch, F—appears prominently in measure 7 (held G♯ in the violin with first three pitches in the bassoon, with A also in harp), in measure 8 (last two notes of solo violin G♯–G, harp F♯, and F in French horn), measures 9–10 (G–F in glockenspiel, F♯ in harp, and G–A♭ in trumpet), and in the small "ostinato" in measures 5–6 (B♭–B–C–D♭ in "inner" voices, E♭–E–F–F♯ in "outer" voices); the tetrachord (0126) found in the viola, measure 2 (starting on D♭) is heard again in the descending violin line measure 8; the two descending lines in measure 3 and measure 9 are linked by the tetrachord (0134) (last four notes in the clarinet, last four notes in the glockenspiel), a unique example here of direct connection between gestural and intervallic contents; the trichord (015) appears in measure 8 in the first three pitches of the solo violin and again in measure 9 at the beginning of the glockenspiel descent; and finally, the trichord (026), a subset of the (0126) noticed above, and therefore emphasizing the relations drawn out of the opening viola line, is found as the three lowest notes of the trumpet chord in measures 1–2 and is heard again in the beginning of the clarinet descent in measure 3. All these connections signal a very tight network of pitch sets, while most of them are active in total independence from any motivic association.

The timbral dimension further emphasizes the symmetry noted in other domains, if in an inverted manner. Most evident in this respect is the combination string/brass in measures 1–2 (melodic line in viola, repeated chord in trumpets), which is found again in the last two measures, as brass/string (melodic line in trumpet, repeated F♯ in harp). The exchange between the continuous string sound (viola) and the resonant string sound (harp) in this passage is paralleled by a similar variation in the two descending lines, placed in symmetrical fashion: measure 3 in clarinet (continuous) and measure 9 in glockenspiel (resonant). One last type of inverted timbral exchange is visible around the central section of the piece, and provides a transition into and out of that section: a low rumble in the bass drum connects measures 4 and 5; it is the lowest sound of the piece. Similarly, a high G♯ harmonic, the highest sound, is played throughout measures 6–8.

It is now apparent that, in spite of the absence of any thematic relationships, this work nevertheless exhibits a remarkable formal process, through the interaction of false (or "inverted") symmetrical arrangements with variations of motivic elements. The most visible of these motives is the rhythmic pattern of 3–3–2 eighth notes, as noted above. Other motives include the timbral motif made up of the mixture of string and trumpet that frames the piece, and the contour motif in arch shape, whose intervallic and rhythmic contents are always variable, yet related. These motivic elements all stem from the initial viola line and trumpet chord. In that sense, the first two measures of the piece can be defined as one of the "centers" of the work, in that they generate several different fields (rhythmic/metric, intervallic, timbral) that are revisited farther on in the piece. Other centers are formed along the way, at points where some of these fields meet again, as if forming a node, for example at measures 5–6, where the initial durational pattern is found again, supporting another presentation of the chromatic set (0123). The connections that these two centers share are of a motivic, not thematic nature. In this work, centers are by and large nodal points, where motivic threads meet and create a perceptibly self-contained unit. This is not always the case, as centers can appear without any connection to their surroundings.[39] Most of the motives mentioned above are actually not necessarily perceptible, because they have a somewhat abstract nature (for example, the rhythmic pattern or 3–3–2 eighth-notes that takes an entirely different form in the middle section), but they powerfully inform the undercurrents of the piece. This view also offers a possible link to the idea of "subthematic" structure introduced by Dahlhaus and discussed in Appendix A. The use of the 3–3–2 pattern, in the way it is found in various situations (even in the metric proportions of the last three measures), bears resemblance to the observation made by Dahlhaus when discussing the role of the chromatic fourth-progression in Beethoven's Piano Sonata Op. 81a:

> The chromaticism intervenes in the evolution of the main musical idea, in a constantly changing relationship to it—as a counterpoint to the continuation of the theme (bar 3) and to the theme itself (bar 17), as a generator of melodic coloration and transformation (bar 37), or as the background for modulating motion underpinning thematic development (bar 77).[40]

The same small- and large-scale activity is visible in the rhythmic motif of Webern's piece. This is the kind of property that one can expect to find in a motif, rather than a theme, in that it affects in perceptible and non-perceptible ways the unfolding of the form.

Notes

1. Luciano Berio, *Two Interviews with Rossana Dalmonte and Bálint András Varga,* trans. and ed. David Osmond-Smith (New York: Marion Boyars, 1985), 79.

2. Lars Ulrich Abraham and Carl Dahlhaus, *Melodielehre* (Cologne: Gerig, 1972), Foreword. "Eine Melodielehre, die 1972, in der Epoche der Klangkomposition und der elektronischen und aleatorischen Musik, erscheint, kann keine Unterweisung in der Komposition von Melodien sein (es sei denn im Bereich der Schlagerproduktion), sondern lediglich eine Anweisung zum Analysieren."

3. "In Beethoven formal ideas and melodic detail come into being simultaneously: the single motive is relative to the whole." Dahlhaus, *Between Romanticism and Modernism,* trans. Mary Whittall (Berkeley: University of California Press, 1980), 42.

4. "In his program notes of 1933, Webern stressed especially the novel aspect of continual change in the *Pieces for Orchestra,* Op. 6: 'A thematic connection does not exist, not even within the individual pieces. I consciously avoided such connections, since I aimed at an always changing mode of expression.'" James Baker, "Coherence in Webern's Six Pieces for Orchestra Op. 6," *Music Theory Spectrum* 4 (Spring 1982): 2.

5. This dialogue of the composer with the processes that he/she creates is discussed at length elsewhere in this volume. See Durand, "In the Mirror Land: Reflections on a Self-Reflection," Part 3, where the notion of *environment* is treated. [The phrase *"au fil de la plume"* is difficult to translate. It means something like "as it comes under the pen," referring to a spontaneous decision at the moment of writing. –Ed.]

6. Thomas Kabisch, "Dialectical Composing—Dialectical Listening," in Kabisch, *Helmut Lachenmann's Compositions for Piano (1956–1980),* trans. Hans-Niklas Kuhn (liner notes to Helmut Lachenmann, *Klaviermusik,* performed by Roland Keller, Col Legno CD 429 356-2, 1989), 43.

7. The notion of contour as an analytical category has been generated some interest in recent American music theory, as introduced in particular by Michael L. Friedmann in his article, "A Methodology for the Discussion of Contour: Its Application to Schoenberg's Music," *Journal of Music Theory* 29, no. 2 (Fall 1985): 223–48. See also:

Elizabeth West Marvin and Paul A. Laprade, "Relating Musical Contours: Extensions of a Theory for Contour," *Journal of Music Theory* 31, no. 2 (Fall 1987): 225–67; Friedmann, "A Response: My Contour, Their Contour," *Journal of Music Theory* 31, no. 2 (Fall 1987): 268–74; Robert D. Morris, "New Directions in the Theory and Analysis of Musical Contour," *Music Theory Spectrum* 15, no. 2 (Autumn 1993): 205–28; and Ian Quinn, "Fuzzy Extensions to the Theory of Contour," *Music Theory Spectrum* 19, no. 2 (Autumn 1997): 232–63.

8. The question of speed also leads to consideration of further psycho–acoustical phenomena, such as streaming. See, for example, Robert H.P. Platz, "More than Just Notes: Psychoacoustics and Composition," *Leonardo Music Journal* 5 (1995): 25.

9. On a related note, one can find interesting examples of the relationship between melodic contour and speed, as expressed by rhythm, where there seems to be a correlation between the size of intervals and the speed at which they are presented. In "Eusebius" from Schumann's *Carnaval*, for example, the varied repetition of the original septuplet figure shows a remarkable feature: it is repeated in the second period (measure 9, with one added note) in quintuplet sixteenths followed by triplet eighths; the first half of this measure is faster than the original septuplet, while the second half is slower. In the slower half, the last interval is much larger than the original one—a move caused as much by the new harmonic context as by a desire for a heightened expressivity. Another, more systematic correlation between space and time is found in Béla Bartók's *Mikrokosmos* No. 141, "Subject and Reflection": in the second-to-last section of the piece (measures 63–73), the main theme and its reflection are in canon (instead of in rhythmic unison, as in the beginning). As the voices drift apart temporally, their interval content is also altered—in this case reduced, to become more and more chromatic, so that the temporal dissonance created by the increased shift between the voices is enhanced by the growing chromatic dissonance.

10. Dahlhaus, *Between Romanticism and Modernism*, 57.

11. See Appendix A for a discussion of this problem.

12. See Appendix B for a brief analysis of Webern's *Sechs Stücke für Orchester*, Op. 6 no. 3, that explores this motivic aspect.

13. One example of recent music that relies almost exclusively on the use of themes is the work of Takemitsu from the late 1970s on.

14. Brian Ferneyhough, "Il Tempo della Figura," in Ferneyhough, *Collected Writings*, ed. James Boros and Richard Toop (Amsterdam: Harwood, 1995), 33–41.

15. Ferneyhough, "Shattering the Vessels of Received Wisdom: In Conversation with James Boros," in Ferneyhough, *Collected Writings*, 386.

16. It is clear that these categories do not exist solely as linear events. Their inclusion in this context is justified to the extent that they can possess a melodic nature.

17. Kabisch, "Dialectical Composing," 43.

18. "Without exaggeration, we could even maintain that the melodic style of Bellini's arias, above all his slow cantabiles, was the quintessence of what the nineteenth century, with astounding unanimity, understood by melody in the strong sense of the term." Dahlhaus, *Nineteenth-Century Music*, trans. J. Bradford Robinson (Berkeley: University of California Press, 1989), 117.

19. It is in precisely such a context that Dahlhaus, strangely enough, calls a melody a "theme" when assessing a vocal line in Meyerbeer's *Les Huguenots*. Dahlhaus uses the two terms interchangeably, even though he writes: "Despite its brevity, a quality it shares with Beethoven's themes, it is thoroughly appropriate to call Meyerbeer's idea a theme: the four measures into which the musical substance has been compressed are self-sufficient, neither requiring a continuation nor even compelling development." (Dahlhaus, *Nineteenth-Century Music*, 12.) A little farther on, he states: "Unlike thematic ideas, the aim of a melodic idea does not lie in the consequences to be drawn from it, thereby revealing its potential." (13) In other words, a melodic idea can only be repeated, not transformed, a characteristic which, in fact, does not belong to the theme.

20. Although it is clear that the quantitative aspect of this approach can be useful (for example, by relying on spectral analysis), it is not my primary purpose here to imply that it is the only valid approach. Certainly, quantifying parameters in this situation can prove necessary in order to guarantee a level of structural control, but they do not constitute an aesthetic choice.

21. For an exposition of the formal process at work in this and other pieces of the same period, in which the original material of a piece appears only at the very end, see Durand, "In the Mirror Land," Part 2 (21–6).

22. For an explanation of this technique, see Jackson Mac Low, *Words nd Ends from Ez* (Bolinas: Avenue B, 1989), Afterword (89–93).

23. The use of this term here should not be understood literally, as a form of linguistics applied to musical discourse, in spite of the references to syntactic and semantic meaning. Music is language, but its objects never reach the level of precision and conceptualization of the spoken word. Here and below the term is used metaphorically in reference to the construction of the musical phrases, not as an object of meaning in itself. Having said this much, I see no need to shy away from the ambiguity inherent in the question of context and material in the establishment of musical meaning. Contextual and individual meanings constantly interact with each other. If this were not the case, then there would be no need to pay attention to either the musical objects themselves (with their inherent presence) or to their temporal placement in a piece of music.

24. The technique I used for *She or not*, a simpler version of Mac Low's "diastic" reading, is explained in Durand, "In the Mirror Land," Part 4 (63–5).

25. The actual quotation and contextual discussion appear in Dahlhaus, *Schoenberg and the New Music*, trans. Derrick Puffett and Alfred Clayton (Cambridge: Cambridge University Press, 1987), 160–1.

26. The question, then, is not whether the melodic line of the piccolo piece is a *melody*, rather than a motivic, thematic, or figural construct, but in what way the melody, as an independent, even outside entity, is being used to generate an entirely separate, self-reliant organization. The two constructions share the same origin, and *La Terre et le feu* is a commentary on the piccolo piece rather than a development of it. Although there is no room here to examine the orchestral parts, it could be shown that the soloist and the ensemble entertain relations of the same kind as those between the piccolo piece and the oboe part—but by completely different means. Notice that this approach, where melodic units come back with little transformation but are set in constantly varied contexts, bears some resemblance with the use of motives in Berg's operas—which in turn owes a debt to Wagner—but here in a purely instrumental context: an opera without text.

27. It must be added here that for listeners familiar with Stockhausen's use of melody for large-scale organization, this type of perception of the melody is actually possible. In that case, the experience of the whole piece is one in which time is at first considerably dilated and,

by the end of the work, contracts to a more normal scale: a decrease in tension, in effect. This temporal phenomenon of large-scale relaxation is supported by the process of unveiling of the melody and of the main pitch center of the work, as shown below.

28. Pierre Boulez, *Jalons (pour une décennie): Dix ans d'enseignement au Collège de France, 1978–88* (Paris: Christian Bourgois, 1989), 167–290.

29. Ibid., 175. "Chez Berg, la conception thématique de la musique vis-à-vis du contenu dramatique est tout à fait explicite aussitôt que dans les *Altenberglieder*. Il change le nom: au lieu de leitmotiv, il préfère parler d'*Erinnerungsmotiv*. Mais la fonction par rapport à la mémoire est bien évidemment la même. Le motif est lié à un personnage, à un sentiment, à une situation. . . . Les motifs sont de plus ou moins grande envergure: il y a des motifs généraux qui circulent dans toute l'œuvre et des motifs locaux qui ne sont liés qu'à une situation spécifique. Certains participent à un développement; d'autres ne participent qu'à une mise en place de signaux. On pourrait les appeler: *variants* comme les thèmes de sonate, de rondo, d'adagio et *invariants*: ces motifs sont cités avec leur contexte ou hors de lui."

30. Ibid., 170. "Mais ce mot thème est aussi synonyme d'illustration. C'est ainsi qu'un homme de théâtre peut, s'il désire définir une musique de scène, parler du thème de l'angoisse, du thème de la joie, de l'orgueil . . . Dans cette descendance du leitmotive wagnérien, nous trouvons le mot de thème lié à la description d'un personnage, d'un type, ou d'un concept."

31. This confusing terminology does not prevent Boulez from making, in this lecture, some remarkably insightful comments on the notion of *theme* in Debussy's music (ibid., 224–30).

32. As suggested by the Grove Dictionary in its definition of leitmotiv: "In its primary sense, a theme, or other coherent musical idea, clearly defined so as to retain its identity if modified on subsequent appearances." (*Grove Music Online*, <www.grovemusic.com>, s.v. "Leitmotif.")

33. Jonathan Dunsby and Arnold Whittall, *Music Analysis in Theory and Practice* (London: Faber, 1988), 156. The quotations are taken from Schoenberg, *Fundamentals of Musical Composition* and *Models for Beginners in Composition*.

34. Dahlhaus, *Ludwig van Beethoven: Approaches to His Music*, trans. Mary Whittall (Oxford: Clarendon Press, 1991), 203.

35. Ibid., 204.

36. See Appendix B for an analytical application of this definition of the term.

37. This is in contradistinction to Boulez's statement: "Le thème a tendu avant tout à formaliser les procédés de développement: d'où sa brièveté qui permet une exploitation systématique de ses ressources." (Boulez, *Jalons*, 170.)

38. The idea of center is introduced in a more general context in Durand, "In the Mirror Land," Part 3 (48–53).

39. Ibid., 50–1.

40. Dahlhaus, *Ludwig van Beethoven*, 210.

ON SOME ASPECTS OF THE PIANO CONCERTO: TIME AS GENERATOR OF SPACE THROUGH MELODY AND HARMONY (1996)

JOËL–FRANÇOIS DURAND

IN THE COURSE of musical history, the concerto for soloist and orchestra, as a form, has witnessed the progressively stronger imposition of a certain type of dramatic conception, owing to the large potential for musical and extramusical relationships between the soloist, perceived as an individual, and the surrounding instrumental mass. This development reached a high point during the nineteenth and early twentieth centuries, when the idea of an individual consciousness arose, separate from and more and more in opposition to the collectivity embodied, for instance, in the state, or in history. The soloist then often came to represent the expression of the "inner" world of the individual, which the orchestra opposes as "outer" world. But the paradox is that these two opposites, the inner and outer worlds, have of course a common and unique source in consciousness—and, because of this fact, the opposition, strictly speaking, results from an inner conflict between two representations that fail to come to terms with each other.

Recognition of this situation served me as impetus to create a musical form for the Piano Concerto in which the orchestra did not need to have a constantly identifiable role in relation to the soloist; instead, its dramatic function could include a large range of structural and/or expressive relationships with the soloist. In this respect it was justifiable to present the orchestra at times either in a completely different world from the piano, emotionally as well as structurally, and at other times interacting more directly with it.

In contrast to the traditional concerto, in which the two forces are brought into some kind of extended dialogue in which they share more or less the same materials, my own Concerto has very little actual dialogue, and most of the moments at which the two protagonists seem to communicate are moments of strong opposition. To realize this basic situation, I decided to create two worlds based on entirely different structural premises (different use of musical space, sense of time, even structural conceptions). This lack of direct structural relationships between the two forces shifts the focus away from the material relations to a more diffuse type of interaction: a qualitative type of interaction rather than the measurable rapport of intervals and rhythms.

More specifically, one of the major aspects of the Concerto is the exploration of the dialectical relationships between harmonic construction and melodic writing. I have long been fascinated by the opposition between these two dimensions, and the opportunity to combine the orchestra and the piano allowed me to expand the scope of this tendency in my works. For example, in the first half of the piece, harmonic blocks in the orchestra are often used to mount violent attacks on the piano's attempts to elaborate its melodic lines. In this situation, the piano cannot be allowed to express its subjectivity, to "sing."

Because of the inherent quality of the materials used in each part (such as very dense orchestral chords against melodic lines in the piano), the orchestra often obliterates the melodic detail of the piano part. In consequence, the need to identify motivic or thematic relationships between the two protagonists, even though they might actually exist at some level, is largely irrelevant. This violence eventually leads to a partial annihilation of the discourse of the soloist and its subsequent self-destruction in the first half of the work. But beyond this constant conflict at the surface, there emerges a sort of gestural unity which is sufficient to support the formal fabric.

Musically, the vertical dimension is the symbol of conflict, of confrontation; it is also the collective, the superimposition of individual notes, of individual identities within the whole. The more notes are piled on top of each other, the less they retain their individual character and the more they become undifferentiated parts of a general color. The horizontal line is the expression of individual freedom, of the individual consciousness which lies in and exists through time.

The piano part was written almost entirely before any work on the orchestral part was started. Its first half results from improvisations, which were extensively reworked and developed in order to elaborate a network of motivic relationships. These improvisations provided a gesturally idiomatic quality to the piano writing directly linked to a kind of subjective expression typical of piano concertos of the late nineteenth and early twentieth centuries: cantabile melodic lines, runs spanning the keyboard, polyphonic textures, and so forth.

A few representative passages of piano writing in the Concerto could be mentioned at this point. The first is a kind of quasi-improvisando discourse (see Example 1, measures 20–35). The next passage (measures 36–49) presents a more affirmative quality, exposed through a continuous polyphonic texture in the low register, largely based on (1) the same minor-third–minor-second constellation at the beginning of Example 1 (here in the right hand: E–F–G, then F–A♭–G, etc.), followed by (2) a fixation on one note, here C: measures 38–42, as the line tries to rise in register but falls back each time. This polyphony becomes one the most important elements of the piano part in the first half of the work, through its numerous and varied repetitions. It exemplifies the tendencies of the soloist's melodic lines toward obsessive repetition and self-destruction. A quick look at a few other occurrences reinforces this impression: measures 88–91 ("sombre et obstiné" = dark and obstinate); measure 102; measures 105–6 ("pesant, avec effort" = heavy, with effort); measure 128; measures 192–3, after the long passage of chords in opposition with the orchestra (fewer notes here; it sounds much more fragmented); and finally measures 198–9, which conclude the first half of the piece: the original polyphony is almost completely destroyed, and only fragments of it are still recognizable.

Furthermore, the piano part in the first half of the work shows a general inclination toward the kind of massive and brutal textures that characterize the orchestra. It is as if the piano were trying to enter into communication with the orchestra on the latter's own terms, which is inherently impossible in this context because of the basic inequality of sound potential. The piano is trying to take on the character of the orchestra, and in doing so reduces itself to silence. Fundamentally, the first half of the piece is a failed attempt at bringing together two completely mismatched instrumental forces.

It is now clear that the piano does not simply express itself in melodic lines. Within its own world there already exists a tendency to oppose

EXAMPLE 1: DURAND, PIANO CONCERTO, MEASURES 15–49

"vertical" elements to the horizontal ones. This does not represent just an attempt to match the two protagonists, because the piano part exhibits within its own melodic texture a dramatic evolution, indicating further its inability to assume an individual identity.

EXAMPLE 1 (CONT.)

After a short piano solo in which the melodic and chordal tendencies are once again opposed (see Example 2, measures 201–9), the second half of the work appears at first to demonstrate a more successful "fusion" between piano and orchestra, as they both seem to share the same gestural language. The irony of this fusion is that, in order to arrive

EXAMPLE 1 (CONT.)

at it, the piano has had to abandon the subjective individuality which characterized it at the beginning of the piece, in the form of melodic expansion. It has now destroyed its capacity to sing. The possible recovery of this capacity will be the subject of the last large section of the work.

EXAMPLE 1 (CONT.)

In opposition to the piano part, the organization of the orchestra part shows a concern for a more arbitrary type of control over the pitch and time parameters. The pitch material of the orchestra is derived from the introduction of the Concerto, which also forms the rhythmic basis of the whole piece. Five rhythmic layers are superimposed, four of them containing almost nothing but the note D: three layers in the piano, two in the orchestra. These layers are then used as rhythmic cycles, each of

EXAMPLE 2: DURAND, PIANO CONCERTO, MEASURES 200–9

them controlling one section of the piece (see Example 3). The rhythmic cycles thus generate the divisions of the whole piece, from a temporal as well as harmonic point of view.

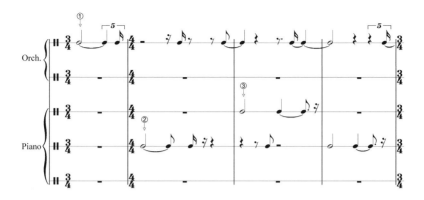

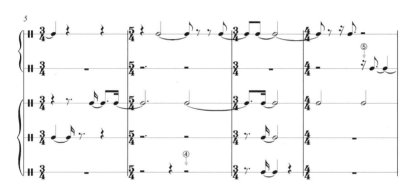

EXAMPLE 3: INTRODUCTION, MEASURES 1–19: RHYTHMIC LAYERS

One example of the use of these cycles is shown in Example 4, in which rhythmic layer 2 is repeated seven times throughout measures 77–200; the rhythms of the cycle serve as time-points to delimit harmonic changes. As for the chords, they are derived from a reading of the five rhythmic layers. By a ninety-degree rotation of the paper, the space of pitches becomes time, and the original rhythms become pitches (see Examples 5A and 5B). The apparent arbitrariness of the process is already alluded to at the beginning of my exposition, where I mentioned the fundamental opposition between the two protagonists ("two worlds based on entirely different structural premises"). The compositional approach involves radically independent methods of organization, as if each of the two worlds knew nothing of the other. Of course, this also means that, at least statistically, they could at times end up with very similar

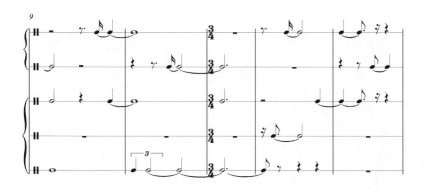

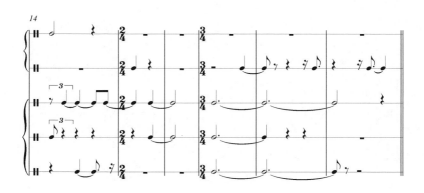

EXAMPLE 3 (CONT.)

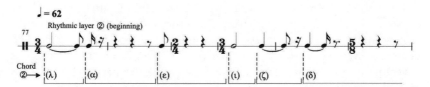

EXAMPLE 4: BEGINNING OF CYCLE 2: USE OF VERSIONS OF CHORD ② IN
RHYTHMIC LAYER ②

characteristics—and this does indeed occur. When it happens, no unnec-
essary effort is made to hide the fact. Previously, I made brief mention of
one of these moments: it is at the beginning of the second half of the

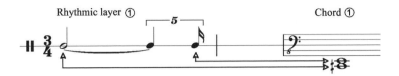

EXAMPLE 5A: CORRESPONDENCES BETWEEN DURATION AND PITCH INTERVAL: FIRST
MEASURE OF RHYTHMIC LAYER ① AND LOWEST INTERVAL OF CHORD ①

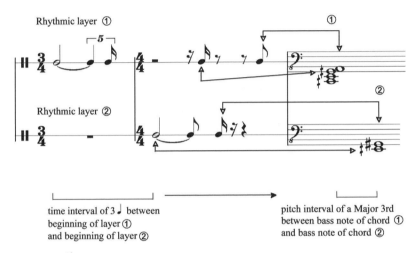

time interval of 3 ♩ between
beginning of layer ①
and beginning of layer ②

pitch interval of a Major 3rd
between bass note of chord ①
and bass note of chord ②

EXAMPLE 5B: CORRESPONDENCES BETWEEN DURATION AND PITCH INTERVALS:
RHYTHMIC LAYERS OF CHORDS ① AND ②

piano part, when the piano enters in a kind of fusion with the orchestra
(measures 210 ff). The gestural unity achieved here points for a moment
toward the deeper agreement between structural strata. But most of the
time this kind of fusion does not occur, and the structural distance
between the results of the two methods of organization allows for a wide
range of interactions between piano and orchestral instruments. The
chords have all different densities (corresponding to the number of attack
points in the five rhythmic layers): ① has fourteen notes, ② has eleven,
③ sixteen, and ④ and ⑤ seven each (see Example 6). The transpositions
are realized on each successive note of the chord, starting from the bottom pitch, so that the chord progressively "disappears," as its density
decreases (see Example 7). In the piece itself, the chords are mostly not
used   in   this   order   of   "disappearance."   They   are   chosen   in

correspondence to the type of density needed in each specific situation, in relation to the activity of the piano. In Example 6, note also the progressive ascent toward the higher registers as the later rhythmic layers enter.

EXAMPLE 6: HARMONIC MATERIAL

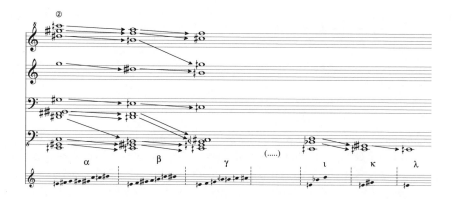

EXAMPLE 7: VERSIONS OF CHORD ② PRODUCED BY SUCCESSIVE REDUCTION

After the introduction, the rhythmic layers are rarely used in a direct way. One instance, however, is found in the section after the introduction, where the first layer is presented as a melody (in the orchestra) and at the same time generates the chords of that first section (measures 20–76). In each cycle, the rhythmic attacks trigger the use of a different transposition of the basic chord used in that section. In Cycle 2, the Greek letters under the rhythmic patterns of Example 4 correspond to the transpositions at the bottom of Example 7. The chords are also used as pitch "reservoir" for melodic purposes. To that effect, they are written in scalar form at the very bottom of Example 7 (all their forms are written starting on E♮, bass notes of all the forms of chord 2; this pitch acts as something like a "tonal" center for the whole section). Cycle 2 starts with a low E♮ in the trombone, followed by Chord 2 in its original, complete form. The role of this "tonal center" is visible also in the inner voices, where it acts as a pedal; see measures 80–91 for example, where the E♮ circulates throughout all the registers.

Going back to the introduction of the work (measures 1–20), we can now see how the time element serves as generator to both worlds in different ways. The basic gesture of the repeated D at the beginning of the work is pregnant with two potential progressions. On the one hand, it can generate a linear flow by becoming a melody; this is what the piano does after measure 20. In doing so, it keeps its dwelling in time. Its original horizontal dimension is maintained. On the other hand, it can become a harmonic construction: now time is made abstract and, by being measured, becomes space. As musical material, time is objectified by the negation of its experiential dimension. It serves as generator for the harmonic content of the orchestra, and then re-infuses the horizontal dimension by being organized as a system of repeated cycles controlling the use of these harmonies. The experiential dimension of time is first taken away from itself, then given back in a double movement of laying down (*legen*), then filling in, or collecting (*sammeln*).[1]

It is at that deep and abstract level of correspondences that the piece reveals a unity of conception, even though most of the musical elements derived from it seem to act against any possible coherence. These correspondences come more clearly to the fore in the second half of the piece, after the final violent opposition between piano and orchestra. During the last ninety measures, the piano attempts to free itself from a durational grid composed of a superimposition of the original rhythmic cycles. Starting at measure 256, the piano seems to be melodically blocked, getting "stuck" on D and C♯ in particular, at first. At this point, the orchestra takes advantage of the situation by bringing back a number of musical elements exposed in the first half by the piano, but in a very deformed manner, mainly because of the pitch and time constraints to which it is subject. The roles played by piano and orchestra in the first half are, so to speak, reversed here: the orchestra trying some of the melodic statements of the piano, the piano being by now far away from any capacity to create melodic lines—with a very different overall result.

This new type of opposition creates a more pronounced feeling of isolation, and it is only after the orchestra has left the field that the piano is able to indicate a new direction, reaching back to the beginning, as well as pointing forward. This is finally attained at the end of the Concerto, when the piano climbs to its highest register, and ends with a series of chords. Now, in that register, the notes can be perceived both as individuals and in their collective sounding together, offering a possible reconciliation of the basic conflict. The tones can be perceived in their individual identity, as well as in their togetherness, as community, without one dimension taking preeminence over the other. Silence is then the place where the collecting can occur.

NOTES

1. The Heideggerian overtones of this image are not unintentional; see Heidegger's essay, "Logos" on Heraclitus' Fragment 50 (*Diel*), which I first read in 1984, in *Early Greek Thinking*, trans. David Farrell Krell and Frank A. Capuzzi (New York: Harper & Row, 1984, pp. 59–78). The whole idea of formal revelation as I envisioned it in the mid-1980s was fundamentally also based on this same conceptual world of "collecting and selecting." Here again, the spiritual dimension, in the widest sense, is constantly present, although only in *my* reading of Heidegger.

IN THE MIRROR LAND

JOËL-FRANÇOIS DURAND

for Brian Ferneyhough on his 60th Birthday

IN THE MIRROR LAND

pour flûte et hautbois

Joël-François DURAND

2003

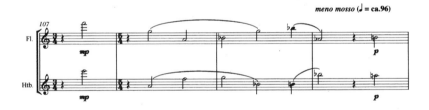

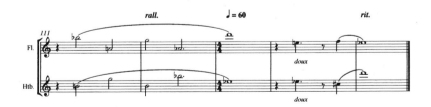

THEMATIC ADAPTATION IN RECENT WORKS OF JOËL-FRANÇOIS DURAND

ERIC FLESHER

THE RECENT MUSIC of Joël-François Durand has shown a remarkable, deepening ingenuity, reflecting a maturation of the composer's
style. One trait that has emerged in recent years is a penchant for re-
using older musical material, discovering its new, expressive potential by
recasting it in a variety of inventive ways. Engaging in more than a
simple act of recycling, Durand breathes new life into such musical ideas
in the ways he adapts them to their new contexts; although this process
may leave recognizable musical traces, the new works sound entirely
fresh, never derivative.

This approach to revisiting finished works is quite different from the
process of disassembly and reconstruction that Durand formerly
employed to create new works from old. For example, in two cases the
composer has applied a type of "diastic" reading to his earlier works,
defining a new syntax by applying a specific grammar. Moreover, while
earlier recompositions such as *Par le feu recueilli* were intended for the virtuoso performer, in his more recent works Durand tackles a variety of

ensembles—even dealing with performers of varying levels of technical accomplishment—shaping his ideas to meet the specific demands of each ensemble. To demonstrate this adaptational flexibility, I shall trace the development of common thematic material between three works of the late 1990s: *Au-delà* for solo piccolo, *Five Musical Tales* for orchestra (*Five Tales*), and *La Terre et le feu* for oboe and chamber ensemble (*La Terre*).[1]

Au-delà, composed in 1997–8, is the earliest in this series. It consists of five short etudes, the first and third of which deal with idiomatic aspects of piccolo writing, employing changes of register, glissandi, and other technical devices. The second and fourth etudes are less concerned with technical issues, focusing more on the use of motivic development to create a sense of form.[2] The fifth movement balances compositional technique and idiomatic piccolo writing, with its motivic development expressed through agile passages in detached articulation. Since the second, fourth, and fifth movements do not focus on technical devices per se, their presence is much more clearly felt in *Five Tales* and *La Terre*. The most notable adaptations the composer makes in creating these new pieces occur in his transformation of pitch and rhythmic material; the means Durand uses to achieve these ends is directly related to the ensembles for which they are scored.

Understanding the pitch language Durand uses in *Au-delà* is of preliminary importance in considering the reappearance of material in *Five Tales* and *La Terre*. Four of the five etudes employ microtonal inflections: the first, second, and fourth etudes are of greatest interest here, using alternate fingerings to produce discrete quarter-tones as well as lip glissandi to create microtonal shading.[3] The second etude contains the greatest density of quarter-tones, which must be produced at a moderately fast speed, often in irregular subdivisions of the beat; the fourth etude also makes prominent use of microtones, albeit at a slower tempo that somewhat facilitates their production.

La Terre, written in 1999 and premiered by the Ensemble Intercontemporain, recasts the fourth movement of *Au-delà*. Although traces of the earlier work can be found in the ensemble parts, there is a much clearer connection with the oboe part, much of which was directly generated from *Au-delà*. There is a deepening of complexity in both pitch and rhythmic language, with many of the seemingly spontaneous moments in *Au-delà* newly configured as structural events, influencing the development of musical ideas.

In adapting the original piccolo material in the oboe part of *La Terre*, Durand employs two main kinds of transformation. First, he makes more consistent use of quarter-tones. Comparing the first twenty-five measures of *La Terre* with its progenitor, we find that although the fourth movement of *Au-delà* contains both a higher number and a higher percentage of quarter-tones (twenty-two quarter-tones among 251 discrete pitch entrances, or 9%), the opening of *La Terre* (thirteen quarter-tones among 166 discrete pitch entrances in the oboe, or 8%) makes earlier and far more consistent use of microtonal shadings. In *Au-delà*, only five quarter-tones are encountered in the first twenty measures—and all of these occur in measures 1–9. The fourth movement's closing music, however, becomes far more saturated with quarter-tones, seventeen of which occur in the final nine measures.

In the opening twenty-six measures of *La Terre*, quarter-tones are heard with regular frequency following the entrance of the first micro-tone, E♯ in measure 5. Eight out of the twenty-one measures of the opening contain quarter-tones in the oboe line; discounting the two full measures of rest (measures 9 and 16, respectively), nearly one of every two measures (42%) contains microtonal shadings, creating the perception that quarter-tones are an integral aspect of the melodic language of the opening oboe solo.

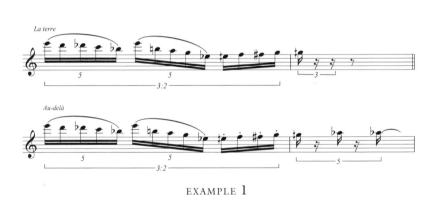

EXAMPLE 1

EXAMPLE 2

Moreover, quarter-tones take on a motivic function in this opening passage: the first occurrence of microtonal intervals occurs in measures 5–6 of *La Terre*, corresponding almost exactly to measures 2–3 of *Au-delà* (Example 1).[4] The subsequent usages of E♯ and G♯ develop their

EXAMPLE 3

original motivic appearance: their second occurrence in measure 20 is similar to their initial appearance, with the F♮ omitted. After the larger quarter-note triplet has been removed, the original sixteenth-note value is lengthened to an eighth, while the phrase-articulating triplet sixteenth note is lengthened to a triplet eighth (see Example 2). The last occurrence of the pitch G♯ appears in measure 24 without the E♮. Again, the motivic similarity is maintained by preserving most of the intervallic motion of the original: only the final interval has been altered from a quarter-tone to a semitone (Example 3).

EXAMPLE 4

EXAMPLE 5

The remaining quarter-tone pitch in this passage, A♮, has a more structural melodic function. In measure 10, it serves twice as a tone of figuration, initially with a quarter-tone alternation around A♭, followed by a quarter-tone trill on A♭ (Example 4). The subsequent appearance of A♮ in measure 12 is similarly a quarter-tone trill. All other occurrences of A♮ (measures 8, 14, and 18) serve as the closing pitch for phrases or phrase segments (Example 5).[5]

Compared to the rhythmic language of *Au-delà*, that of the opening of *La Terre* has likewise become more complex, favoring a greater concentration of irregular beat subdivisions. The fourth movement of *Au-delà*, at 126 eighth notes in length, contains forty eighth notes' worth of rhythmic dissonance; approximately 68% of the rhythmic information in this movement is irregular.[6] *La Terre*, however, contains thirty eighth notes' worth of rhythmic dissonance for an introduction of only 117 eighth notes in length; the percentage of odd-number subdivisions is increased to 74%.

There is, moreover, an audible difference: *Au-delà* begins with five full bars of rhythmic dissonance, and it is not until beat two of measure 6 that a regular subdivision of the thirty-second note is encountered. Since regular beat divisions seldom last longer than a quarter note in duration, the instability of such rhythmic language may pose difficulties for the listener in judging the actual speed of the music. In *La Terre*, however, the rhythmic complexity is more readily audible, as the rest of the ensemble plays predominantly in regular beat subdivisions; when departures from this norm are encountered, they are never more complex than triplets. The impression is therefore one of a relatively stable rhythmic background, contrasting with a complex and highly irregular oboe solo.

The composer's skills of adaptation were faced with a different type of challenge in the work preceding *La Terre*. *Five Tales* was written for the Seattle Youth Symphony at the request of its conductor at the time, Jonathan Shames. The realities of writing for a youth orchestra are quite immediate: one cannot expect developing musicians to execute complex rhythms with perfect consistency, nor should one expect such players to be familiar with microtonal intonation and the special techniques needed to produce such pitches. Three of the work's five movements have direct ties to *Au-delà*; the first movement, "Village Dance," will serve as a representative illustration of Durand's adaptation of his ideas to fit the technical limitations of writing for youth orchestra.

The movement's first forty-three measures correspond roughly to measures 1–22 of the second movement of *Au-delà*, whose melodic line is read through, with a few interruptions, to create most of the dance's melodic material. The changes made to the original material can be broken into two categories: a "tempering" of microtonal pitches, and "regularization" of rhythmic dissonance. The pitch material Durand uses is tempered in one of two ways, both of which take technical concerns into consideration. The first method adjusts the original quarter-tone line to twelve-tone pitch space by rounding off intervals to the nearest (smaller or larger) semitone.

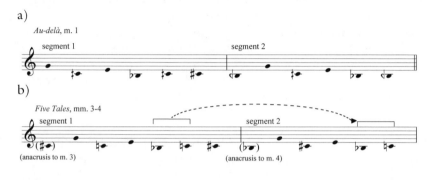

EXAMPLE 6

   Example 6 compares the pitch material of the first melodic phrase of *Five Tales* with its corresponding passage in *Au-delà*, dividing the larger, two-measure phrase into two-beat segments, labeled "1" and "2." The composer allows himself flexibility in choosing whether to round up or down to the next semitone: the C♯, found twice in the first measure of *Au-delà* (Example 6a, segment 1) is first rounded down to C♮ in *Five Tales* (Example 6b, segment 1). Its next occurrence (Example 6a, segment 2) is rounded up to C♯ (Example 6b, segment 2), creating a more balanced melodic line, shifting the initial tritone between the anacrusis and downbeat of measure 3 to the downbeat of measure 4, contrasting with the perfect fifth on the downbeat of measure 3. This shifted dissonance is immediately followed by the tritone E–B♭, propelling the phrase to its cadence on C. This cadence is itself the product of a freer semitonal rounding of the B♮, which is found twice in the original passage (Example 6a, segment 2). While its first occurrence is rounded down "normally" to B♭, its final instance is rounded up by three quarter-tones to C at the end of the phrase (Example 6b, segment 2). The local-level decision to use an interval larger than a quarter-tone for rounding further allows Durand to preserve the motivic B♭–C in the preceding segment of the phrase (Example 6b, segment 1).

Au-delà, m. 2

EXAMPLE 7

The phrase ending at measure 7 shows a different type of pitch adjustment, which, while possibly being mindful of the young interpreters, maintains the integrity of the original line. This passage corresponds with the end of measure 2 of *Au-delà* (Example 7), where a quarter-tone enlarged minor ninth (E♯–F♯) is preceded by a similarly enlarged tritone (B–E♯). Durand rescores this cadence for the violin by altering the E♯ up to G.

This not only preserves the contour of the original phrase, but also renders the line more easily playable by placing the lowest note on the open G string, allowing the violins to easily place the F♯ on the D string. A more explicit semitone rounding would change this note either to E or F♮; either way, the line would have to be rescored for an instrument capable of playing below G3, or it would have to be transposed to a higher octave. In either case, intonational problems could arise with the resultant ninth, especially among young musicians with different-sized hands.

Five Tales, mm. 2-7

Au-delà, mm. 1-3

EXAMPLE 8

The main change in rhythmic language in *Five Tales* is the composer's removal of most irregular beat subdivisions. *Au-delà* makes extensive use of triplets and quintuplets, which Durand has largely avoided in *Five Tales*. This process of rhythmic transformation manifests itself in two ways. First, rhythms are sometimes rewritten with regular beat subdivisions, with an attempt to preserve the rhythmic proportions of the original music. This is shown in Example 8, where the opening three measures of *Au-delà* are given with the corresponding passage from *Five Tales*. The first two triplet figures in measure 2 of *Au-delà* are converted to rhythms with sixteenth-note subdivisions. The impression of long and short rhythmic values is maintained, with the dotted-eighth–sixteenth figure at the end of the triplet on beat one almost literally transferred to the dotted-eighth–sixteenth figure at the beginning of measure 5 in *Five Tales*.

This is followed by a slightly freer rhythmic interpretation on beat 2, where a triplet sixteenth note is followed by the value of a full quarter note. This initial short value becomes a regular sixteenth-note pickup to the following quarter note; only at the end of the phrase is the triplet sixteenth speed preserved between the two passages.[7]

EXAMPLE 9

The other means of rhythmic simplification entails the removal or the addition of pitches. One example of the former occurs at measure 16 in *Au-delà*, where a series of sixteenth-note quintuplets is converted to three and one-half beats of sixteenths (*Five Tales,* measures 32–4). The fifth quintuplet sixteenth note of the original phrase is removed (Example 9), converting the remaining pitches into a regular grouping of four sixteenth notes. The following downbeat is preserved, with the phrase continuing a further three beats, ending on a final eighth-note value.

A more complex example of rhythmic transformation, involving pitch addition, is shown in Example 10. An E♭ is added to the final two beats of the new passage, converting the original triplet eighths into a group of four sixteenths. As he did in the passage quoted in Example 3 above, the

EXAMPLE 10

composer has sought to maintain the rhythmic proportions of the original phrase, converting the triplet figure on beat 2 of measure 8 into part of a sixteenth–eighth–sixteenth syncopation, whereas the eighth note of the following syncope on beat 4 is converted to a dotted eighth (measure 17, beat 2). The longest rhythmic value in the original phrase, a sixteenth tied to a dotted eighth (measure 9, beats 2–3) is shortened to an eighth note on beat 2 of measure 18.

One feature common to all these instances of rhythmic transformation is a flexible sense of downbeat: Durand does not attempt to keep pitches originally occurring on the beat in similar metrical positions. Instead, downbeats occur at new points within the phrase. In Example 10, for instance, the B♮ on beat 3 of the original becomes a sixteenth-note pickup to the second measure of the corresponding passage in *Five Musical Tales;* similarly, the B♭ in measure 9 of the original is also converted to a sixteenth-note pickup to the third measure of the corresponding passage.

The challenges Durand faced in recomposing ideas from *Au-delà* must have been daunting, and one could easily imagine a simpler, more formulaic approach that would generate numerous offspring from a single work. Indeed, his diastic readings of earlier works could easily have devolved into such mechanical derivation. It is characteristic of real composers, however, to maintain their artistic standards, regardless of the method by which their ideas are generated; it is the hallmark of *artists* to maintain these standards, regardless of medium for which they write. In responding to the compositional exigencies arising from both a new compositional grammar as well as the necessity of modifying musical language to suit his performers, Durand has proven himself to be a true artist.

Notes

1. The composer went further in his process of adaptation, creating *La Mesure de la terre et du feu* for oboe and viola from material contained in *La Terre*. Since this is, in a sense, a "second-generation" piece, it will remain outside the scope of this analysis.

2. Composer's performance notes for *Au-delà*.

3. The third etude also contains occasional microtonal shadings, produced by overblowing certain fundamentals at the third partial.

4. The only differences here are the missing staccato articulations on the last four sixteenth notes of the quarter-note triplet in *La Terre*, as well as the ending rhythm, which has been changed from a quintuplet *(Au-delà)* to a triplet sixteenth. See also Durand's essay in this volume, "Melody—Three Situations," which includes a complete score of the fourth piccolo etude as Example 10 (pp. 106–7).

5. A phrase segment here can be seen as an internal division of the larger phrase, marked either by a rest immediately following the segment or by a change in articulation, as shown by the end of the slur in measure 14.

6. Rhythmic dissonance here is defined as an irregular division or subdivision of the beat.

7. This is one of only two places in the entire movement where odd-number subdivisions are encountered, the other being the literal repeat of the last four notes of the cadence in measures 42–3.

Centers, Fields, and Cracks: Some Solutions to Problems of Contemporary Composition in the Music of Joël-François Durand

Ryan M. Hare

No one who has been an active participant in the creation, performance, or study of contemporary music, in this new century or in the previous one, has escaped the debate over its accessibility and relevance. This debate, like an invasive undergrowth, infests every forum for new music: its tangles have ensnared, agitated, and sometimes enraged almost everyone involved at one time or another. People who might otherwise be united in their enthusiasm for the art form are all too often cruelly divided by aesthetic or ideological differences. These differences are made all the more stark by a basic lack of agreement as to what to do about the central and by now quite chronic problem of the reception of new music among general audiences. Few, it seems, even those outside its avid fan base, would deny that contemporary music is important; yet many are dissatisfied with what actually makes its appearance under that name. It therefore suffers from a lack of popularity, even by the somewhat tame standards of "popularity" in the world of so-called art music; and living composers are regularly called to account for being out of touch with the public, for not caring what audiences want to hear.

In considering just what it is about this music that has contributed to the problem—what features of the music itself make it difficult for audiences to accept—the point is not to assign blame for the situation, or to condemn some particular body of works. Rather, I would prefer to suggest some paths that new music might follow in the future that would approach the problem differently from the way it has been done in the past, and that would do so without compromising artistic and aesthetic ideals. To ask that new music remain intrinsically new and challenging yet at the same time appeal, at least potentially, to a broader range of the listening public is, I realize, to ask a lot; but it is hard to imagine any other way out of the present crisis.

Part of the problem, certainly, is that the extraordinary diversity of contemporary music during the past century has itself exacerbated the situation to a level well beyond any historical precedent. The widespread confusion in the musical culture at large over just what contemporary music is, and whether its perceived "accessibility" is at all relevant to its worth, has confronted its promoters with an apparently Sisyphean struggle—one that composers too are drawn into whether they like it or not, with often detrimental effects on their creative energies. The diversity of the present-day musical scene unhelpfully presents the developing composer in particular with a bewilderingly vast range of compositional options, something that I can attest to first hand. This is particularly an issue for a composer who seeks constructive, non-polemical solutions that do not vitiate the essence of what contemporary music is: new music clearly belonging to these first years of the twenty-first century.

There is no universal solution, of course, and obviously no composer alive today can single-handedly resolve all these difficulties. However, in his recent music Joël-François Durand has taken some noteworthy steps toward doing so. A brilliant example of his success in this regard is provided by his oboe concerto, *La Terre et le feu* (1999). What is different about this work, by comparison to Durand's earlier compositions, is not at all that it adopts a more conservative musical vocabulary (it doesn't), or that Durand has in any way simplified or "dumbed down" his complex musical ideas (he hasn't), but that he has achieved a kind of clarity that was never as fully realized previously. It is the nature of this clarity which is of greatest interest: on the one hand, the familiar fingerprints of Durand's style, and some traditional elements of European-style modernism, are present: one finds complex rhythms, quarter-tones, and of course a non-tonal harmonic structure. On the other hand, the coherence of the ideas is never lost, the momentum of the musical argument is always clearly perceptible, and the musical expression itself is consequently that much more palpable. There is an impression of mystery, of an unfolding in the dramatic sense, and the musical structure in its complexity enhances this quality. The music is certainly new—one can make adequate comparisons only to other works in Durand's own oeuvre—but it is also holds the promise of being more approachable by a wide spectrum of the concertgoing public than one typically expects of contemporary music that is not blatantly retrogressive.

While the internal construction of a piece of music (its framework, its sources of material) is of vital concern to composers and analysts of music, and often to performers as well, few would argue that it holds much appeal for a general audience. The typical concertgoer may have relatively little interest in how a piece of music is made yet be deeply fascinated by what it means, what it expresses, what its connections to life are or might be, why it is beautiful, evocative, or profound. Knowing the twelve-tone row used in the composition, for example, isn't going to help him or her with such questions; composers need to recognize when it is time to set the shop talk aside. In Durand's case, the insights he offers into his own musical thought in his self-interview, "In the Mirror Land," are eminently suited to an audience with a broad range of musical knowledge and understanding, in that he does not avoid difficult ideas about music but does avoid specialized technical language. Most significant of all, his self-reflective dialogue communicates on a very personal level.

Advocates of contemporary music have been saying for decades that one of the principal obstacles to the appreciation of new music on the part of audiences is simple lack of familiarity. Undoubtedly this is true to a degree: music that seems prickly and incomprehensible at first often becomes far less daunting after repeated hearings. Much of the responsibility for facilitating such multiple exposure rests with performers of new music and the administrators of musical institutions—but it has to be shared by the composers themselves. One would hardly want to see the uncritical resuscitation of older musical styles and idioms—even though some composers seem to be attempting just such a "safe" route to gaining favor for their music—but one contributing factor to the perennial unfamiliarity of much new music stems from the opposite extreme, the riskiest imaginable behavior, on the part of composers who seek innovation almost every time they sit down to write a new piece.

Although, as John Rahn puts it, "In losing originality art loses itself,"[1] composers might do well to regard their efforts as contributing to innovation in a more general sense, relieving themselves (and the audiences) of the pressure to produce something totally different every time and increasing the likelihood that audiences will actually become familiar with their work. I would suggest that the music of Elliott Carter exemplifies the virtues of this approach. Carter's mature idiom has been well established for over fifty years, and while his style has certainly gone through some significant metamorphoses during that time, his musical personality has remained consistently and immediately recognizable. More important, while the forbidding density of the earlier music of his mature style has started to sound much more familiar, even somewhat "old-fashioned," it has also given way to a remarkable clarity of expression and gesture in his compositions of the past fifteen years or so. One might argue that this would not have been possible had Carter not had such a long career, writing so much music in a consistent, ever fruitful idiom.

Durand's account of his earlier career in "In the Mirror Land" reveals his struggles with the demands of innovation. Fatigued by a self-imposed compulsion to invent a different, elaborate precompositional structure for each new piece, he began to think, half-seriously, of doing the exact opposite, emulating the architect Roithamer in Thomas Bernhard's novel *Correction:* "I thought I should spend all my life just rewriting the same piece over and over, until I got it right."[2] The musical world should be grateful that he did not set out on that path after all—Roithamer's obsessive quest ends with his suicide—but eventually, Durand found that the right solution, for him, lay between the extremes of constant innovation and constant repetition, in an exploration of new ways to manipulate the musical structures of earlier compositions in order to create new ones.

Much more could be said about the contest between perpetual innovation and the need to create an integrated body of works, but what I would prefer to focus on here is the nature of the difficulty of the compositions themselves. Along with unfamiliar musical language and style, in much contemporary music the listener is also confronted with a formidably difficult musical surface. The sheer density of surface elements can confuse the listener, who is left frustrated, aurally grasping for something to follow. In the words of Pierre Boulez, "Beyond a certain complexity perception finds itself disoriented in a hopelessly entangled chaos . . . it gets bored and hangs up."[3] Can repeated hearings ever overcome the challenges posed by such complexity? Conditions that preclude easy apprehension of a work's form include rapid changes of texture, orchestration, or surface detail; texture or form with no immediately obvious hierarchy highlighting "important" musical elements for the listener to grasp; and a lack of repetition. None of these difficulties is unique to contemporary music, but in much of the standard repertoire the inherent compositional difficulties are more easily overlooked, and consequently are less of an impediment to appreciation, owing to the familiarity of common-practice tonality. Or, to put it another way, without the distraction of an unfamiliar style, listeners' ears may be directed more readily toward the other aspects of a score's complexity. Nevertheless, I suggest that composers would do well to think more carefully about how to make listeners aware of what they should be listening for.

Durand's recent music, and the ideas he has expressed in "In the Mirror Land," suggest some useful approaches to this problem, particularly his idea of musical centers and the fields within which they resonate. In Durand's words, "The idea of center inside a field, or rather of center generating a field, is usually a musical idea chosen by the composer for specific, personal reasons . . . active in the sense of creating a certain impetus, a movement forward, or a certain affective resonance."[4] Essentially, Durand's notion of musical centers allows a remarkable flexibility, in that it can apply to many different musical objects, and a freedom from the traditional concepts of musical texture which are, after all, primarily the legacy of tonal music. It is often problematic to make use of traditional terms such as "polyphony," "homophony," or even "heterophony" in describing the texture of much contemporary music, and for good reason. Along with the dissolution of traditional triadic harmony came a dissolution of conventional ideas of textural hierarchy, disorienting listeners who had been accustomed to rely on such conventions and were left mostly unable to discover a sense of direction in musical textures that lacked them.

For example, in the music of Anton Webern, applying terms such as "melody" and "accompaniment" is simply not very useful. His twelve-tone music is certainly more clearly "polyphonic" than his pre-twelve-tone works, but one distinctive attribute of Webern's style is that the polyphonic strands are not projected by single instruments, contrary to traditional polyphonic practice; the polyphonic "voices" are distributed in the ensemble according to musical logic which is structured independently from the instrumental parts themselves. This stylistic feature of course made possible Webern's *Klangfarben* orchestration of the *Ricercata à 6 voci* from J. S. Bach's *Musikalisches Opfer*. Further, in the pre-twelve-tone compositions, formal hierarchical distinctions can be tricky indeed. As Durand puts it, "In the early atonal music of Schoenberg and Webern . . . it sounds as if everything is essential, until you become quite familiar with it, though analysis."[5] I take it that "analysis" in this sense can be done informally on the part of a listener not otherwise trained in the vocabulary of contemporary music. One can grasp intuitively that certain elements of the musical texture, from the perspective of fields resonating from their centers, are salient and provide direction or a sense of momentum or "happening" in the musical form. A center can be virtually any sort of musical object: a melody, a theme, a motive, a chord, a texture, even a single note; the distinctive element of a center is the meaning it creates/inhabits within the large-scale musical structure. Durand's own discussion of what constitutes a center is thorough and interesting, so I will leave it to the reader to consult directly.[6] Its applicability to much contemporary music is readily apparent, and is even relevant to the realm of electronic and computer music, where so often the music consists of gestures and events that have little or no apparent relation to the traditional tonal sound world—yet one cannot deny the musical impetus of meaning in time that such gestures and events create.

The idea of musical centers has considerable significance for the function and hierarchy of texture in much contemporary music, for flexibility in the creation of new music, and even for new approaches to the understanding of structure from the point of view of performance. In the words of conductor Daniel Barenboim, "Music is not about statements or about being. It's about becoming. It's not the statement of a phrase that is really important, but how you get there and how you leave it and how you make the transition to the next phrase."[7] Barenboim's topic is performance interpretation, but his statements apply as readily to composing. This musical space, where the center—a phrase being one possible kind of center—becomes something, and where it came from, and where it goes, is aligned with Durand's notion of a musical field. As Durand writes, "As soon as something enters the realm of time, it is bound to *become* something else."[8] This is liberating as well as clarifying. It affords the composer (and the performer, and the listener) a path of discovery into musical structures in which the old terms for musical texture are misleading or simply not operative at all, and can also renew an understanding into the forms and idioms of traditional tonal music which are far more familiar. Barenboim, after all, is speaking in general terms, not specifically about contemporary music. A refined sense of musical structure by way of this dynamic concept of centers and fields leads to a superior apprehension of the important structural elements of the composition, particularly in contemporary compositions.

The tendency of much new music to be characterized by rapid and unpredictable surface change surely reflects the nature of contemporary society. In an era characterized by a greatly increased pace of change, it would be futile to demand of composers that their art remain impervious to its effects. The real issue here is: What are the threads connecting the things that are changing, or—to use Durand's terminology—what are the centers of the musical objects, and how are they related? How does one center become something else? How do these situations recur, or do they recur at all?

The lack of repetition as a general condition of contemporary music was extensively discussed from the 1950s on; it was one of the factors that provoked the development of minimalism, which offered a seeming superfluity of repetition in place of the modernist tendency to repeat nothing literally. The extremity of this reaction could be taken as symptomatic of the failure of contemporary post-tonal music, by and large, to replace much of what recurrence and repetition meant in tonal music. Some interesting solutions to this problem are to be found in Durand's thoughts on new roles for melody in contemporary composition.

In "Melody—Three Situations," Durand describes a compositional situation in which elements of the musical past may be transformed to achieve new meaning in the musical present and future, in this case regarding both melody and recurrence. Durand acknowledges the typical rejection of melody (in the way it was understood in common-practice tonality) by many contemporary composers, but points out as well that "It is still a fact that the need for linear organization of the musical discourse stubbornly survives," and "Fortunately, the state of composition has largely changed since the 1970s, and it is now again quite relevant to approach the subject without recourse to past compositional techniques and aesthetics."[9] Much of modernism has been characterized by the rejection of the past. One notion of what post-modernism could be is the recovery and reconsideration of some aspects of the musical past: not by regressing to some hopelessly anachronistic style, but rather by integrating those aspects with some of the notable artistic achievements of modernism without resort to ironic, self-referential commentary.

Therein lies Durand's interesting solution: he proposes and creates musical lines which can be clearly understood as melodies on some level, but whose importance in the musical structure is fundamentally different from that of melodic ideas in older music. In essence, the melodies in the three pieces Durand analyzes form centers of fields, with distinct meanings in the compositions, the identity of these centers having been reevaluated uniquely according to the structural principles governing each composition. In addition, the meaning (identity and function) of melodic lines is permitted to change through the course of the composition, not necessarily by way of standard types of development or sequence, but through unique and ever-changing interactions with the structure of the composition. Each of the three examples from Durand's own compositions makes use of different strategies, but the common thread between them is clear, as is its contribution to the expressive clarity of Durand's recent music. One can readily imagine the coherence that such an approach to melody might foster, coherence that meets listeners more than half way without sacrificing compositional creativity or originality.

Durand does not explicitly mention recurrence in "Melody—Three Situations"; nevertheless elements of recurrence are relevant to these concepts of new possible functions of melody in a composition. Of course, in a sense, the changing function of a melody as it recurs is a phenomenon already witnessed in the common-practice period: after all, when the first theme of a sonata-form exposition reappears in the recapitulation, even if literally, it does not function the same way—is not perceived to have the same meaning—as it did in the exposition. Or consider Bach's *Goldberg Variations:* one experiences the Aria very differently once one has taken the time to listen through all the variations that separate its first and second appearances. This basic premise is well understood, but Durand takes it several steps further by allowing a melody (its center and its field of resonance) to assume even more elaborate, and potentially ever-changing, structural roles. As a consequence, with this expansion of meaning and function on the part of melody, recurrence itself can also take on a renewed position of prominence, thereby enhancing the listener's apprehension of the work's discrete structural elements.

One further, intriguing feature of Durand's music is what he terms the "cracks": places in the musical fabric where something foreign, spontaneous, or generally unexpected is allowed to appear. Such moments may be governed purely by intuition: the music which enters a composition through a crack generates its own field and can determine a special meaning in the larger structure for itself as a center; thus such "inserts" can "project an aura beyond themselves within a piece."[10] The effect can be constructive or subversive, or something more ambiguous. Whatever their qualities, these cracks allow unexpected connections to be made between other fields and centers already operating within the piece. Thinking in terms of the fields projected by such events potentially enriches musical meaning, and encourages a dynamic understanding of musical structure on the part of the listener. It affords an opportunity to elucidate the intuitive.

Composers who desire their music to be challenging and original, or as John Rahn puts it, composers "whose musical minds are bent on exploration rather than colonization,"[11] are probably always going to face obstacles of one kind or another to widespread appreciation of their art. Every such composer's way of dealing with this problem will be different, no matter how willingly he or she does so. Durand's music offers persuasive solutions in part by allowing the integration of reconsidered musical elements, which enhance the coherence and, consequently, the directness of expression of his musical thought. Most appealing of all is that, with disparate concepts of music—concepts that were once thought incompatible—synthesized into something new, Durand's music shows one path away from some of the trends of contemporary music that have caused difficulty for many audience members. Notably, he achieves this without resorting to polemics, and all the while remains utterly true to an awareness of new art as something that should be at once challenging and inspiring.

NOTES

1. John Rahn, "What Is Valuable in Art, and Can Music Still Achieve It?," in *Perspectives on Musical Aesthetics,* ed. John Rahn (New York: Norton, 1994), 63.

2. See Joël-François Durand's "self-interview" elsewhere in this volume, "In the Mirror Land: Reflections on a Self-Reflection," 16.

3. Michel Foucault and Pierre Boulez, "Contemporary Music and the Public," trans. John Rahn, in *Perspectives on Musical Aesthetics,* 89.

4. Durand, "In the Mirror Land," 48.

5. Ibid., 49.

6. See, in particular, 49–52.

7. Daniel Barenboim and Edward Said, *Parallels and Paradoxes: Explorations in Music and Society* (New York: Pantheon, 2002), 21.

8. Durand, "In the Mirror Land," 45–6.

9. See Durand's essay elsewhere in this volume, "Melody—Three Situations: *Un Feu distinct, La Terre et le feu, Athanor,*" 89–90.

10. Durand, "In the Mirror Land," 52.

11. Rahn, "What Is Valuable in Art?," 56.

"As If to Illustrate the Process of Creation Itself": Joël-François Durand's *Lichtung*

Christian Asplund

Written in 1986–7 for string quartet with alto flute, clarinet, horn, trumpet, piano, and contrabass on commission from the Ensemble Intercontemporain, *Lichtung* is one of a series of compositions that Durand wrote during the years 1984–91 exploring the dynamics of presenting essential thematic material at the end rather than the beginning of a piece. Instead of presenting a pair of ideas that are then developed in the middle, then returned to at the end, *Lichtung* reveals an essence at the end, after a complex clearing process pursued throughout the course of the piece.

I. The Ur-Chords Narrative

This "essence" is a series of thirty-two pitch classes, called the "*Ur-Melodie*" in Durand's sketches (see Example 1).[1] From this series, Durand

generated thirty-two different series of chords that he called *Ur*-chords, numbered from U1 to U32 (Example 2). The U-number is more than an ordinal position in the collection of *Ur*-chords; it also indicates how many chords are in the series. U32 is actually the *Ur*-melody itself, consisting exclusively of monads. The *Ur*-melody folds in on itself in stages to form the successively shorter and denser *Ur*-chords from U31 (a succession of thirty-one dyads and monads), to U15 (a succession of fifteen trichords and dyads), to U11 (a succession of tetrachords and trichords), to U1, which is a single huge chord containing all twelve pitch classes.

Durand uses this collection of chord series throughout the piece to generate melodies, chords, textures, and even rhythms, but it also guides the underlying form of the whole piece. *Lichtung* begins in pyramiding fashion, revealing the first *Ur*-chord (U1) at measure 2 (see Example 3). Its voicing is highlighted by an all-interval tetrachord, A♭3/D4/G4/E5 (T_n type [0256]), played by the winds and vibraphone, that foreshadows the fundamental structure both of the *Ur*-melody and of the entire piece. From this point until rehearsal letter Q (measure 176), the piano and percussion, often doubled by the strings, play a straightforward statement of all the *Ur*-chords in order from U1 to U32, as other material is played by other instruments. From measure 172, U32, or the *Ur*-melody itself, played by the piano, leads to a climax of a tutti U1 at measure 176 (see Example 4).[2] This is followed by *Ur*-chords U2 through U8 in rapid succession, as tutti simultaneities.

Then, beginning with U9 in measure 185, the *Ur*-chords begin to splinter into multiple strata, divided among different instrumental groups. This proliferation reaches an apex at measure 193, where U19 (violin and cello), U20 (flute and clarinet), U21 (trumpet and bass), and U22 (viola and horn) appear simultaneously in different irregular subdivisions of the beat. From that point on, the textural complexity thins, little by little, until measure 203, where the violin begins a frenetic transposed version of U31, almost as if in defiance of something—a gesture that continues until the last few notes of the piece. In measure 209, the flute and horn begin the final statement of U32: the essence that is uncovered. This melody is exposed in long notes with varying unison orchestrations in the winds, while the violin, accompanied by its less

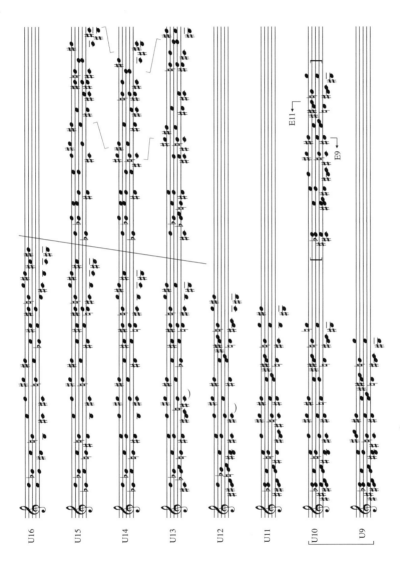

EXAMPLE 2: *LICHTUNG*: THE THIRTY-TWO SERIES OF *UR*-CHORDS

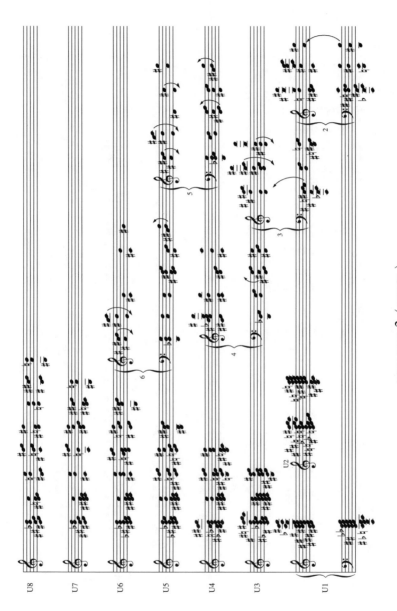

EXAMPLE 2 (CONT.)

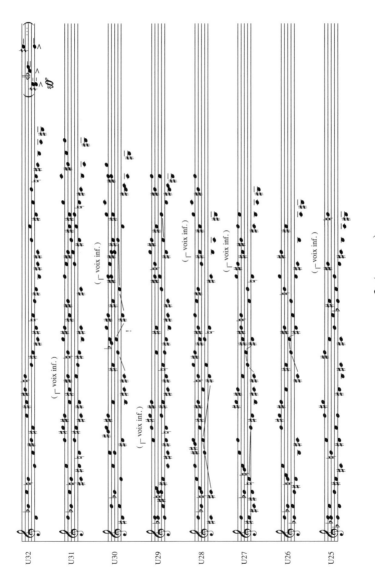

EXAMPLE 2 (CONT.)

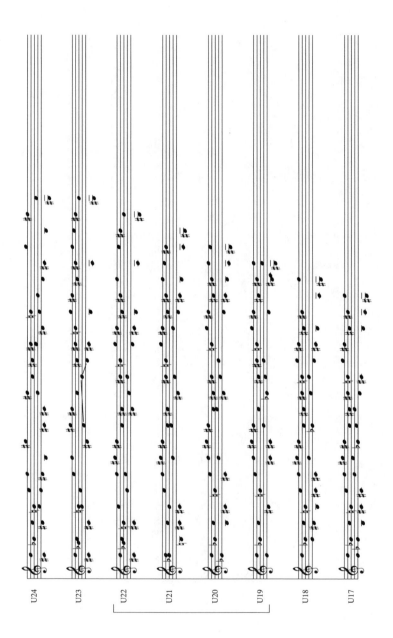

EXAMPLE 2 (CONT.)

Lichtung

Joël-François Durand

(1987)

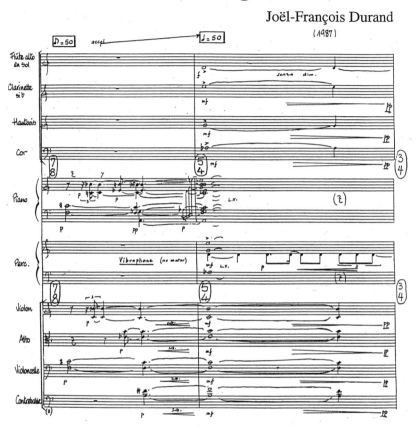

EXAMPLE 3: *LICHTUNG*, MEASURES 1–2

urgent partner, the viola, is sawing away on U29. The defiant gestures become more sparse and brief while the viola joins in with the sustained U32, until the last measure of the piece where, after a final burst from the violin, the clarinet takes over from the viola and gives the last fading tones of U32 (see Example 5).

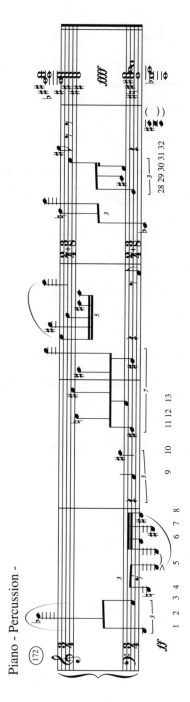

EXAMPLE 4: *LICHTUNG*, MEASURES 172–6

EXAMPLE 5: *LICHTUNG*, MEASURES 220–2

II. SECTIONAL NARRATIVE

Some of Durand's sketches suggest a seven-part division of the piece, marked with roman numerals I through VII and independent of the articulations signaled by rehearsal letters in the score—but without providing most of the specific boundaries for the sections. I have made my own seven-part division based on what information I can derive from the sketches, coupled with what seem to be logical structural divisions of the piece. Section Ia comprises measures 1–3, in which A♭3 and D4 emerge from U1 as the central pitches of the piece. Section Ib comprises measures 4–45, in which the alto flute moves gradually through an embellished chromatic ascent from D4 to C♯6. Section II begins at measure 43, before Ib ends, as the woodwinds begin "fighting" with each other, playing complex micropolyphony with intermittent chords in the strings, often in trills. The winds build to a fortissimo at measure 72, whereupon a sudden shift to *molto espressivo* muted strings brings in IIIa. Measure 83 is the first of two "chorale" intrusions in which the strings play a slow, quiet melody in octaves against the winds' harmonies, essentially in unison rhythm. Section IIIa ends in measure 106, shortly after the rhythmically complex string texture has ceased. In measure 107 the strings join in the more sustained texture of the winds that began IIIb in measure 96. This texture is dominated by a long melody in quarter-tone stepwise motion; it is passed around among the winds, which often play in and out of various stepwise and unison simultaneities, with crescendos and diminuendos. It has the effect of a kind of moaning. Durand's sketches suggest that this melody is derived from a version of U32 that is diminished by half in pitch space—that is, with minor seconds becoming quarter-tones, major seconds becoming minor seconds, minor thirds becoming three-quarter-tones, and so forth. The moaning becomes more urgent until measures 119–20, when a jerky piano and clarinet figure takes over, immediately followed by the second chorale intrusion in measure 121.

Section IV begins in measure 122 with a brief piano cadenza, which is answered by similar gestures in the winds. The dialogue continues with another piano cadenza beginning at measure 128 and a response from the winds beginning at measure 129. At the pickup to measure 132, the piano joins the winds in a kind of synthesis of the preceding dialectic that continues through measure 136. Throughout the passage, the strings provide an underpinning of sometimes widely spaced, sustained chords in crescendo. At measure 137 the ensemble divides into two ensembles that share downbeats of measures but have different meters. The winds and piano are in $\frac{2}{4}$, while the percussion and strings are in $\frac{3}{4}$. The split ceases at measure 148 (rehearsal N) when section V begins what might be called the piano-dominated portion of the piece. The piano is forced to play fast, dense passages with little or no silence because it has reached the last few *Ur*-chords, where the series are twenty or more chords in length. This leads naturally to a harmonic and rhythmic intensification, in the course of which (rehearsal P, measure 165) the ensemble again splits metrically. The reunion occurs at the climax (rehearsal Q, measure 176), the beginning of Section VI and a tutti presentation of U1 at *ffff*. A rapid statement of tutti *Ur*-chords in rhythmic unison follows; VIIa begins on measure 199 when the flute begins a transition to the final statement of U32, which begins VIIb in measure 209.

This narrative reveals the three crucial moments of *Lichtung*: the beginning, in which A♭3 and D4 emerge from U1 (see Example 3); measure 176, where U32 seems to give birth to U1 in a violent and powerful gesture (see Example 4); and the ending, in which a peaceful, dying gesture reveals the essential character of U32 (Example 5).

III. Discussion of the Reductions

After listening to *Lichtung* many times, both with and without score, I began to feel that I was experiencing an unfolding of pitches over long spans of time that could be elegantly communicated in a reductive notation borrowed from the graphing techniques of Schenkerian analysis. Such an analytic strategy seems uniquely appropriate to this work, since "*Lichtung* means 'clearing'. . . and that refers to Bernhard's *Korrektur*, which is about the process of constantly revising a work to the point where it is reduced progressively (by eliminations) to a very short, 'essential' version."[3]

In each phrase or section, at each level, I have used the listening process to intuit a hierarchy of notes, guided by some very basic principles of melodic design. For the "foreground" and "middleground" layers, I have indicated what seem to be the more structural notes with stems. Notes interpreted as embellishments are slurred to the stemmed notes they apparently prolong. The basic paradigms of passing tone, neighbor, and consonant skip are thus operative in this process, if in vestigial form. To move to the next stage of reduction, I have removed unstemmed notes and then selected even more structural notes from among those remaining. I have performed this process repeatedly until arriving at what could plausibly stand as the "background." In keeping with the graphic conventions of Schenkerian notation, open noteheads represent the most fundamental layer of all. This approach is very efficient, assuming that an analysis can reveal *a* truth (a way of hearing or interpreting a piece) rather than *the* truth about a piece (the only way of hearing or interpreting a piece), whether "correct" or "incorrect." The unity of musical space (in multiple dimensions), which is operative in *Lichtung*, allows for multiple interpretations. As with any object of three (or more) dimensions, perception depends upon perspective.

WHY A REDUCTION THAT IGNORES THE MIDDLE OF THE PIECE?

The reader will notice that my graphs focus on the first and last sections, I and VII. After many listenings, I found that VII seemed to answer the question asked in I by the alto flute, and by the U1 in measure 2. Moreover, faced with the considerable expanse of the score, I sought an analytic strategy that would enable me to examine the pitch organization of specific sections of the piece (in the context of more general narratives of the entire piece) and the way in which this pitch organization reinforces motivic and tonal tendencies of U32. The beginning and ending were natural choices.

The reduction of section I reveals an epic-length chromatically ascending line that composes out U1, "the big chord." We then find that this line, together with the unison statement of U32 (in VIIb) with its descending arc, form an antecedent-consequent pair, the many measures of intervening music notwithstanding. Therefore, sections II through VI are appropriately bracketed in this pitch reduction as explorations in a more open musical space, opened up by the ascending alto flute span. The newly revealed U32 in VII represents the actual destination of the alto flute line in Section I.

Two PITCHES

As mentioned earlier, D4 and A♭3 are the primary pitches of *Lichtung*, the tonic dyad as it were. As the first and last pitches of U32, their importance is unavoidable. The following narrative will discuss the way in the which the graph reveals these pitches at the top of the hierarchy. (In fact, a cursory glance at the graphs will reveal these pitches to be primary.)

Two INTERVALS

This pitch pair gives us our first structural interval, the tritone. The second is the semitone. In *Lichtung*, the roles of the tritone and the semitone, and their relationship to each other, are analogous on some levels to that of the perfect fifth and the step in tonality. The semitone is not as pitch-specific as the tritone; it appears prominently in U32 and in all the graphs, but, more important, it is composed out on multiple levels in the chromatic double-neighbor motive discussed below.

Two MOTIVES

The reduction reveals two motives, found on more than one structural level, that are present already in U32. These motives are identified throughout the graphs with square brackets. The first motive is the chromatic double neighbor (often labeled "DNM" or double-neighbor motive) $<+2,-1>$ (or its inversion, $<-2,+1>$) that we find in order numbers $<2,3,4>$, $<10,11,12>$ of U32 (see Example 1). A less important motive, with several intervallic manifestations, consists of two steps in the same direction. The most frequently occurring is the one consisting of one semitone and one whole tone. It is found in U32 at order numbers

<30,31,32>, <28,29,30>, <25,26,27>, <15,16,17>, <9,10,11>, and, as compound melody, <1,5,6> (see Example 1).

GRAPH NARRATIVES

The analysis is conveyed in five graphs:

Graph 1 (Example 6) concerns section Ib (measures 4–45) and encompasses a total of five layers, from a foreground to a deep middleground (Layer 4).

Graph 2 (Example 7) reduces section VII (measures 199–end), four layers from the foreground to Layer 4.

Graph 3 (Example 8) combines Layers 4 from Graphs 1 and 2 into what I call Layer 3. Layer 3 is reduced to Layers 2 and 1 and finally to a background that is further reduced to a generating sonority, functioning analogously to Schenker's tonic triad. An alternative reduction of Layer 3 is also given.

Graph 4 (Example 9) begins with the last page, the "essence" spoken of, as an independent foreground. It is reduced along three different pathways to arrive at the generating sonority.

Graph 5 (Example 10) takes the idea of Graph 3 a step further and hollows out even more of the middle of *Lichtung*, leaving only Ia and VIIb.

GRAPH 1 NARRATIVE

SECTION IA

This opening simultaneously contains the piece's structure in microcosm and exemplifies Durand's stated conception of revealing an essence from a more complex, developed structure, as opposed to the more traditional approach of stating the thesis in the beginning and developing or varying it from there. U1 is the final product of a series of precompositional transformations that leads from a thirty-two-note melody (U32, the *Ur*-melody) to a single huge chord. Yet U1 is presented first in *Lichtung*, "struck" like a rolled chord, after which certain tones are revealed as fundamental once others decay. These tones fulfill the Schenkerian role of the triad in the fundamental structure of *Lichtung*. In the last page of the score (VIIb) a silence of two and a half beats precedes the similarly intense and concentrated close of the piece. In this case, it is not a chord and its important tones that are exposed, but rather the final phrase of

U32, the *Ur*-chord that is a melody and the first stage in the genesis of *Lichtung*. This closing also contains a strong resolution to D4 and A♭3, as revealed in each background. It also points up Durand's tendency to use semitone or quarter-tone upper and lower leading/neighbor tones to reinforce important pitches.

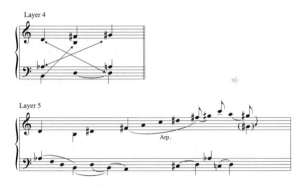

EXAMPLE 6: GRAPH 1 (LAYERS 4 AND 5)

Section I*b*
In measures 2–3, D4 immediately begins to emerge as a pitch center as all instruments but the vibraphone and alto flute that are holding this pitch begin to fade out. The vibraphone's lowest note, A♭3, also becomes significant when it is allowed to resonate along with G4 and E5. However, since it is the lowest note in the chord, it naturally sustains for a longer duration. Consequently, A♭3 is prolonged as a bass tone through measure 5, where it is reiterated in the piano. The D4 is also reiterated repeatedly by alto flute and piano in measures 3–5, and reinforced by a variety of neighbor/leading tones in the alto flute, often a quarter-tone away from D4. The opening ends on measure 6 with a "half-cadence" with the virtual bass and treble voices in unison on a C4, which is held in diminuendo by the alto flute. In the measure before rehearsal A (measure 13), there is a full cadence on the D4/A♭3 dyad.[4] In the process of unfolding this tritone, certain similarly symmetrical patterns start to form. One such symmetry lies in the use of B3, equidistant between A♭3 and D4, as a prominent resting tone.

An important cadence on B3 occurs in the last beat of measure 21 with a fermata. Consequently, the diminished triad becomes, by extension, an important fundamental sonority. In Layer 5, we notice that a diminished seventh chord is formed in the bass using A♭, F, D, and B. This sketch

EXAMPLE 6 (CONT.): GRAPH 1 (LAYERS 6, 7, AND FOREGROUND)

also reveals a diminished seventh chord as a means for the soprano to fill in an octave leap from F♯4 to F♯5. Note how the foreground presents a soprano that undulates around certain pitches in quarter-tones and gradually rises. Layer 7 reveals a chromatic rise from D4 (or, under a slightly different interpretation, B3) to C♯6, occurring in mm. 3–39, which in Layer 5 reduces to a rise through minor thirds, or an arpeggiated

EXAMPLE 6 (CONT.): GRAPH 1 (LAYERS 6, 7, AND FOREGROUND)
(CONT.)

diminished-seventh chord from D♯ through to C6, with the A5 resolving
down to G♯. An initial ascent of a tritone from the central D4 to the G♯4,
an octave above the important G♯3, emerges in Layer 4.

Layer 6 reveals a convergence on a cluster (beginning of measure 8)
with C, C♮, and C♯ which soprano and bass approach by contrary

EXAMPLE 6 (CONT.): GRAPH 1 (LAYERS 6, 7, AND FOREGROUND)
(CONT.)

motion. This convergence points up a tendency throughout the analysis for the soprano and bass to hand off pitches, to cross, and to move generally in the same register.

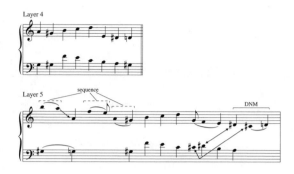

EXAMPLE 7: GRAPH 2, SECTION VII (LAYERS 4, 5, 6, AND FOREGROUND)

EXAMPLE 7(CONT.)

GRAPH 2 NARRATIVE (SECTION VII)

The graphs of Section VII (Example 7) reveal a more tightly concentrated melodic structure characterized by a more traditional curve rather than a long upward sweep. Note the prominence of C♯ and G as "leading tones" to D and G♯, as well as the "phrygian" leading tones, E♭ and A, that lead to D and G♯ from above. Note also several sequential or semi-sequential figures (marked by dotted square brackets). Again, the double chromatic neighbor motive is crucial. Soprano and bass overlap frequently and trade pitches freely. Notice especially the foreground of measures 217–8. The elegance of the final two measures as a distillation of *Lichtung* is illustrated in this graph, in which the final tones of U32 outline a perfectly balanced cadential formula. We find indeed that the chord formed by G♯3 and D4 is the fundamental sonority from the final background of the sketch for the last page (Graph 4, Example 9; see below).

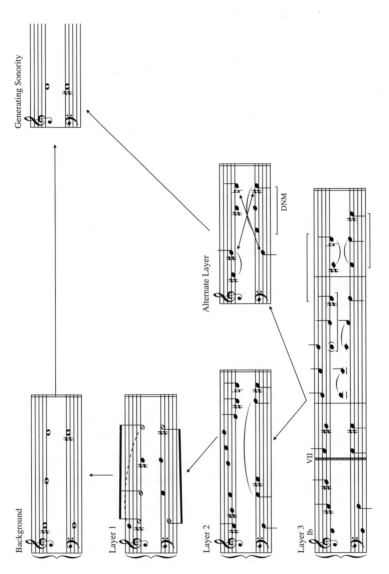

EXAMPLE 8: GRAPH 3 (BACKGROUND AND LAYERS 1, 2, 3)

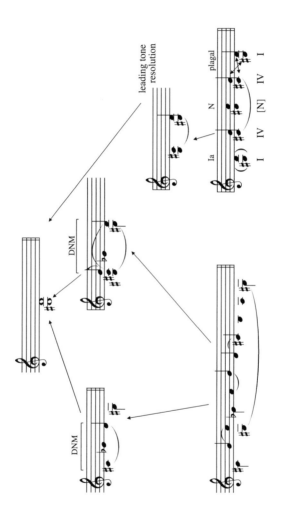

EXAMPLE 9: GRAPH 4: VIIB "ESSENCE"

GRAPH 3 NARRATIVE (SECTIONS IB/VII)

This sketch (Example 8) brings together the background levels of Sections Ib and VII. We find that VII picks up the melodic motion stepwise where Ib left off. The background looks strikingly similar to the most common Schenkerian *Ursatz*. The soprano moves down in two whole steps like a "three-line" and the bass ascends by a fourth, albeit an augmented one. As the final chord, the tritone seems to function in this atonal space as an octave does in tonal space.

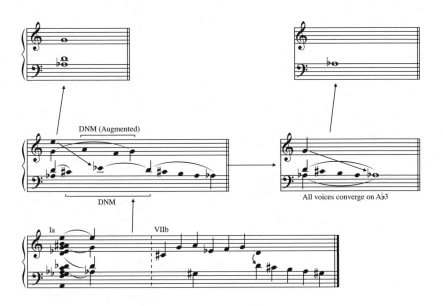

EXAMPLE 10: GRAPH 5: OUTER EDGES (IA–VIIB)

GRAPH 4 NARRATIVE (VIIB)

In the three different interpretations of the foreground shown in Example 9, we notice the prominent hallmarks of this piece: the chromatic double neighbor and the G♯3/D4 sonority. The problem here is how to deal with G4. Each of the first two solutions (from left to right) has its own merits. The first proposes a "monophonic" interpretation, where the skip from D4 to G♯3 is preceded by a double neighbor that prolongs D4. In the second, the G♯3 is heard as a pedal tone throughout the passage, and the G4 is bracketed as an important but not structural descant. The third interpretation reevaluates the role of G4 as part of a passage of parallel tritones that includes an upper neighbor and a descending ("plagal") perfect fourth. An additional association is presented as a register displacement and a notation that looks and functions something like a voice exchange. This third interpretation has an additional layer before the shared generating sonority in which the register displacement is taken away and the soprano G4 appears as the alto G3. The C♯4–D4 leading-tone figure is now all in the soprano, yielding parallel tritones ascending by half step: a double leading tone.

GRAPH 5 NARRATIVE (IA/VIIB)

The final sketch (Example 10) takes the idea of hollowing out the middle, found in Graph 3, a step further. This graph of Ia and VIIb, the outer edges of the piece, tests their unique background, which naturally reinforces most of the background conclusions of the other sketches but has, to some extent, its own logic.

The most foreground layer shows all of the notes heard in Ia and VIIb in sequential order in two parts. The middleground puts all of these notes in four parts, which reveals a very elegant prolongation of a "Viennese" chord in fourths, A♭3/D4/G4. The chromatic double-neighbor motive in the tenor and an augmented, whole-step version of this same motive (that is, <–4, +2> instead of <–2, +1>) firmly imprint the D4 and G4. The A♭3 is always present as pedal. This level leads to two possible paths, one suggesting an immediate background consisting of the A♭3/D4/G4 sonority, the other an additional middleground level in which all three remaining voices converge at A♭3. Both paths lead to a background of the A♭3 monad.

We have, then, graphs that reduce different quantities of music that result in different, though related backgrounds. The fact that three different generating sonorities are represented (A♭3, A♭3/D4, and A♭3/D4/G4) suggests a hierarchy for the three pitches, with A♭3 being the most fundamental, followed in importance by D4 and then G4. However, I would suggest, rather, that D4 assumes more prominence in the beginning (section I) while A♭3 becomes more important in the last section (section VII). This would suggest a unifying paradigm of the descending tritone skip, D4–A♭3.

CONCLUDING COMMENTS ABOUT THE REDUCTIONS

The understanding of a piece such as *Lichtung* can benefit greatly from a hierarchal sifting of its multitude of sounded pitches. The graphing process reveals both the underlying voice leading of specific passages and, ultimately, voice-leading paradigms that may be unique to the piece or repertoire. With non-tonal music, we cannot use the tonic triad and the descending scale as the underlying structural frame. We can instead find a unique harmony and/or melodic sequence that form the piece, as with the D4–A♭3 dyad in *Lichtung*.

This approach to atonal music enables us to hear melodies that we may otherwise miss, at least on a conscious level. Besides making us aware of an overall motion that underlies a piece, it can also free us from the kind of note-counting that can bog down the listening experience with a piece of this scale and complexity, rather than open it up. This is especially true of music with a substantial precompositional element, where the analyst may feel obliged to decode the poietic while neglecting the aesthetic.[5] Finally, such an analysis provides one possible route to a better understanding of the continuum (albeit a problematic one) between non-tonal music and tonal music.

IV. REVERSAL OF POIETIC AND ESTHESIC

In writing this essay, I was confronted with multiple and multiply-layered narratives:

Lichtung
Score of *Lichtung*
Recordings of *Lichtung*
Recollection of a live performance of *Lichtung*
Durand's meta-narrative of the piece's genesis
Durand's own analytical illustrations (including the *Ur*-chords) of
    Lichtung
Durand's sketches
An early draft of my own paper
Durand's comments on my draft
Bernhard's *Correction*, the last word of which provided the title of this
    work
Durand's interpretation of *Correction*
My recollection of Durand's interpretation of *Correction*

Durand's correction of my recollection of Durand's interpretation of *Correction*

Durand's revision of the structural meta-narrative of *Correction* that provided the structural meta-narrative for *Lichtung*

The poietic meta-narrative of classical music comes to us from a multitude of sources, including (especially) the Beethoven sketchbooks (perhaps as mediated by Leonard Bernstein and others). In this meta-narrative, the music emerges from murky origins through layers of revision, finally to reveal a finished product, a composition of structure and complexity, such as the second movement of the *Eroica* Symphony. The aesthetic meta-narrative of classical music is the familiar account of sonata form, which itself models the "organic," "creative-process" meta-narrative of romanticism more generally. Two (contrasting but related) ideas are presented as germ and seed which couple, grow, develop, and flower, finally to produce seed and germ, which are somewhat different from the original elements.

Lichtung reverses these. On the composition side, the sketches and recollections of the composer suggest an initial composition of two contrasting but related ideas, the U1 *Ur*-chord and the U32 *Ur*-melody. These are transformed through developmental processes into thirty other sequences of pitches or chords, which are themselves developed into the passages of music that make up the score. The finished product models a different process: that of the progressive revelation of an essence. The essence is always present—that is, it does not evolve or grow. Rather, it goes from being partially hidden to being gently but clearly open to view in the final measures, "as if to illustrate the process of creation itself."[6]

V. The Essence of a Meta-Narrative of *Correction* and *Lichtung*

Lichtung, or "clearing," is the final word of Bernhard's *Correction*, a novel that deeply influenced Durand during the 1980s. In *Lichtung* and in his texts about it, Durand revises two concepts underlying *Correction*: "correction" and "clearing."

CORRECTION:

Bernhard's idea of "multiple revision resulting in an 'essential' version: . . . the ultimate 'correction' or revision being [a] suicide," is revised in *Lichtung* in such a way that "the origin of the work is progressively revealed to the listener, as if to illustrate the process of creation itself, in which ideas are discarded, others are kept, in order to get to the essence of the work . . . , as if one were wandering in the forest, passing through various densities of textures until one gets to the center, the light, the clearing." [7]

CLEARING:

"[*Correction*'s] trajectory leads . . . closer and closer, not just to the clearing . . . , but to a clearer understanding of what the clearing means . . . , as the place where something terrible happened . . . a suicide. . . . [B]ut that morbid occurrence has nothing to do with my piece! I actually turned the metaphor around and associated the idea of clearing, as the end of a process of discovery, to the idea of birth, of creation (the origin of the piece)." [8]

Notes

1. Joël-François Durand, sketches for *Lichtung*. I am grateful to the composer for letting me borrow these sketches for study.

2. Durand, lecture handout for *Lichtung*.

3. Durand, private communication to the author, June 1996. "Bernhard's *Korrektur*" is a reference to Thomas Bernhard's 1975 novel, trans. Sophie Wilkins as *Correction* (Chicago: University of Chicago Press, 1990). I should also mention that in later correspondence (3 May 2004), Durand stated that "[t]hat idea of revision is not at all part of the conception of . . . the piece. . . . There is no sense of going over and over the same things, then correcting them by reduction, or anything like that." Whether or not there is a "sense" of revision in the piece, the role that *Correction* played suggests the aptness of this analytic strategy.

4. The cadences mentioned here and later obviously do not use the harmonic vocabulary of tonality. But they do represent, not only textural points of repose, but harmonic ones as well. I am proposing a pitch relationship that is analogous to the I–V dialectic. The C4 monad functions here as an intermediate and somewhat unstable resting place, while the D4-Ab3 dyad is the generating or "home" sonority.

5. Arnold Schoenberg's words from a letter to Rudolf Kolisch (July 1932) come to mind: "You have rightly worked out the series in my string quartet. . . . But do you think one's any better off for knowing it? . . . This isn't where the aesthetic qualities reveal themselves. . . . I can't utter too many warnings against overrating these analyses, since after all they only lead to what I have always been dead against: seeing how it is *done*; whereas I have always helped people to see: what it *is*!" Schoenberg, *Letters*, ed. Erwin Stein, trans. Eithne Wilkins and Ernst Kaiser (Berkeley: University of California Press, 1987), 164.

6. Durand to the author, 3 May 2004.

7. Durand to the author, June 1996.

8. Durand to the author, 3 May 2004.

DURAND, BERNHARD, AND FORM

JONATHAN W. BERNARD

THE RELATIONSHIP BETWEEN LITERATURE and music has a venerable place in Western cultural history, but it is only in relatively recent times that it has received sustained attention from either artists or critics, in detailed or appreciably technical terms. That there are by now so many examples to be cited of the impact that a novel, play, poem, or philosophical treatise has had on a musical composition may be assessed as one of the more significant legacies of modernism—which, among its many other effects on the arts of the twentieth century, greatly stimulated their mutual influence. And it is to modernism, most likely, that we owe as well our awareness of this influence and the impetus to talk about it—something that, to judge from the work of many a contemporary composer, may turn out to be one of its most lasting effects.

Readers of Joël-François Durand's self-interview "In the Mirror Land," elsewhere in this volume, can already appreciate that this composer, for one, is a serious reader, with eclectic and wide-ranging tastes; but among the authors from whom he has drawn instruction and artistic nourishment, surely the postwar Austrian novelist and playwright Thomas Bernhard (1931–1989) must stand in first place. Durand's encounter with Bernhard, which began with Bernhard's novel *Correction* (*Korrektur*,

1975) in 1978 and has been renewed continually since then, registers most strongly, perhaps, in pieces written during the 1980s, starting with the earliest works he now acknowledges as his. Even over the past decade, though, it is clear that the influence of Bernhard continues to resonate for Durand, and remains special for him even beyond that of the numerous other authors to whom he accords more than passing mention.

Before discussing what Durand has absorbed from Bernhard, in ways that are specifically reflected in his compositions, it is worth considering what there is about the work of this writer that might be of special interest to a composer. The plot details in some of the novels, of course, seem almost guaranteed to attract the attention of musicians: the fictional Glenn Gould in *The Loser* (*Der Untergeher*, 1983), for example, who resembles the real Glenn Gould in certain respects, but in others decidedly not; the narrator of *Concrete* (*Beton*, 1982), who has been working for ten years on the definitive study of Mendelssohn but who has yet to write a word of it, owing to an inability to think of the right opening sentence. (The type of character represented by the latter, the blocked writer monstrously exaggerated, appears in many of Bernhard's works: someone whose creative efforts produce only pathological effects, and whose portrayal cannot help but evoke a response of morbid fascination from anyone who has ever felt the afflictions, be they mild or severe, of artistic blockage.)

But the first thing that probably strikes any reader picking up a book by Bernhard for the first time is, simply, the unusual appearance of the text on the page: the prose unrolls in sentences that are often extremely long even by the standards of the German language—sometimes going on for a page, or even more—and often without paragraph or chapter breaks. The novel *Correction* falls into two sections, the first of which in the English translation runs to 138 pages, the second 131, with not a single paragraph break in either section; the novel *The Lime Works* (*Die Kalkwerk*, 1970), after an opening, fairly brief passage in which ellipses mark several line breaks (not quite paragraphing), proceeds for the remainder of its 239 pages with no breaks at all. This format alone might well suggest the idea of *flow*, in the musical sense; but it is the qualities of Bernhard's diction that are particularly suggestive of an analogy to music. The "seamless" look of the text is not, after all, simply the author's stylistic conceit: often cast as an interior monologue, whether in first or third person, the narrative is possessed of a remarkable continuity that quite readily brings music to mind for anyone, it would seem, with the least sensitivity to that art. Bernhard himself vouched for the analogy on several occasions; for example: "I would say, [writing, for me,] is a question of rhythm and has a great deal to do with music. Yes, what I write can be understood only if one gets it clear that the musical element counts first of all, and that only in second place comes what I am narrating."[1] The encouragement supplied by such statements has led some literary critics to note, for instance, Bernhard's "speech analogous to music, in which words seem to metamorphose into tones."[2] This quality comes across even in English translation, if not with quite the vividness of the original; it is difficult to give an accurate impression of it in a short excerpt, but here is one that may serve, the opening sentence of *Yes* (*Ja*, 1978):

> The Swiss and his woman friend had appeared at the real-estate agent Moritz's place at just the moment when, for the first time, I was trying not only to outline to him the symptoms of my emotional and mental sickness and eventually elucidate them as a science, but had come to Moritz's house, who in point of fact was then probably the person closest to me, in order quite suddenly and in the most ruthless manner to turn the inside of my, by then not just sickly but totally sickness-ridden, existence, which until then he had known just superficially and had not therefore been unduly irritated let alone alarmed by in any way, turn that inside of my existence out, and thus inevitably *alarmed and appalled* him by the very abrupt brutality of my undertaking, by the fact that, on that afternoon, I totally unveiled and revealed what, over the whole decade of my acquaintance and friendship with Moritz, I had kept hidden from him, indeed concealed from him throughout that period with mathematical ingeniousness, and kept continually (and pitilessly towards myself) covered from him, in order not to grant him, Moritz, even the slightest glimpse into my existence, which profoundly horrified him, but I had not allowed that horror to impede me in the least in my revealing mechanism which had, that afternoon and of course also under the influence of the weather, gone into action, and step by step, that afternoon, I had, as though I had no other choice, all of a sudden pounced upon Moritz from my mental ambush, unveiling *everything* related to myself, *un*veiling everything that there was to unveil, *revealing* everything there was to *reveal*; throughout the incident I had been seated, as always, in the corner seat facing the two windows by the entrance to Moritz's office, to what I always called his box-file room, while Moritz himself, after all this was the end of October, sat facing me in his mouse-grey overcoat, possibly by then in a drunk state, which in the falling dusk I had been unable to determine; I had not, all that time, let my eyes leave him, it was as if that afternoon, after many weeks when I had not been to the Moritz house and had completely been on my own, which means reduced to my own head and to my own body, for a very long, though not

yet nerve-wrecking, time in a state of utmost concentration *about everything*, resolved to do *anything* that promised me salvation, and finally, leaving my damp and cold and dark house and crossing the dense and sombre wood, pounced on Moritz as though on a life-saving sacrifice in order, as I had determined on my way to Moritz's house, to persist in my revelations and therefore downright improper hurts until I had reached a tolerable degree of relief, which meant until I had unveiled and revealed as much as possible of my existence which for many years I had concealed from him.[3]

One notices immediately the way in which the sentence seems to keep extending itself, encompassing within its arc what more "normal" prose might have broken into a dozen or more separate sentences. The flow is by no means steady: some phrases advance the narrative, others dwell upon or circle about what has just been said, repeating, elaborating, or varying it, often almost obsessively—or come back after a certain interval to ideas previously exposed—before the narrative can continue once again. This process is implemented in part by the emphasis on certain words through immediate repetition and unpredictable underscoring ("unveil," "reveal," "everything"/"anything"), and their return later in the sentence, as well as words that receive no particular emphasis when first used that nevertheless register as repetitions when re-used, at widely varying intervals ("sickness"/"sickly" recurs right away; for "concealed" we wait much longer; "existence" is repeated once in the short run and once in the long). Also noteworthy is that several of these repetitions occur right at the end of the quoted sentence, almost as though their disparate periodicities had synchronized at that point.[4] Schenker's assertion that all great musical composition originates in extemporization comes to mind, for there is something of the performed, even the improvised, in prose like this, a quality that has not been lost on the keenest observers of Bernhard's art: "Bernhard's texts read as if he spoke them out loud into the typewriter. He performed himself in the act of writing."[5]

There is also something virtuosic about the passage quoted above, a quality that hints at another possible link to music. Stephen D. Dowden has pointed out that, while in a way it trivializes Bernhard "to reduce his . . . art to its technical virtuosity, customarily celebrated as 'musical,'" still "this virtuosity is surely the key, its role is specific and identifiable."[6] As Dowden adds, though, virtuosity need not *necessarily* be interpreted specifically as musical. Partly for that reason, it seems, the various attempts that have been made to pin down the putatively musical quality of Bernhard's prose with analogies to specific musical forms, devices, or repertoires have usually missed the mark. To speak of the word repetitions identified above, for example, as if they were "motifs" in the musical sense is only to engage a metaphor that leads nowhere and is, as a result, unconvincing. To locate the "developmental spiral" of Bernhard's writing, in the words of one critic, "somewhere between Bach's *Art of the Fugue* and the twelve-tone repetitions of Schönberg and Webern" is to clarify very little.[7] Jonathan J. Long remarks that the "fetishizing or absolutizing of musical terminology" evident in characterizations of Bernhard's repetitions of words or phrases as akin to rondo, or in the description of one section of *Old Masters* (*Alte Meister*, 1985) as a double fugue, is best set aside in favor of more general analogies, such as those ventured by Gregor Hens in his analysis of *Old Masters* invoking the metaphor of three voices in counterpoint, or the idea of polyphony inherent in a character saying one thing and thinking something quite the opposite at the same time.[8] But this approach is not quite satisfactory, either. True, it avoids the pitfalls posed by overly specific analogies; but the kind of connection proposed in their place is *so* general that it might as easily apply to many other works of literature, leaving the special stylistic qualities of Bernhard's prose—the ones that make him instantly recognizable—completely out of account.

One other aspect of Bernhard's writing that does hold some promise for an analogy to music lies in its larger dimensions: what could be called its form. Comparisons of Bernhard's novels to fugues and rondos are flawed not only because they are too specific, but also because they are anachronistic. Why should musical forms of this kind, already outmoded well before the close of the nineteenth century, be particularly germane to *any* art of the late twentieth? Form, I would suspect, is as problematic a topic in literature of the past half-century as it is in music of the same period. To the extent that theorists and analysts have been able to get anywhere with the idea of form in late twentieth-century music, they have done so by appealing to the idea that every individual work "discovers" its own form—which is not to say that every work by a given composer is necessarily radically different from every other, but simply that nothing, when it comes to form, can ever be taken for granted, even in its most general outlines. Having established that basic principle, it is usually possible to find "typical" ways in which individual composers arrive at the form of their compositions, even if (as is often the case) these ways change from time to time.

Likewise, writers about Bernhard have identified certain narrative strategies that seem to be of general, if not absolutely universal import in his works. One, certainly, is repetitive narration, in which the same event is recounted more than once, changing its significance for the narrator (and the reader). For example, in *Yes*, the narrator states that he wants to

tell the story of what happened after his meeting with Moritz's clients—
and yet, as he keeps coming back to this meeting, it becomes ever clearer
that he is actually fixated on his life *before* that meeting, and on his state
of depression (this process of clarification is begun in the very first sentence, quoted earlier in this essay). "The circular movement of the narrative, which always returns to the same point in time and space, is a
formal analogue of the self-absorbed, even solipsistic existence that the
narrator leads, and provides a vivid illustration of his inability to break
out of it."[9] Another strategy is the fragmentary or self-contradictory
presentation, in which some critics have found evidence of nihilism: a
mismatch between language and reality, in which the characters can convey "only fragments of experience, which the reader must integrate as
best he can."[10] In *The Lime Works*, this effort is doomed, ultimately, to
failure, because the narrator is not fully in control of his own narrative
and presents a mass of information in which the factual discrepancies fail
to add up to a coherent picture.[11] In the second part of *Correction*, fragmentary presentation plays a role in the form of excerpts from
Roithamer's (by this time) hopelessly mixed-up papers (already in a
somewhat disordered state at the beginning of the novel, toward the
end of the first part they are unceremoniously dumped out of the knapsack containing them, in a seemingly deliberate attempt by the narrator
to avoid ever being able to sort them out successfully). A third strategy
is the construction of multiple time levels, which considerably complicates the narrative in many of Bernhard's works, sometimes compromising it to the point that the reader cannot be absolutely sure just when
certain events took place in relation to others. In the first part of *Correction*, for example, there are three such levels: (1) the time spent by the
narrator in Höller's attic, sorting through Roithamer's papers; (2) a time
further in the past, in which the narrator recalls other events; (3) the
time in which the narrative is actually being written down.[12]

Emphasis on fragmentation and ambiguous temporal structuring,
however, should not come at the expense of noticing that, despite the
fact that the *completed* details of the story being recounted, in all their
multifarious particularity, can never be known with absolute accuracy, still
their general import, often at first somewhat shrouded in mystery,
becomes ever clearer as the narrative advances. And it is this inexorable,
irreversible development that gives Bernhard's narratives a good deal of
their enormous and ominous power. One finds some acknowledgment of
this in the critical literature: Dowden, for instance, mentions the "incrementally gathering clarity" of the second part of *Extinction* (*Auslöschung*,
1986), which proceeds, as he puts it, by way of the "manic flow of words
and thought . . . , developing the characters and ideas with increasing

insistence."[13] It should be obvious, in the second part of *Correction*, that while the narrator may never manage to put more than a tiny fraction of Roithamer's text fragments into any kind of plausible order, still the main development becomes ever clearer: Roithamer, trapped by his own ideas and the failure of his great project to fulfill its intended purpose (quite devastatingly the opposite, in fact: the cone-shaped house he built for his sister to provide her with the most blissful existence imaginable instead precipitates her death), travels in a metaphorical spiral that is echoed in his final, literal path to the clearing in the middle of the forest, the site of the abandoned cone house and his suicide.

Ultimately, perhaps, there is no way to explain the "musical" effect of Bernhard's writing except by reference to the creative work of artists who are known, from extrinsic evidence, to have been influenced by him. Some, at least, of Durand's compositions are examples of such creative work. The question for us—since ultimately, in this connection, we are more interested in Durand's music than Bernhard's prose—is: How might Durand be "read" through Bernhard, in a way that would shed some light on how his pieces came to assume their definitive shape, without raising the expectation that *every* salient feature of Bernhard's prose is faithfully reflected in these pieces? For if indeed Durand did learn from Bernhard, his method was hardly one of slavish adoption. Some of the formal devices mentioned in the previous paragraphs are highly suggestive for analysis of Durand's own forms; but others, it is quite clear, were firmly rejected, if in fact they were ever even considered.

As mentioned earlier, the experience of reading Bernhard's prose left traces in Durand's music from the beginning of his career. Durand has mentioned that the "relentless continuity" he grew to admire in Bernhard served as a model as early as the String Trio (1981).[14] Not much later comes his "German trilogy," comprising *So er* (1985), *Lichtung* (1987), and *Die innere Grenze* (1988), the first two of which signal a direct relation to Bernhard in the choice of title. *Lichtung*, as noted elsewhere in this volume, refers specifically to *Correction*, "Lichtung" ("clearing") being the last word (and last sentence in its entirety) of that novel, emblematizing the ever-intensifying focus upon "correction"— that is, the process of revision that leads to a single word—and also denoting the clearing in the forest where the culminating act of Roithamer's life (his suicide) takes place.[15] The title *So er* alludes to a kind of rhetorical device found in many of Bernhard's works, but it could be taken to point specifically to the second part of *Correction*, "Sifting and Sorting," which is the narrator's attempt to put into some meaningful order a selection from the vast, completely disorganized pile of jottings that constitute Roithamer's *Nachlaß*: every so often, as if to remind the reader that these are really not his, the narrator's, words, the phrase "so Roithamer" is interjected, usually although not always at the end of a sentence. Thus Durand's title removes the character's identity from this punctuating phrase to lend it a meaning something like "so he wrote" or "so he spoke."

The very striking opening of *So er*, with its rhythmically gnarled phrases in the low winds and brass separated by measures of complete silence, has, to my ears, an almost rhetorical quality. There is no perceptible regularity to the durations of the phrases; all are fairly short, but they range between two and thirteen beats in length through measure 21, after which the separating silences cease (the latter vary less: between one and a half and three beats). They do have other features in common, however: all but one ends at a loud dynamic, either in crescendo or *senza diminuendo*; and almost all of them end with a (vertical) interval of a tone, a semitone, or a cluster involving both. The clear articulation supplied by these common features does not make the phrase endings identical, but they are close enough in effect to make the possibility that an analogy is intended here to the recurrent "so Roithamer" of *Correction* too strong to overlook.

Of course, Durand does not continue in this fashion all the way through his piece the way Bernhard does in "Sifting and Sorting." Starting in measure 25, sounds begin to seep into the spaces between the phrases, as notes from these phrases are sustained, then begin to take on a kind of minimal development of their own (measures 30–2), then produce phrases in their own right simultaneously with the sustained notes (41–3). Up until this point, we have heard only the instruments in Group 2; now Group 1 joins in. Both are confined to woodwinds and brass (each also including one percussionist on pitched and unpitched metallic instruments), but the makeup of each is distinctive (only the horn is found in both), and they are spatially separated in the stage seating plan. The increase in timbral diversity brought about by Group 1's entrance goes hand in hand with an increase in rhythmic/contrapuntal complexity, eventually coming to something of a climax in measures 82–3, where every instrument of the two groups is playing *f* or *ff* in a different rhythm; after an extremely quiet fermata chord in measure 84, this rhythmically saturated texture reenters with redoubled force in measure 85, then dwindles away over the next couple of measures as Group 3 (all strings, also separated spatially from the others) makes its first appearance, ushering in a new phase of the piece.

From about Rehearsal J (measure 123) on—approximately the last third of *So er*—one begins to notice a gradual change in the rhythmic quality, as rhythmic unison becomes an ever more dominant feature of the texture. The bass clarinet and trombone of Group 2 (also in pitch unison) and the piccolo of Group 1 play continuously from measure 123 to measure 152 in rhythmic unison, a line broken only occasionally by rests that are also taken mostly in unison. While this is going on, establishing a basis for "common purpose" between the two wind groups that has not heretofore existed explicitly, the other, essentially accompanying parts are beginning to coalesce rhythmically as well. This development is manifested at first mainly by separate rhythmic unisons in the two different groups that are also separate from the continuing piccolo/bass clarinet/trombone line; but as the strings reenter, at the upbeat to measure 143, rhythmic agreement becomes closer between the two wind groups, in part by way of synchronization with the solo instruments. Following the momentary blurring (return of rhythmic complexity) in measure 153, trombone and piccolo coordinate for one more phrase, after which (measure 158 on) they begin to pull apart—again, a change seeming to occur in response to the reentry of the strings after a long hiatus. The pickup to measure 160 is a synchronization of eight instruments (two each from the two wind groups, four from the strings), after which a more heterophonic texture reasserts itself for a short time—except that in each group the endings are still synchronized (measures 161–3). In measure 164 the texture is clearly stratified into just two rhythmic planes, joining the two wind groups; this situation continues for the next few measures, with some instruments switching planes and new ones entering. By measure 168 there are four planes—but this seems to be a mere bump in the road toward unanimity, for in measure 170 a two-plane system is once again in place, again also joining instruments from the two wind groups.

At measure 174 another string entrance signals the next phase: all instruments in the three groups coordinate here, and from here until the end (measure 198) the texture is given over entirely to chords. The strings, in keeping with their special role, play in a kind of antiphony to the two wind groups until dropping out for good after measure 192, leaving the winds to finish the piece with a series of quiet, irregularly spaced chords. Example 1 presents a series of "snapshots" that summarize rhythmic developments over these last seventy-five measures of the piece: in 1a, the two-voice melody in rhythmic unison with subordinate parts in their independent organization; in 1b, the closer coordination of these subordinate parts with the two-voice melody; in 1c, the first clear instance of two planes; in 1d, the synchronized entrance of all winds and strings; in 1e, an example of wind/string antiphony; in 1f, the final four chords.

The gradual process of rhythmic simplification carried out over this stretch of music is probably the most immediately audible measure of the

EXAMPLE 1A: DURAND, *SO ER*, MEASURES 123–7

motion towards the center, the gradual revelation of the basis of the
work, and is also one means by which Durand realizes the idea of *distance,* "a key word in my conception of the piece," as he asserts in a program note. Distance has four aspects in *So er:* spatial, structural, symbolic,
and pure. Rhythmic development, especially in terms of the tendency
toward unison textures and verticalization that becomes ever stronger as
the piece approaches its conclusion, could be said to draw on at least
three of them: spatial (the division of the ensemble into groups and sub-
groups, which makes it possible to hear the rhythmic stratification as it
emerges); symbolic (which "refers to the process by which the music
slowly approaches its original material—the piece approaches its center");
and pure (having to do mainly with the string group, the sound and
expression of which is quite different from that of the wind groups, but

EXAMPLE 1B: *SO ER*, MEASURES 133–7

whose material nonetheless "is as close as can be to the heart of the piece" and that therefore never quite merges with the other groups: "it keeps its distance").[16]

As for structural distance, under Durand's definition it is specifically relevant to the harmonic plan (the "accords de base" and their slow emergence as the piece progresses)—less aurally obvious, perhaps, than the rhythmic dimension, but no less important. Example 2 reproduces this scheme of fundamental chords as Durand has outlined it: eight in all, only seven of which are actually used for the most part; the eighth, shown in parentheses, is saved for the very final sonority and comes into play, somewhat obscurely, a little earlier in the final passage. The seven chords are organized, according to the composer, with "each of them controlling a

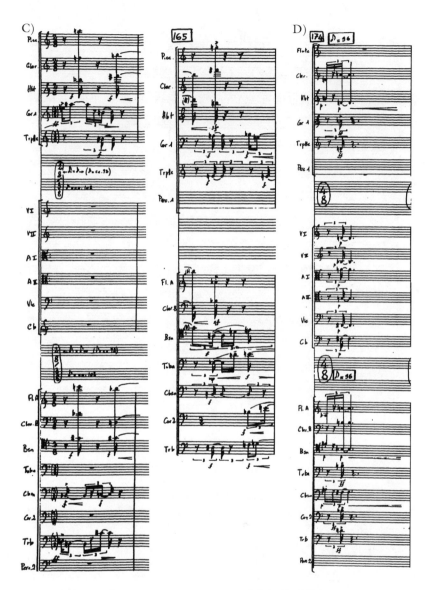

EXAMPLE 1 C–D: *SO ER*, MEASURES 164–5, 174

different section of the work while undergoing various transformations."[17] Durand's scheme also presents twelve melodies (not shown in
Example 2), each tracing a specific "path" through the sequence of chords

EXAMPLE 1 E: *SO ER*, MEASURES 182–4

and each assigned to one of the wind instruments. (There is no hint of "traditional" voice leading here: the flute does take as its melody all the highest notes of the chords, but the oboe proceeds C–G♯–C♯–E–F♯–D– B♭, the clarinet has F♯–C–G–F–A–D♯–E, and so on.) A note in the sketches indicates that while the music of Group 2 concentrates on the

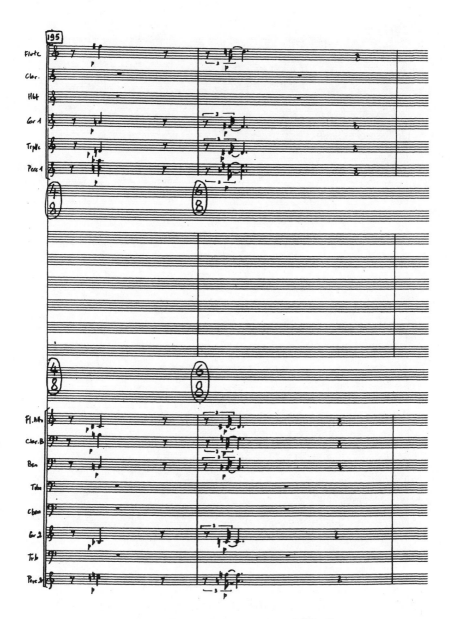

EXAMPLE 1F: *SO ER*, MEASURES 195–8

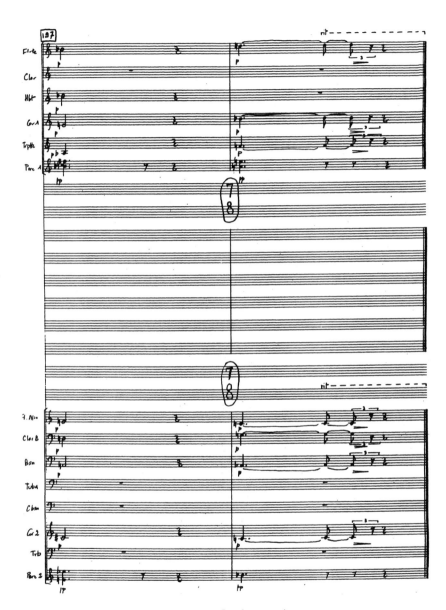

EXAMPLE 1F (CONT.)

fundamental chords, that of Group 1 deals more with the melodies—the implication being, apparently, that as the end of the piece approaches these two aspects of structure will come into an alignment that more and more resembles the model in Example 2. An examination of the opening (Example 3), where Group 2 is heard exclusively and Chord 1 is the controlling sonority, suggests that the assigned melodies are nowhere to be found, on the surface at least, even if some short fragments seem almost recognizable. Harmonically speaking, however, the texture is absolutely saturated with the whole-tone sound of Chord 1, with a strong emphasis on trichord (026), the uppermost three notes of the chord, and its inversion (046), in various of their transpositions. Complete forms of the chord do not turn up for a while: the first is the rather obliquely presented [0,2,4,6,8] in measure 10, with 3 as a "passing tone," interlocked with [2,4,6,8,10] (measures 10–1); then [1,3,5,7,9] in measure 11. Here at the beginning of the piece, these formations are very far from the point where they will be presented explicitly as *chords;* instead, they occur as collections dispersed over several beats.[18]

EXAMPLE 2: *SO ER*, SOURCE CHORDS (FROM COMPOSER'S NOTES)

Turning now to the final twenty-five measures of *So er*, where as noted the texture has been taken over entirely by chords, we find Durand's scheme being realized, although not in quite as neat a form as we might have expected. Example 4 displays the entire final passage in harmonic reduction, with the chords labeled according to the numbering in Example 2. While every vertical formation can be traced, in some fashion, to the scheme, there are a few "wrinkles" that persist right to the end of the piece. Measure 173—actually a kind of large upbeat to the major structural articulation in measure 174—provides some idea of the intricacies involved. The first four numbered chords occur here in order, but in the first, the F must be ignored; the instance of Chord 2 is actually an

EXAMPLE 3: *SO ER*, MEASURES 1–11 WITH ANALYTIC OVERLAY

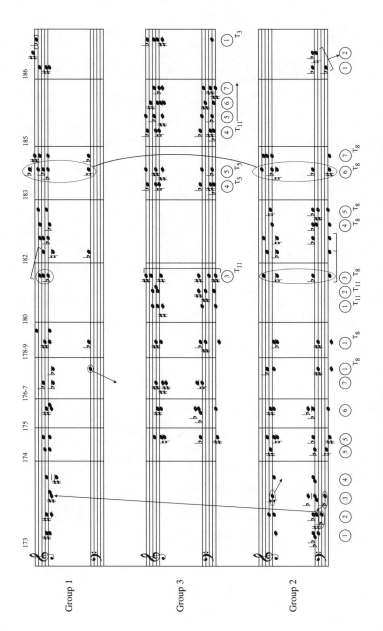

EXAMPLE 4: *SO ER*, MEASURES 173–98, HARMONIC REDUCTION

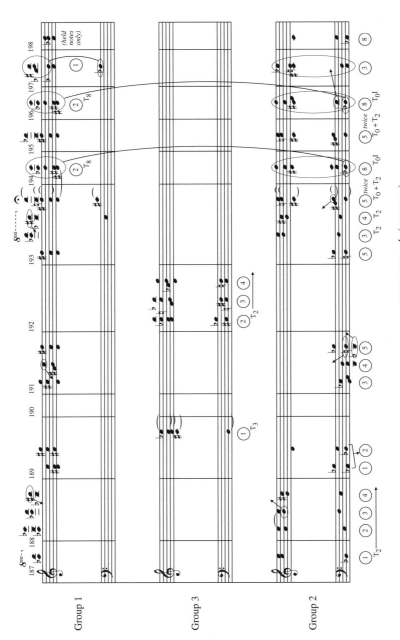

EXAMPLE 4 (CONT.)

amalgamation of its original pitch content and its inversion; Chord 3 has an extraneous B♭ that really belongs to the previous chord; and Chord 4 lacks an E, which must be supplied by Chord 3 (the circled pitches are directed by arrows to their "proper" locations). In a way, this makes sense, for throughgoing verticalization has just begun to be established here; but adjustments of this and other kinds continue to be necessary for a successful reading of the harmonies.

A survey of Example 4 shows that the chords generally appear in numerical order, as if by way of several complete or partial passes through the scheme, with an occasional momentary doubling back—as for example at measure 183, where Chord 5 (measure 182) is followed by Chord 4, after which Chords 5, 6, and 7 complete the sequence. There is frequent recourse to transposition, at different levels that are usually maintained for several successive chords. The final measures present the greatest analytical challenges of all: here the combination of different forms of the same chord or even different chords, a possibility already hinted at in previous measures, is made extensive use of; Chord 8 appears twice in inversion before sounding, "upright" and untransposed, as the last sonority. As for the melodies, some, at least, emerge explicitly—though it is clear that the extensive reworking of the harmonies by comparison to the scheme of Example 2 somewhat complicates the proceedings. The flute does manage a complete version of its melody from measure 189 to the end (with one pitch pair repeated); horn 1 and bass clarinet do the same, but include one extra pitch each; trumpet and horn 2 also do the same, but each with one pitch omitted. Others seem to occur only in fragments—some of them, by proxy as it were, in the strings, where they are also transposed.

In short, although this aspect of compositional structure remains somewhat enigmatic, enough of its components fall into conformity with the process of clarification delineated by the rhythmic developments previously discussed to allow us to draw provisional parallels with that "incrementally gathering clarity" in Bernhard. To me, what is most striking about the resemblance, particularly when the comparison is made in terms of the rhythmic aspect of Durand's scores (this one as well as others), is the sense of irrevocability at each turning point, when a palpably new stage is entered into. Some of the effect (in Bernhard at least) is attributable to the fact that the reader does not consciously register the fact that a change is happening until some time after it has begun; but it is precisely this use of the device that heightens the growing sense that the circle is closing, that complete understanding will arrive only once it is too late to escape.

In the second part of *Correction*, there are numerous such turning points. The Roithamer we first encounter through the mediation of the narrator's "sifting and sorting" of his fragmentary texts is, to all appearances, very much an outwardly directed person, acting quite aggressively in the world at large: conducting scientific research in Cambridge and traveling back and forth between this professional base and his native territory in upper Austria in order to see to two other matters occupying his attention: building the cone house for his sister and making arrangements to sell off the family estate that he grew up loathing. He does not yet seem much of a victim (although the reader knows, from the first part of the book, of his eventual end), even if he is evidently suffering under a rather pronounced persecution complex. This aggressive, confident stance, however, is all a façade, in which cracks soon begin to appear. One of the first is his passing remark that he was capable of building the Cone, as he calls it, in which he has he has invested so much time and money, "though it runs counter to my mind and counter to all, even my, reason." Another, not many pages later, is a detailed description of the interior of the Cone itself, supposedly a gift of love to his sister, which quickly begins to sound crazily oppressive, more like a prison than a place where any sane person would want to live.[19] Gradually, Roithamer's focus shifts from the outer world, turning inward to his recollections of life as a child growing up at Altensam; his animosity toward everything and everyone narrows to a more or less exclusive focus upon his parents (especially his mother), whom he blames for his self-acknowledged "monstrousness"—and, as the appalling details come to light, bit by bit, one can hardly blame him. Clearly, however, something is wrong here, for his parents have both been dead for some time, yet he cannot seem to shake free of their grasp.

The next stage in Roithamer's progress toward self-understanding is his recognition that this monstrous quality in him was essential to launching him on the Cone project, *"this terrifying idea,"* as he calls it, which became a way of conquering his monstrousness before it destroyed him. Yet in the end it's a no-win situation, for "once we've reached our aim, we no longer know anything about the way to our aim and we keep finding it impossible to believe, for the rest of our lives our doubt keeps increasing and we can't believe that we have reached our aim . . . even if this aim is the building of a so-called work of art, we find ourselves frightened by it."[20] During the six years that this project requires for its realization, the turning inward intensifies with Roithamer's retreat from his foothold at Altensam and his taking of lodgings in Höller's attic when visiting the region. The attic, in fact, becomes a kind of womb for gestation of his project, papered from floor to ceiling with plans and drawings for the Cone and with texts of importance to him.

Meanwhile, the subject of suicide has made its first appearance in Roithamer's writings, in the context of his mother's manipulative behavior, a threat she frequently held out to get her way in disputes with his father.[21] Eventually we hear about two relatives who actually have committed suicide; and it is at this point that Roithamer is impelled to make the fatal connection between correction and negation:

> Actually I'm shocked by everything I've just written, what if it was all quite different, I wonder, but I will not correct *now* what I've written, I'll correct it all when the time for such correction has come and then I'll correct the corrections and correct again the resulting corrections andsoforth, so Roithamer. We're constantly correcting, and correcting ourselves, most rigorously, because we recognize at every moment that we did it all wrong (wrote it, thought it, made it all wrong), acted all wrong, how we acted all wrong, that everything to this point in time is a falsification, so we correct this falsification, and then we again correct the correction of this falsification and we correct the result of the correction of a correction andsoforth, so Roithamer. But *the ultimate correction* is one we keep delaying, the kind others have made without ado from one minute to the next, I think, so Roithamer, the kind they *could* make, by the time they no longer thought about it, because they were afraid even to think about it, but then they did correct themselves, like my cousin, like his father, my uncle, like all the others whom we knew, as we thought, whom we knew so thoroughly, yet we didn't *really* know all these people's characters, because their self-correction took us by *surprise,* otherwise we wouldn't have been surprised by their *ultimate essential correction, their suicide.*[22]

Having arrived at this stage, one has no meaningful choices: "If we don't, every time, involve ourselves in the most problematic undertakings, we're lost, there's nothing left, so Roithamer." But: "What then follows is the catastrophe of breakdown, whatever our idea was about deserts us when we sleepwalkers awake in the middle of what we were doing, so Roithamer. Once we recognize the process, it's already broken off, nothing's left but a man who's been destroyed, killed."[23] Unable to correct the Cone once it has been built, unable to undo his sister's death, Roithamer turns to an enormous manuscript that he has previously written on Altensam and its relation to the Cone and proceeds to "correct" it mercilessly, reducing it from its original eight hundred pages to two hundred, and then to twenty, turning everything he had said into its exact opposite—and then, finally, turning the process of "ultimate correction" on himself. The inexorable closing of the circle—suggesting, in this situation, the tightening of the noose—reduces his previously manic creative activity to paralysis, until there's but one thing left that he can do.

Durand has mentioned that he still esteems *Correction* as his "highest model" among Bernhard's novels, "because it's so perfectly focused and proportioned."[24] Recognition of the regard in which Durand holds this text leads us back to a consideration of his own title, *So er.* Is Durand referring to someone specific with this "he"? Is it, perhaps, Bernhard himself? This might seem implausible on the face of it; but the idea is interesting, especially if we consider that in the second part of *Correction* the narrator does not continually interject "so Roithamer" simply for the sake of orienting the reader properly. The whole performance wears an eerie psychological aspect; for while he is at obvious pains to distinguish his identity from Roithamer's, he has become completely enmeshed in Roithamer's work and thought, having admired him, almost to the point of being in thrall, for most of the time he has known him—and now he sits self-imprisoned in the attic where Roithamer lived for so long, his own literary aspirations (if in fact he ever had any) co-opted by the near-impossible task of putting his late friend's papers in order. Thus the "so Roithamer" is effectively a gesture of desperation. In reality, all those thousands of fragmentary texts are the narrator's now, and he must do the best he can with them. It is possible that Durand has turned this gesture into one of homage, acknowledging Bernhard's special impact on him while writing something that is very much his own piece—divorcing, that is, the qualities of Bernhard's narrative flow from the morbid associations that they develop in this novel (as they do in almost all of his writings) and concentrating on their great potential, from a technical standpoint, for controlling, in an exacting way over appreciable spans of time, the process of clarification. Durand, after all, by his own account did something very similar in *Lichtung*, declining to see the ultimate clarification as death and recasting it as a process of discovery that connotes creation, revealing the generating kernel of the piece.[25]

Die innere Grenze is another work in which the concluding measures function as a kind of distillation of all that has preceded them, although the details are quite different from those of *So er.* For this string sextet, Durand composed six chord progressions—strict note-against-note writing—of varying length. Unlike the chords of *So er*, these progressions are never heard explicitly as such, although we do get pretty close in that final section of *Die innere Grenze,* where in six phrases of a few measures each the progressions are given a kind of polyphonic treatment, seriatim.

EXAMPLE 5A: DURAND, *DIE INNERE GRENZE*, SOURCE PROGRESSION 1
AND DERIVATIONS (FROM COMPOSER'S NOTES)

(It is as though one were just verging on hearing them clearly, the outlines still ever so slightly fuzzy.) Example 5a, excerpted from Durand's
lecture notes, presents the first of these progressions ("accords") below a
kind of voice-leading reduction of the corresponding passage in the initial measures of the final section (measures 241–4). (The remainder of
this example will be explained shortly.) Example 5b displays measures
241–4 as they actually appear in the finished score of the work. The
impression of growing clarity in the final section is further promoted by
the fact that, in the succession of six progressions, the longer ones (thir-

EXAMPLE 5 B: *DIE INNERE GRENZE*, MEASURES 241–4

teen and seventeen chords) occur at the beginning, the shorter ones (six
and ten chords) at the end—a tendency that is reinforced by the progressively shorter phrases in the final section that correspond to these

progressions (from twenty quarter-note beats for the first progression, in measures 241–4, to nine for the sixth progression, in measures 256–7).

A	**B**	**C**	**D**	**E**	**F**	**G**
mm. 1–14	mm. 15–59	mm. 60–99	mm. 100–73	mm. 176–225	mm. 226–40	
1.	4. 5. 2.(chords)	1. 2. 3.	4.	5.(⌈ 6 ⌉) 4.(⌈ 5 ⌉) 6.(chords)	5.(⌈ 6 ⌉) 4.(⌈ 5 ⌉) (⌈ 7 ⌉)	1. mm. 241–4 2. mm. 245–8 3. mm. 249–51 4. mm. 252–3 5. mm. 254–5 6. mm. 256–7

EXAMPLE 6: *DIE INNERE GRENZE*,
FORMAL OUTLINE (FROM COMPOSER'S NOTES)

This last section is the seventh of the piece, according to Durand's formal plan, reproduced in Example 6; in the previous six sections, he uses the progressions both separately and in combination to develop a wide variety of textures, often in ways that effectively obscure their origins. Durand refers to one technique he frequently employs in this development as *lecture diagonale*, or "diagonal reading," in which an instrumental line is extracted from the order of chord progression according to no readily inferable rules; this is tantamount to treating the notes of each chord as a pitch-class collection rather than as a pitch collection, since the original registers of the notes read on a path zig-zagging through the texture are then adjusted for the sake of melodic considerations. The lower half of Example 5a, to be read against the chord progression in the upper half, reveals how diagonal reading yields the violin melody that opens the work, measures 1–2.[26] The corresponding excerpt from the score, as ultimately notated, appears in Example 7. Overall, it would appear, the aim of diagonal reading (together with more conventional melodic and harmonic reading, carried out simultaneously) is to "use up" the contents of each progression, spreading it in more or less abstract form over several sections of the work.[27]

Another type of effacement is evident at the beginning of the fourth large section of *Die innere Grenze,* starting at measure 100. The source progression (no. 4 of the six), as transcribed from Durand's sketches for the work, appears in Example 8a; this is developed into the six-line reading shown in Example 8b (again from the composer's lecture notes). Notice that none of the six lines so extracted exactly follows the "voice

Commande de l'état français

pour le SEXTUOR SCHOENBERG

dedié a Maryvonne Le DIZÈS-RICHARD

JOËL-FRANÇOIS DURAND

"Die Innere Grenze"

pour sextuor à cordes (1988)

EXAMPLE 7: *DIE INNERE GRENZE*, MEASURES 1–3

EXAMPLE 8A: *DIE INNERE GRENZE*, SOURCE PROGRESSION 4
(TRANSCRIBED FROM COMPOSER'S SKETCHES)

leading" of the original chords; in this sense they are diagonal readings, although by and large the lines remain in the general region in which they began. (The procedure is quite similar to the process of extraction of lines noted above for *So er*.) In the transference to the finished score (Example 8c), several other factors come into play that further blur the relationship to the source progression. First, notes are omitted and registers radically revised; see, for instance, violin 1 in measure 102, which lacks a C where it "ought to" occur. Second, one of the six lines is left out, replaced by a sustained note (assigned to cello 2) the function of which will be explained in a moment. Third, the assignment of lines to instruments changes with each successive measure of rhythmic unison: for example, violin 1 keeps to the top line in measure 102 and 104, then switches to the second line in 106; violin 2 takes the second line in 102, the third line in 104, the fourth in 106; and so on. Fourth, the entire assemblage of lines is transposed in each successive occurrence according to a scheme determined by the intervals in the sustained-note part played by cello 2; this line, noted in Example 8b, is actually the lowest strand of the original chord progression, read as strict voice leading. That is: because the second note of this sustained-note part is E, a major second above the first note, D, the lines in measure 104 (to which E corresponds) are transposed up a major second; measure 106, "controlled" by F♯, is transposed yet another major second higher; and so forth.

EXAMPLE 8B: *DIE INNERE GRENZE*, LINES EXTRACTED FROM
SOURCE PROGRESSION 4 (FROM COMPOSER'S NOTES)

Although one cannot really say that the derivation of material from the six source progressions becomes more transparent as the piece progresses (before, that is, the near-perfect clarity of the final section, from measure

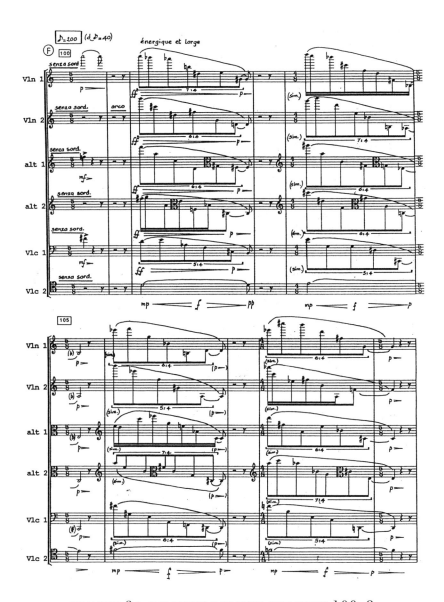

EXAMPLE 8C: *DIE INNERE GRENZE*, MEASURES 100–9

241 on), nevertheless there *is* a sense in which the piece becomes more assuredly "itself" as it comes closer and closer to its conclusion. As

Durand mentions in his self-interview, the composition of *Die innere Grenze* began in what seems a consciously chaos-inducing act: cutting apart the score of the earlier String Trio with scissors and pasting together the resulting fragments to form, as it were, accidentally "found" sextet (trio × 2) textures—something that might very well remind the reader of the narrator of *Correction* dumping out the contents of Roithamer's knapsack. Yet, in Durand's case at least, there was a method to this apparent madness: by taking up these fragments into a separate compositional scheme that, as one can see from the outline in the preceding paragraphs, had nothing to do with the Trio per se—allowing the inevitable disruptions to occur, working through and around them— Durand hoped to test the strength of his scheme, to discover the "inner boundaries" of its coherence, "beyond which it would collapse."[28] As things turned out, the test was successful: as the piece goes on there are fewer and fewer such disruptions, and they make less and less of an impression on the surface. Such a strategy might plausibly have been inspired as well by reading Bernhard; for there can be no doubt that many of his characters do deliberately confront madness (mental chaos) in their conscious actions, something which provides (whether they survive it or not) a harrowing experience, but one which in any case cannot be avoided.

Again by his own account, Durand made use of the end-clarifying scheme in two more of his pieces, *L'Exil du feu* (1989–91) and *Un Feu distinct* (1991), before beginning to branch away from it. The Piano Concerto (1993), extensively discussed by the composer in an essay elsewhere in this book, is already quite different in conception: although there is a revelation of sorts at the end of the piece, it doesn't work in quite the same way as it did in the pieces of the preceding decade; the path to it is quite a bit more complicated—in part, one must gather, because the "original material," so to speak, emerged only as Durand was writing the piece; he didn't actually have it in hand, or even in mind, ahead of time.[29] But one has the impression that Bernhard has remained a kind of *point d'appui* for Durand, in one sense or another, right up to the present day. By way of conclusion, then, I'd like to point out two examples from relatively recent works that seem to me to illustrate it, in different ways: one having to do with what could be called the "local" quality of Bernhard's prose; the other more a matter, again, of form.

The first example is found in *La Terre et le feu* (1999), for oboe and ensemble of twelve instruments. In this work, the oboe has a particularly active and virtuosic part to play; one is tempted also to characterize it as loquacious or voluble, recognizing at the same time the risk of reading too much into its possible resemblance to speech. This speechlike quality may owe something indirect, at least, to the "diastic" method by which the solo line was constructed, as explained by Durand in his own essay, "Melody—Three Situations," elsewhere in this book. In any case, it does not really come close to the manic, obsessive quality of the typical Bernhardian monologue—except in one passage, headed "sauvage" (measures 128 ff.; see Example 9). From here to measure 174, the oboe part explodes in a furious rant that is as different in expression as can be imagined from the character, by turns blossoming, searching, or meditative, that it exhibits elsewhere in the piece. This is partly a product of the rapid passagework, although as mentioned there is plenty of virtuosity on display throughout *La Terre et le feu*. It also derives in part from the narrow pitch range of phrases such as measures 132–4 or 140–5, and to the fact that there seems to be a ceiling of sorts at E♭6 for a time, only occasionally broken through to E6; to the way that certain figures recur, such as the material in measure 137 recapitulating that of measure 132; to the further intensification and attenuation that occurs with the rise in tessitura of measures 153–4—and, most of all, to the fact that it goes on as long as it does. The listener might expect the passage to be coming to a close by measure 155, where the solo part pauses—but this turns out to be only a short break; the oboe then continues for another twenty measures, again with (mostly) the same narrow repertoire of figures that characterized the first part of the passage.

EXAMPLE 9: DURAND, *LA TERRE ET LE FEU*, MEASURES 129–37, OBOE

My second example comes from the orchestral work *Athanor* (2001), also already discussed in "Melody—Three Situations." Here it is the overall conception of form—which points to the exposure of a long melody at the end of the piece that is present already earlier, but in a concealed, "purely structural" function—that seems to owe something to the idea of a clarification that can come only once the ambitus is already closed. What is different in *Athanor*, by comparison to Durand's earlier work with progressive clarification, is the unmistakable emergence of multiple time scales, as the tones of a melody, widely dispersed and in some cases only implicitly present in the earlier sections of the work, are finally pulled together and made into an explicit line. Does this have any connection to multiple time *levels*, in the sense discussed by Long among others, in the narrative tissue of Bernhard's novels? Probably not—but the sense alone, conveyed more and more definitely by repeated hearings of *Athanor*, of negotiating a long passage from opacity to transparency through a graduated series of light values of near-infinite fineness in between, makes as convincing a "proof" of Durand's continued meditation upon Bernhard as any music of his that I can think of. Given these qualities, and given reports from the composer that his most recent work, *Ombre/Miroir* (2004), follows a similar plan,[30] we can probably expect this fortuitous literary-musical cross-pollination to bear a good deal more fruit in the years to come.

NOTES

1. Thomas Bernhard, interview, quoted in Jonathan J. Long, *The Novels of Thomas Bernhard: Form and Its Function* (Rochester: Camden House, 2001), 11; my translation. "Ich würde sagen, es ist eine Frage des Rhythmus und hat viel mit Musik zu tun. Ja, was ich schreibe, kann man nur verstehen, wenn man sich klarmacht, daß zuallererst die musikalische Komponente zählt und daß erst an zweiter Stelle das kommt, was ich erzähle."

2. Hermann Helms-Derfert, quoted in Long, *The Novels of Thomas Bernhard*, 2; my translation. "das musikanaloge Sprechen, das die Wörter in Töne zu verwandeln scheint."

3. Thomas Bernhard, *Yes*, trans. Ewald Osers (Chicago: University of Chicago Press, 1992), 1–3. All emphases marked with italics are the author's, although some italicizations of word prefixes in the original have evidently proved impossible to carry over into the translation with perfect accuracy.

4. The only repetitions noted here are instances that correspond to the original German, in which at least the root of the word is preserved. The translation of this sentence introduces several repetitions that are not found in the original, and obscures some that are clearer in the original. However, the basic effect of such repetitions should be clear enough from reading just the translation.

5. Gitta Honegger, "Language Speaks. Anglo-Bernhard: Thomas Bernhard in Translation," in A *Companion to the Works of Thomas Bernhard*, ed. Matthias Konzett (Rochester: Camden House, 2002), 169–85 (171). The quoted passage is attributed by Honegger to Austrian writer (and 2004 Nobel laureate) Elfriede Jelinek, in private conversation.

6. Stephen D. Dowden, "A Testament Betrayed: Bernhard and His Legacy," in A *Companion to the Works of Thomas Bernhard*, 51–67 (63–4).

7. See Mark M. Anderson, "Fragments of a Deluge: The Theater of Thomas Bernhard's Prose," in A *Companion to the Works of Thomas Bernhard*, 119–35 (120).

8. Long, *The Novels of Thomas Bernhard*, 14. Here Long cites Gregor Hens, *Thomas Bernhards Trilogie der Künste: "Der Untergeher," "Holzfällen," "Alte Meister"* (Rochester: Camden House, 1999). See

also Long's general discussion of "'Musical' Prose," 11–5 passim. Others too have taken up the idea of "polyphonic spaces" in Bernhard's work, for instance Uwe Betz, *Polyphone Räume und karnevalisiertes Erbe: Analysen des Werks Thomas Bernhards auf der Basis Bachtinischer Theoreme* (Würzburg: Ergon, 1997).

9. Long, *The Novels of Thomas Bernhard*, 81.

10. Charles W. Martin, *The Nihilism of Thomas Bernhard: The Portrayal of Existential and Social Problems in His Prose Works* (Amsterdam: Editions Rodopi B.V., 1995), 24.

11. Martin, *The Nihilism of Thomas Bernhard*, 27; Long, *The Novels of Thomas Bernhard*, 57–8.

12. Long, *The Novels of Thomas Bernhard*, 65. Long identifies the presence of three time levels as well in *The Loser*, *Cutting Timber* (*Holzfällen*, 1984), *Old Masters*, and *Extinction* (*Auslöschung*, 1986).

13. Dowden, "A Testament Betrayed," 55.

14. Durand, private communication to the author, 25 July 2004.

15. See Christian Asplund's essay for the present collection, "'As If to Illustrate the Process of Creation Itself': Joël-François Durand's *Lichtung*," for an analysis of that work.

16. Durand, "Texte de présentation/note de programme" for *So er*, included among the composer's sketch and manuscript materials; used by permission. All translations are my own. The composer's generosity in sharing these materials is hereby gratefully acknowledged.

17. Ibid.

18. There is some suggestion as well in Durand's sketches that the successive transpositions of chords in each instance of Group 2 material are controlled by the successive intervals of one of the melodies, which is thereby registered implicitly. For example, in the opening, if the contrabassoon's melody (which in Durand's scheme simply takes the lowest note of each of the seven chords) is the control, then the initial T_0 should be followed by T_2, T_1 twice, T_3, T_2, and T_1, in that order. The exact time frame for this series, however, remains unclear to me; further, it would appear that some of the chords (here articulated as collections) under this interpretation would have to be incomplete. Such matters, obviously, offer rich possibilities for further study.

19. Bernhard, *Correction*, trans. Sophie Wilkins (Chicago: University of Chicago Press, 1990), 152, 163–4.

20. Ibid., 202–3.

21. Ibid., 183.

22. Ibid., 242. The word "andsoforth" is the closest possible equivalent to Bernhard's unusual formation *undsofort*. In the last sentence, the translator has rendered Bernhard's "wesentliche" as "existential," which I have replaced with the more accurate "essential."

23. Ibid., 248.

24. Durand, private communication to the author, 25 July 2004.

25. Durand, private communication to Christian Asplund, 3 May 2004; used by permission.

26. The entrance of viola 1 in measure 3 with a different diagonal reading that is also transposed by a tritone represents another type of development, ranging even farther afield from literal statement of the contents of the chord progressions.

27. Durand's lecture notes for his composition master classes at Royaumont in 1993, where he discussed *Die innere Grenze* at length, intimate as much: "lecture pratiquement exhaustive des lignes polyphoniques."

28. Durand, private communication to the author, 9 March 2005.

29. Ibid.

30. Ibid. This characterization on Durand's part is borne out by examination of the score, specifically the rather subdued, elegiac final section (measures 232–61).

JOËL-FRANÇOIS DURAND

BIOGRAPHY

1954   Born in Orléans (France), 17 September.

1960–72   Elementary, middle, and high school in Ville d'Avray and Saint-Cloud (in the suburbs of Paris).

1972–75   Mathématiques Supérieures–Mathématiques Spéciales.

1975–78   Studied music education at University of Paris VIII (Vincennes), piano and clarinet at the Ecole Normale Supérieure de Musique.

1979   Attended master classes with György Ligeti at the Centre Acanthes in Aix-en-Provence.

1980–84   After a year of private study with Brian Ferneyhough, left Paris to study with him at the Musikhochschule in Freiburg im Breisgau, Germany. Received a scholarship from the DAAD, 1981–82.

1982   Premiere of the String Trio by the Arditti Quartet at the Summer Courses in Darmstadt, 25 July.

1983   Attended master classes with Luciano Berio at the Centre Acanthes and with Luigi Nono at the Freiburg Musikhochschule.

1984   Left Europe to pursue a Ph.D. in composition at the State University of New York at Stony Brook; studied with Bülent Arel. Scholarships from the Fulbright Foundation (1984–85) and the French Ministry of Culture (1985–86).

1985   Chosen by György Ligeti to represent France in a series of master classes given to young composers from the European Community in Asolo (Italy), where the premiere of the first version of *So er* took place on 10 April. Premiere of final version by the ASKO Ensemble (under Denis Cohen) at the Venice Biennale, 1 October.

1987   Premiere of *Lichtung* by Ensemble Intercontemporain (under Lothar Zagrozek) in Paris, 9 March. Followed the computer course at IRCAM.

1988   Premiere of *Die innere Grenze* by the Sextuor Schoenberg at the Maison de Radio France in Paris, 27 November.

1990   Received the Kranichsteiner Musikpreis from the Summer Courses in Darmstadt, after a performance of *Die innere Grenze*. Invited to teach at the Darmstadt Summer Courses (and again in 1992 and 1994).

1991   Premiere of *L'Exil du feu* by the Ensemble Itinéraire (under Mark Foster) in Paris, 23 May. Moved to Seattle to take up a teaching position in composition and theory at the University of Washington.

1992   Premiere of *Un Feu distinct* by the Ensemble Contrechamps (under Farhad Mechkat) in Geneva, 27 March.

1993   Co-director of the Composition course at the Centre de la Voix in Royaumont in September. Premiere of *La Mesure des choses I. La Mesure de l'air* at the Musica Festival (Strasbourg), 18 September.

1994   Premiere of the Piano Concerto at the Présences Festival in Paris, 12 February. Visiting Assistant Professor at the University of California at San Diego (autumn).

1995   Gave master classes at the Civica Scuola di Musica, Milan.

1997   Premiere of *Les Raisons des forces mouvantes* at the first Internationale Woche für Neue Orgelmusik in Trossingen

(Germany), 8 May. Gave master classes at the Royal Academy of Music, London.

1998   Gave master classes at the eighth Internationaler Meisterkurs für Komposition des Brandenburgischen Colloquiums für Neue Musik, Rheinsberg (Germany). Premiere of *She or not* at the Colloquium, 20 September; premiere of *Five Musical Tales* by the Seattle Youth Symphony in Benaroya Hall, Seattle, 22 November.

2000   Premiere of *La Terre et le feu* by the Ensemble Intercontemporain (Didier Pateau, oboe, under Patrick Davin) in Paris, 9 March.

2002   Appointed Associate Director of the University of Washington School of Music.

2003   Premiere of *Athanor* by the BBC Symphony Orchestra (under Pierre-André Valade) in London, 5 December. Awarded the Donald E. Petersen Endowed Professorship.

2004   Premiere of *Ombre/Miroir* by the ensemble musikFabrik (Helen Bledsoe, flute, under James Wood) in Cologne, 19 September.

2005   Premiere of String Quartet by Quatuor Diotima in Bonn, 24 September.

Joël-François Durand

List of Works

1980–81 String Trio

7 min.

Premiere of first version: Internationalen Ferienkurse für Neue Musik, 25 July 1982, Darmstadt (members of the Arditti Quartet). Premiere of final version: Dieppe, 18 April 1984 (Trio à Cordes de Paris)

Publisher: DURAND Editions Musicales, Paris, 1990

1982 Roman

solo violin; 8 min. (revised 2000)

Premiere: 6 September 1982, Turin (Roger Redgate)

DURAND, 1990

1983 . . . d'asiles déchirés . . .

solo piano; 12 min.

Premiere: 8 June 1983, Bergamo (Antonio Bacchelli)

DURAND, 1990

1984–85 So er

20 instruments; 11 min.

Commissioned by the European Community Youth Orchestra

Premiere of first version: Asolo, 10 April 1985 (European Community Youth Orchestra, conducted by Lutz Köhler). Premiere of final version: Venice Biennale, 1 October 1985 (ASKO Ensemble, conducted by Denis Cohen)

1986 Trois Mélodies

mezzo-soprano, clarinet, horn, percussion, violin, contrabass; 6 min.

Texts by Yves Bonnefoy

Premiere: 15 April 1986, New York (Stony Brook Contemporary Chamber Players, conducted by Joël-François Durand)

DURAND, 1993

1987 Lichtung

10 instruments; 12 min.

Commissioned by the Ensemble Intercontemporain

Premiere: 9 March 1987, Paris (Ensemble Intercontemporain, conducted by Lothar Zagrosek)

DURAND, 1993

1988 Die innere Grenze

string sextet; 23 min.

Commissioned by the French Ministry of Culture, Paris, for the Sextuor Schoenberg

Premiere: 27 November 1988, Maison de Radio France, Paris (Sextuor Schoenberg)

DURAND, 1988

1989–91 L'Exil du feu

16 instruments and electronics; 22 min.

Commissioned by IRCAM

Premiere: 23 May 1991, Centre Pompidou, Paris (Ensemble Itinéraire, conducted by Mark Foster)

DURAND, 1991

1991 **Un Feu distinct**

flute, clarinet, piano, violin, cello; 15 min.

Commissioned by Ensemble Contrechamps

Premiere: 27 March 1992, Geneva (Ensemble Contrechamps, conducted by Farhad Mechkat)

DURAND, 1991

1992 **B.F., Ein Mittelpunkt**

8 instruments; 3 min.

Premiere: 16 January 1993, Amsterdam (Nieuw Ensemble, conducted by Ed Spanjaard)

DURAND, 1992

La Mesure des choses I. La Mesure de l'air

solo clarinet; 12 min. (revised 2002)

Commissioned by the Festival Musica, Strasbourg

Premiere: 18 September 1993, Musica '93 (Armand Angster)

DURAND, 1992

1993 **La Mesure des choses II. La Mesure de la mer**

solo piano; 9 min.

Premiere: 22 November 1993, Meany Hall, University of Washington, Seattle (Laurent Philippe)

DURAND, 1995

Concerto for piano and orchestra

piano and orchestra (2.2.2.2–2.2.2.1–perc.(3)–keyboard–harp–timp.–10.8.6.4.2); 22 min.

Commissioned by Radio-France, Paris

Premiere: 12 February 1994, Festival Présences, Maison de Radio France, Paris (Stefan Litwin, piano; Orchestre Philarmonique de Radio France)

DURAND, 1993

1994   **Le Chemin**

solo piano; 18 min.

Premiere: 3 February 1998, London (John-Paul Gandy)

DURAND, 1994

1995   **Un Chant lointain**

electronic carillon; 4 min.

Written for the dedication of the new carillon at the University of Washington

Premiere: 16 February 1995, University of Washington

1996   **Les Raisons des forces mouvantes**

solo organ; 16 min.

Premiere: 8 May 1997, Internationale Woche für Neue Orgelmusik, Trossingen (Hans-Ola Ericsson)

1997   **Par le feu recueilli**

solo flute; 10 min.

Premiere: 4 June 1998, Meany Hall, University of Washington (Felix Skowronek)

DURAND, 2001

1997–98 **Au-delà, Cinq Etudes pour piccolo**

solo piccolo; 7 min.

Premiere of first version: 3 February 1998, London (Katharina Zahn)

Premiere of final version: 22 May 1999, LandMarks/EarMarks Festival, Duisburg (Camilla Hoitenga)

DURAND, 1998

1998   **Cinq Contes Musicaux (Five Musical Tales)**

orchestra (2.2.2.2–2.2.2.0–perc.(4)–harp–timp.–strings); 14 min.

Premiere: 22 November 1998, Benaroya Hall, Seattle (Seattle Youth Symphony, conducted by Jonathan Shames)

She or not

solo baritone; 9 min.

Premiere: 20 September 1998, Rheinsberg Colloquium for New Music, Rheinsberg (Reiner Holthaus; Neue Vocalsolisten)

1999   **La Terre et le feu**

solo oboe and 12 instruments; 19 min.

Premiere: 9 March 2000, Centre Pompidou, Paris (Didier Pateau, oboe; Ensemble Intercontemporain, conducted by Patrick Davin)

DURAND, 1999

La Mesure des choses III. La Mesure de la terre et du feu

oboe and viola; 12 min.

Premiere: 4 February 2001, Benaroya Hall, Seattle (Alex and Marlise Klein)

DURAND, 2000

Cinq Duos

violin and viola; 14 min.

Premiere: 25 November 2002, Meany Hall, University of Washington (Kyung Sun Chee, Helen Callus)

DURAND, 2000

2001   **Athanor**

orchestra (3.3.3.3–4.3.3.1–perc.(4)–timp.–4.14.10.10.8); 19 min.

Commissioned by Radio-France, Paris

Premiere: 5 December 2003, Maida Vale Studio, London (BBC Symphony Orchestra conducted by Pierre-André Valade)

DURAND, 2001

Tiodhlac

solo clarinet; 3 min.

Premiere: 4 October 2001, The Warehouse, London (Roger Heaton)

2003   **In the Mirror Land**

flute and oboe; 6 min.

Premiere: 22 February 2003, Brechemin Auditorium, University of Washington (Helen Bledsoe, Peter Veale)

2004   **Ombre/Miroir**

solo flute and 14 instruments; 14 min.

Commissioned by musikFabrik and the Kunststiftung NRW

Premiere: 19 September 2004, WDR Studio, Cologne (Helen Bledsoe, flute; musikFabrik conducted by James Wood)

2005   **String quartet**

Commissioned by the Beethovenfest, Bonn, for the Quatuor Diotima

20 min.

Premiere: 24 September 2005, Beethovenfest Bonn 2005, Kunstmuseum Bonn (Quatuor Diotima)

Discography

String Trio

Trio de l'Ensemble Intercontemporain

Auvidis–Montaigne MO 782093

Die innere Grenze

Sextuor Schoenberg

Auvidis–Montaigne MO 782093

Concerto for piano and orchestra

Stefan Litwin, piano; Deutsches Symphonie-Orchester Berlin, conducted by Bradley Lubman

Auvidis–Montaigne MO 782093

Les Raisons des forces mouvantes

Hans-Ola Ericsson

Mode Records 139

La Mesure des choses III. La Mesure de la terre et du feu

Gareth Hulse, Paul Silverthorne

Mode Records 139

La Terre et le feu

Gareth Hulse, oboe; London Sinfonietta, conducted by Pierre-André Valade

Mode Records 139

Athanor

BBC Symphony Orchestra, conducted by Pierre-André Valade

Mode Records 139

FILMOGRAPHY

Roman, for violin: Maryvonne le Dizès, violin. Broadcast by TF1, 4 March 1990

OTHER PUBLICATIONS

1992   "Découvrir la musique de Ruth Crawford Seeger," *Voix Nouv-elles* newsletter, Royaumont (Spring)

1987   "La Sonate pour piano de Jean Barraqué," *Entretemps* 5: 89–117

Contributors

CHRISTIAN ASPLUND is a composer, improviser, and theorist who resides in Provo, Utah where he is associate professor at Brigham Young University. He has degrees from the University of Washington, Mills College, and Brigham Young University. His teachers have included Joel Durand, John Rahn, Stuart Dempster, Bill Smith, Alvin Curran, and Thea Musgrave. He has performed with Christian Wolff, Eyvind Kang, Larry Polansky, and Willy Winant. His compositions have been performed and recorded by Marilyn Crispell, Almeida Opera, the Downtown Ensemble, and others. He is also a co-founder of Seattle Experimental Opera which has produced six of his operas. His compositions are available from Frog Peak Music.

JONATHAN W. BERNARD is Professor of Music (Theory) in the School of Music, University of Washington. He has published widely on the theory and analysis of music of the past century, including the work of Varèse, Bartók, Carter, Messiaen, Ligeti, Feldman, Zappa, and the American minimalists, as well as on the history of theory, the history of twentieth-century compositional practice, and popular music of the 1960s. He is the author of *The Music of Edgard Varèse* (Yale University Press) and the editor of *Elliott Carter: Collected Essays and Lectures, 1937–1995* (University of Rochester Press).

ERIC FLESHER was born in Princeton, New Jersey in 1968. Prior to earning his D.M.A. in Composition from the University of Washington, he studied at the Hochschule für Musik "Hanns Eisler" Berlin, Cambridge University, and California State University, Northridge. His teachers have included Joël-François Durand, Paul-Heinz Dittrich, and Aurelio de la Vega. His works have won numerous prizes, and have been performed widely in Europe, Asia, and the United States. In 2002 he was a recipient of the Franz Liszt Stipendium für junge Komponisten, entitling him to an artistic residency in Weimar, Germany. He currently teaches Composition and Music Theory at Central Washington University.

RYAN M. HARE, originally from Reno, Nevada, is an assistant professor of music and teaches composition, music theory, and studio bassoon at Washington State University. He is also the bassoonist in the Solstice Wind Quintet. He earned a Doctorate of Musical Arts in Composition from the University of Washington; his other degrees include a Master of Music in

Composition from Ithaca College and a Bachelor of Arts in Music from Oregon State University.

Index